The Life
of the Transcendental
Ego

Edited by
EDWARD S. CASEY
and DONALD V. MORANO

The Life
of the Transcendental
Ego

Essays in Honor of William Earle

State University of New York Press

ALBANY

Published by
State University of New York Press, Albany

© 1986 State University of New York

For information, address State University of New York
Press, State University Plaza, Albany, N.Y., 12246

Library of Congress Cataloging in Publication Data

The Life of the transcendental ego.

"Selected bibliography of writing by William Earle": p.
Includes index.
1. Philosophy. 2. Earle, William, 1919– .
I. Earle, William, 1919– . II. Casey, Edward S.,
1939– . III. Morano, Donald V., 1934– .
B29.L524 1986   142   86–5835
ISBN 0–88706–171–0
ISBN 0–88706–170–2 (pbk.)

10 9 8 7 6 5 4 3 2 1

Contents

Foreword

I

It is becoming evident that the continued prospering—indeed, the very survival—of any movement in contemporary philosophy requires an active joining of this movement to other movements or tendencies. We can observe such joining happening even within a given movement. The continental tradition in twentieth century philosophy is a striking case in point: think of the merging of existentialism and phenomenology in the work of Merleau-Ponty and Sartre, or of hermeneutics and Heideggerian thought in Gadamer's writings. The conjoining of entire traditions is evident in the curious but powerful admixture of Dewey, Heidegger, and Wittgenstein that we witness in Richard Rorty's *Philosophy and the Mirror of Nature.* It is also manifest in Paul Ricoeur's assiduous efforts to combine phenomenology, psychoanalysis, and analytical philosophy in his writings on language and metaphor—thereby complementing the attempts of Mikel Dufrenne to bring together aesthetics, Marxism, and phenomenology. Not to be overlooked here is the unique blend of Heidegger, deconstruction, and literary criticism which we find in the pyrotechnical productions of Jacques Derrida. In fact, the situation today—and doubtless for many years to come—is aptly resumed in the title of a book by Morton White that was premature but prophetic at the time of its publication in 1956: *Toward Reunion in Philosophy.*

If a lasting and significant reunion in philosophy is to be effected, however, it will have to represent the merging of more than several strictly contemporary tendencies. This is above all true of continental philosophy, which possesses such profound tap roots in earlier European traditions. Yet, aside from begrudging acknowledgments (for example, on the part of Husserl or Merleau-Ponty) or from deconstructionist and somewhat self-serving readings (that is, as practiced by Heidegger or Derrida), no one has managed fully to reunite these crucial traditions with contemporary continental thought. No one, that is, except William Earle, whose life and work this volume celebrates. For Earle has the singular distinction of being the only philosopher who has put current continental thought thoroughly in touch with its own origins in rationalism (especially Descartes and Spinoza) and in transcendentalism (Kant and Hegel).

In Earle's abundant writings—particularly in the major tetrology constituted by *Objectivity, The Autobiographical Consciousness, Mystical Reason,* and *Evanescence*—we find something quite different from any mere *Nebeneinanderstellung* of these origins with more recent thought. As any reader of these four books knows, there is, instead, a creative conjunction of diverse background elements from within. We say "from within" to emphasize that for Earle it is always of matter of *re-thinking* a given tradition and then of so deeply *assimilating* a line of thought congenial to that tradition as to make it genuinely his own. At the same time, Earle is constantly engaging in original thinking, which is never compromised by any mere wish to "agree" or "disagree" with any other thinker, past or present. It is precisely in doing his *own* thinking that he makes the most meaningful connections with particular traditions—and makes them connect with each other. This is a very rare accomplishment: rarely accomplished at all, and still more rarely accomplished with such memorable style and wit.

The exact manner whereby Earle's own thought merges with that of others is also unique. Take the case of phenomenology and existentialism once more. In Earle's sure vision, these are linked in an altogether new and unexpected way. Rather than being drawn together as they have been by Merleau-Ponty and Sartre in a common project of describing the structures of human existing—in its bodily being or as pure nihilative consciousness—they are accorded respective domains of action and expertise by Earle. Phenomenology is granted priority with regard to "objectivity"—which is explored with nuanced precision in Earle's early book of this same name—while the existentialist emphasis on what is unique and unrepeatable in human existence is given its full due (e.g., in Earle's *Autobiographical Consciousness*). At the same time, the transcendental ego (long since abandoned by Heidegger, Sartre, and Merleau-Ponty in a shared flight from Husserl) is considered indispensable in the understanding of objectivity and subjectivity alike, that is to say, as their all too scarcely noticed source. This ego, unlike its empirical counterparts operative in artistic creation, psychoanalytic therapy, or historical action, is capable of divesting itself of any concrete concerns and living in a timeless realm of its own—a realm most completely treated in *Mystical Reason* and in *Evanescence*. It is just this transcendental factor, "the eternally actual aspect of the self,"[1] which establishes the incursion of certain basic *leitmotifs* of Western philosophy into the evolving Earlian position: for example, freedom, immortality, spirit, "world," God. Once again, there is a transformation of notions first set forth by others—as in Earle's intriguing idea that the transcendental ego is finally to be construed as "God thinking Himself, the self-awareness of absolute reality."[2] In such a circumstance, Husserlian phenomenology and Spinozistic rationalism are shown to be much closer cousins than we might ever have imagined them to be.

II

"The Life of the Transcendental Ego" is at once the title of a now-classic article of William Earle's[3] and of the present collection of essays offered in homage to him on the occasion of his sixty-fifth birthday. In the latter capacity, the title expresses the fact that no American philosopher within living memory has contributed comparably to reviving serious interest in the transcendental dimension of human life, where "transcendental" connotes much more than a Kantian condition of possibility. In fact, as we have just seen, the transcendental bears on what Earle unblushingly calls "absolute reality." Thus its proper province is the metaphysical, not the epistemological or the ethical. It is not surprising that, as a direct consequence, Earle has published a number of ground-breaking studies in a journal entitled *The Review of Metaphysics*.[4] Nor is it surprising that, on the premise that metaphysics touches on every aspect of human being and the universe, he has written so widely on such a wealth of topics, all of which receive illumination in his lucid prose: Spinoza and surrealism, freedom and existence, Hegel and Jaspers, culture and civilization, love and time, the ontological argument for God's existence and the appearance and disappearance of God Himself, film and politics, memory and mysticism. And it is not surprising, either, to find that he has lectured and taught on a still more diverse plethora of subjects in the past several decades, always with eloquence and insight.

What *is* surprising and not entirely predictable from such a commitment to a metaphysical transcendentalism—a transcendentalism that is as existential as it is phenomenological—is William Earle's enormous influence as a teacher of philosophy *par excellence*. As Asher Moore says in his contribution below, "I have not known any one who approaches Earle's life-long involvement, uncompromising and understanding, with his students; mentor and comrade, he has begotten offspring of the mind." Being a student in his classroom was not only unforgettable in itself, thanks to Earle's remarkable elucidations of even the most arcane pages of Hegel's *Encyclopedia* or Jaspers' *Philosophie*. It was also inspiring to be in the presence of a mind that was truly thinking for itself, with ruthless honesty and with an equally ruthless irony. When such experiences are combined with conversations in Earle's apartment that are unforgettable for their freeflowing and yet rigorously probing character, the impact could not be other than profound, both personally and philosophically. It was very much due to this impact, along with that of John Wild and James Edie, that the Northwestern graduate program in philosophy, specializing in contemporary continental thought, entered into a veritable Golden Age in the 1960's and 1970's. For many of those who studied with him during this time, Earle the man was as forceful and salutary an influence as was Earle the writer: which may itself be taken as illustrating his own idea that philosophy is to be considered a species of ontological autobiography.

Everyone contributing to the present volume, former student or current colleague, has found himself transformed as a philosopher and as a person by encounters with William Earle. These encounters were not merely memorable; they called into question quite basic assumptions about the nature of human being-in-the-world and of the cosmos. *And of philosophy itself:* how it has been conceived, how it can be taught, how in sum it can be *practiced* in the most ramified ways as one of the most challenging of human undertakings. Throughout such encounters (and long afterward in recollection) Earle has been an authentic *spiritus rector*, a guide to the philosophically perplexed, someone whose genial words never failed to bring even the most tortuous topics out of Stygian darkness. In his presence and by his very agency, we came to know in person what *Existenzerhellung*—"illumination of existence"—means.

III

The diverse essays presented in this book are dedicated to William Earle as teacher or as colleague—always as friend. This is not to ignore Aristotle's dictum that "we should honor truth over friendship." But there are contexts, including pre-eminently the present context, in which friendship is most deeply honored precisely by the pursuit of truth. Moreover, as Earle himself reminds us, the word "truth" is rooted in "troth," that is to say, in matters of loyalty that are essential to friendship itself.[5] This volume constitutes a collective expression of continuing loyalty to the man from whom the contributors have learned so much of philosophical truth.

Fortuitously, more than by the design of the editors, the essays which are offered here discuss various facets of Earle's philosophy or take up topics and thinkers that are critical to his thought and life. A number of the contributors explicitly acknowledge the importance of Earle in their own philosophical development.

Equally fortuitously, the essays themselves fall into four natural groupings. The first three offerings, under the heading of "Existence, Reason, and Choice," consider Earle's philosophy in its full sweep, setting forth either an appreciative but critical conspectus (as in Asher Moore's opening piece) or engaging issues fundamental to this philosophy (as in James Edie's and Robert Scharff's contributions). In a second section, "Philosophical Vision, the Transcendental, and the Mystical," J.N. Mohanty treats transcendentalism as a basic move in modern philosophy, while Philip Grier and William Langan come to terms with Earle's increasing interest in mysticism. More particular focii are delimited in Part Three, "Art, Ontology, and Consciousness," with individual essays by Forrest Williams on Spinoza's *Ethics* as a form of "edifying ontology," by Erich Heller on Nietzsche as the last philosopher of art, and by William Bossart on hitherto unsuspected correspondences between Sartre and Zen Buddhism. A final section, "Morality and War, Surrealism and Memory," includes a discussion of Earle's critique of ethics as an established enterprise (Hugh Curtler), an evaluation of Earle's views on the morality of war (Errol Harris), a consideration of Earle's active engagement in surrealist film (William Fowkes), and a treatment of the place of memory in Earle's thinking (Edward Casey).

In his "Afterword," William Earle addresses each of the essays in the volume with his characteristic flair for the *mot juste*. As in the acclaimed case of the Library of Living Philosophers, here the honoree answers his admirers and critics candidly and at length. In the instance before us, William Earle not only furnishes us further insight into his own thought but advances this thought itself into new registers. It is as if conversations that began decades ago in Evanston, Illinois (or, more likely, just over the Chicago city limit in Earle's apartment) were still going on in full vigor—as indeed they are in the pages below, where we have the unusual privilege of witnessing an ongoing dialogue between one of the most original thinkers in America today and various of his interlocutors. Just as the life of the transcendental ego does not come to any finite end, so its philosophical powers continue undiminished in these many-sided and open-ended discussions between William Earle and those who here pay him tribute.

We wish to thank the College of Arts and Sciences at Northwestern University, and especially its Dean, Rudolph H. Weingartner, for a grant that aided in the publication of this book.

Edward S. Casey

Donald V. Morano

NOTES TO FOREWORD

1. William Earle, *Evanescence* (Chicago: Regnery, 1984), p. 33.
2. William Earle, *Mystical Reason* (Chicago: Regnery, 1981), p. 71.
3. *The Review of Metaphysics*, Vol. XIII, No. 1 (September, 1959), pp. 3–27.
4. For a list of these studies, see the Selected Bibliography at the end of this volume.
5. See *Mystical Reason*, p. 106.

I

Reason, Existence, and Choice

Reason and Existence: Or, What Spinoza Was Doing Up In His Room[1]

ASHER MOORE

Time and mortality assure that most of the contributors to this volume will be younger than the man it honors. Many of them will be former students.

In Earle's case, the inevitable is appropriate. He intends nothing invidious in citing Nietzsche's dictum that a married philosopher is a joke; still, he has himself remained a bachelor who chooses to live alone, and who, except for a few old cronies, of whom I presume to think myself one, prefers to spend his leisure hours with his students—past and present—in conversation which moves from philosophy to art, from anecdote to travel, from analysis to laughter, from partisanship to the aspect of eternity, personal yet rigorous. I have known more dazzling lecturers, more encyclopedic scholars, and more involved academics, but I have not known anyone who approaches Earle's life-long involvement, understanding and uncompromising, with his students. Mentor and comrade, he has begotten offspring of the mind.

Years ago, Earle and I used to sit side by side at the business sessions of the Western Division displaying our bad manners by snickering audibly over the clichés which, in the obituaries (then delivered orally) of colleagues who had died without leaving behind extensive bibliographies, substituted for references to professional accomplishment—phrases like "dedicated teacher," "loved and respected by his students," "his door always open to students," "long years of faithful service to Alma Mater College." I realize now that my laughter mocked teachers as such, his only the phrases in which we bury them.

Earle is also, I am convinced, one of the outstanding philosophers of our time, a matter which students are less able to judge fairly since it involves the extent to which that which he has taught them was of his own creation, not a product of a school or movement or a variation on what the *Zeitgeist* was up to in his youth. About the formative years, one who shared them enjoys a certain advantage.

Earle and I are contemporaries—he is some three weeks my senior. I met him first in 1948, when both of us assumed our first full-time teaching positions at Northwestern University. In time both of us came to expect that along with Douglas Morgan, who arrived in the same year, we would spend our entire careers together. As things worked out, I left Northwestern in 1961, some two years after Morgan had made a similar decision. For the whole decade of the '50's, however, Earle and I were involved in daily, and often nightly, discussion. After my departure our discussion was necessarily inter-mittent, but I think that both of us were surprised to find that the temporal intervals seemed not to interfere with philosophical con-tinuity, so that we picked up the thread of our discussion almost as easily after a half-year as after a weekend. Not until quite recently did we begin to find reminiscence sometimes more congenial than philosophy. That adds up to some twenty-five years during which, as I esteem it, Earle and I shared the philosopher's search: his were the views I took most seriously, to him I addressed my thoughts, from him I awaited an answer.

At first our dialogue was an argument. I was fresh from Harvard, where I had been indoctrinated into the pragmatic-positivistic-lin-guistic thinking which was the dogma of that time and place—strict adherence was required of all who did not wish to be considered, in the favored term, "muddle-headed." Earle, meanwhile, had been at the University of Chicago. His interests, even if not his sympathies, were less parochial than mine. While I was being taught that Hume was the only philosopher of importance before Moore and Russell, McKeon had taught Earle to respect the past and Hartshorne had taught him that he should not therefore reject the present, especially his own present. Still, he made nearly as much of a point of his loathing for Locke as I made of my ignorance of Hegel, and it was perhaps not wholly the tinting of my own glasses which occasionally led me to suspect that the term "empiricist" called to his mind an image of alchemists at work.

By 1955, when I went to France to study Sartre and Merleau-Ponty (!), our argument had become a shared inquiry from a shared perspective. I will not say that Earle's views did not develop during those years—for him, as for me, existentialism loomed ever larger. Still, the philosophic ground we came to share was *his* ground. He showed me the way out of Harvard; he demolished the caricature of "rationalism" I had been taught; he convinced me that Nietzsche and Kierkegaard were philosophers after all. Later, as I became more adept on the new ground, I like to think that our relation became more equal. But the turf was his.

In a letter of recommendation written in 1957, I said, "I think Earle is . . . the most creative, the most genuinely philosophical, philosopher of my generation. . . . I regard his *Objectivity* as the most important philosophical book published in the United States by a man now under sixty; and I think it may well turn out to be the most important work published since the major books of Dewey, James, Santayana. . . . I have learned more philosophic truth from him than from any other individual."

Many will find this judgment exaggerated, excusable only on grounds of friendship. Among those of the "analytic," "empirical," "anglo-american" persuasion, Earle would not make the top twenty; indeed, he would be fortunate to be thought of.[2]

Through acquaintances at Chicago, through Paul Henle, to a lesser extent through Douglas Morgan and me, Earle came to be on speaking terms with many of the best analysts of the time. He was invited to Harvard as a visiting professor. His friendship with Henry Aiken gave rise to what, had it been published in a professional journal, might have exposed analysts to the kind of critical yet obviously *not* "muddle-headed" assessment which they so successfully manage to tune out.[3] Why, then, is he so little known in those circles, now that those with whom he was personally acquainted have been mostly replaced by their students?

Earle has a genius for the memorable retort. To those who fundamentally share his views, these one-liners seem devastating aperçus. Those whom the shoe fits understandably take a different view of the cobbler. What seems to his admirers the koan-like economy of those tossed-off remarks seems sheer contrariness, wild swings in the bottom of the ninth, to those at whom the remarks are aimed. Those deeply committed to science can hardly be expected to applaud Earle's explosive, "Who *cares* about the stars? We *know* what they are—just a lot of gas!"—this at the top-echelon party at an annual meeting—or to appreciate the occasion when, at a meeting of the Northwestern Department of Philosophy back when the "hypothetico-deductive" model of science was all but unchallenged, we were stunned into silence by his volunteering to teach the course on Philosophy of Science, a silence he finally broke with, "I want to teach *Hegel's* philosophy of science." How can analysts be expected to react when Earle, asked to clarify something he had said (this, too, was at a division-meeting party), replied, with a certain loftiness, "*I* said it; *you* figure out what it means!" Analysts make much of logic (although not so much as to bother to read Hegel on the subject) only to hear Earle say (we are back at a department meeting) that, when it again becomes his duty to teach the logic course he will again use Ruby's textbook "because there are fourteen weeks in the semester and Ruby has fourteen chapters." If *I* demur to Earle's comments on the corpulence and lace cuffs of the man I still think of as "le bon David [Hume]," what must be the reaction at Harvard?

Of course, his friends have only blackened his reputation by repeating these remarks. Here I must count myself among the worst offenders. Now that I am a senior professor, in a position to command at least the appearance of respectful attention from newly recruited instructors, I take pains to impress upon them the extraordinary merit and importance of this philosopher of whose existence their respective graduate schools have often left them ignorant in order to see their incredulity when I finally tell them that he thinks the ontological argument valid. It is the same look of disbelief which must have appeared on *my* face when Earle first told *me* that he thought the ontological argument valid.

Earle's espousal of the ontological argument is crucial. It is one of the two foci of his thought.[4] It threatens analytic philosophy on such a crucial point that, rather than reexamine their fundamental assumptions, analysts usually assume that Earle must be joshing. It was the crucial stage in his influence upon me: when I finally came to agree with him about it, most of what Harvard taught me lay in ruins. It was the crucial *nexus* in the realist/rationalist view set forth in *Objectivity*. It was a brilliant piece of philosophy. And it was uniquely *his*, the most striking evidence of his philosophic power and originality, since, before Earle, even the most died-in-the-wool metaphysicians shied from defending it.

The ontological argument, Earle showed me, is not really an argument—not in the sense of inferring one thing or idea from another, existence from concept, for instance. Nor is reason itself fundamentally a process of inference, of "composition and division." Reason is a clear thought, and the ontological "argument" consists in nothing more than becoming clear about just what it is one is thinking about when one thinks of the infinite whole of Being. If one is thinking about the Whole, then one is not thinking about, or in any sense beginning with or taking as a premise, the concept or idea of the Whole, since that is clearly a finite part of the Whole, *one* thing which is. And that, Earle said, is all there is to the ontological argument.

"But wait," I interrupted, "you are talking about *what* it is you are thinking about, not *that* it is. You are confusing the existential and the predicative sense of the term 'is'."

"No, I am not," he insisted. "The ontological argument does not involve the existential 'is,' only what you call the predicative sense. As I just told you, the ontological "argument" is not an argument which tries to prove the existence of something in the sense in which that chair exists. It is simply and only an explication of what something is."

AM: "But then you are only clarifying your own idea."

WE: "I am not clarifying my own idea; I haven't said a word about my idea—of God or of anything else. I have been talking about God."

AM: "But you have not proved that God *exists!*"

WE: "Maybe I haven't *proved* it in the usual sense of the word, but I've certainly *shown* it. What could be more evident than that Being is. That's what Being is: something which necessarily is."

AM: "But that's *analytic!* In fact, it's a rank tautology."

WE: "Rank or not, it certainly is analytic: that Being does not be is a contradiction. As everyone except empiricists has known since Parmenides."

AM: "But analytic propositions are vacuous. They concern only relations of ideas. They disclose nothing about matters of fact."

WE: "Propositions express thoughts, and, as Plato says, when you think, you think about *something*. And in this case, the something is the infinite Whole. It is not an idea or a term or anything but what it is."

AM: "But . . . but . . . what you seem to be saying is that if we can think about something, then it is real."

WE: "Precisely."

AM: "But then it follows that unicorns and golden mountains are real."

WE: "Have I ever said that the existence of unicorns and golden mountains can be proven *a priori?* The ontological argument holds *only* of Being. It holds of Being because Being *essentially* exists; it is not of the essence of a unicorn or of a golden mountain to exist. Existence is of the essence only of that unique Whole in the absence of which thought would be impossible, having no object."

AM: "But if the existence of the Whole follows from our ability to think it, why *doesn't* the existence of a golden mountain follow from our ability to think *it?*"

WE: "Because when you think of a golden mountain you are thinking of a finite thing which depends for its existence upon *other* things. If you try to think of it alone, as something which necessarily exists by its own nature, you cannot do so, for the thought is self-contradictory, that is, unthinkable. It is like Carnap's asking us to suppose that the universe is an urn containing three black and five red balls, or whatever silly number it was. Who could possibly suppose such a thing? Only the infinite is complete and hence depends upon nothing but itself. Only of the Whole is it true that if you think of it you are *ipso facto* thinking of something which depends upon nothing else and the existence of which follows necessarily from itself alone."

AM: "Ah, now I see the trouble. You said, '*if* you think of the infinite.' But there is, as Leibniz said, the prior question whether you *can* think of the Whole."

WE: "Well, can you?"

AM: "*Can* I?"

WE: "Well then, *are* you? Are you thinking of the infinite Whole or of a golden mountain?"

AM: "Well, I'm certainly not thinking of a golden mountain. But I don't know whether or not I'm thinking of the Whole."

WE: "If *you* don't know what you are thinking of, surely no one else can tell you."

AM: "But how do I *determine* what it is I'm thinking of? What *criteria* do I use? We're talking about 'criteria of meaningfulness,' aren't we?"

WE: "Yes, I suppose so, but since one obviously *knows* what one oneself *means*, to require *criteria* of meaning is to go from the clear to the obscure. As for how you determine what you are thinking about, the only way is to think about it. 'A true idea is its own test,' as Spinoza said."

AM: "But how do I *tell* whether I have a true idea—an idea of Being, for example?"

WE: "Well, if you are thinking about something which necessarily exists by its own nature, then you are thinking of Being."

AM: "BUT THAT'S CIRCULAR!"

WE: "THAT'S THE ONTOLOGICAL ARGUMENT! AT LAST YOU'VE GOT IT!"

I don't suppose our argument went exactly that way, and I can only hope that my reconstruction does not attribute to Earle blunders of my own. But that is essentially the way it went, over and over and over, until eventually I did get it.

After a while I realized why it had taken me so long to see the light. It was because I had brought with me from Harvard not only the standard empirical theory of knowledge but also the assumptions about the nature of cognitive consciousness which underlie that theory and which deny the very existence of light. Except on the level of sensation, cognitive consciousness consisted, according to those assumptions, of beliefs. Since beliefs were self-contained, albeit referential, psychological acts or states, they could, and often did, occur in the absence of an appropriate object, that is, when they were false. Since the occurrence of a belief was thus no evidence of its truth, it followed that all evidence was external and that *self*-evidence was a muddle-headed reference to what was in reality only tenacity of conviction (Hume's force and vivacity). Things were not quite that univocal on the level of sensation, where one did hear talk of "immediate givenness." Even on that level, however, many followed Berkeley in denying any distinction between sensing and the sense-datum, while those who admitted the distinction generally denied that sensing was in itself cognitive, holding instead that the most elementary cognitive element was the "basic proposition" and that the relation between a basic proposition and the sensation verifying it could be construed non-intentionally—perhaps causally, as Russell thought. I certainly never heard anyone speak of immediate givenness as self-evidence.

All of this, Earle said, was standing on its head. There are to be sure beliefs, and beliefs require external evidence, but all evidence, Earle claimed, is derived ultimately from self-evidence, and self-evidence characterizes not beliefs, but reason—reason not in the empiricist sense of a juggling of concepts or beliefs, but in the sense of openness, awareness, disclosure, in the rationalist sense of insight, *inspectio.* Plato and Aristotle were right that clear reason is transparent, without character of its own, nothing but the presence, the evidence, of its object, without which it could not occur. The question is not whether an object exists, but what the object is, and this can be answered only by inspecting the object more intently. There is no escaping the fact that a true idea is its own best test as well as the test of all that is only believed. If "tenacity of conviction" were anywhere relevant to this matter, it would not be at the level of reason but would consist in the sheer unavoidable force of sensation, the psychological duress that sensation places us under. But even sensing, Earle thought, is a light which makes something evident.

The relation of this to Husserl is apparent. Yet behind Husserl stands the "true idea" of Spinoza, especially the true idea of God or Nature. Behind Spinoza stands the "intuition" of Descartes and the rationalist distinction between reason and imagination. Behind rationalism stands the perennial philosophy back to Parmenides. Earle had learned more from McKeon than from Husserl.

Unfortunately, what makes Earle one of the foremost metaphysicians of his time makes him too rationalistic and too catholic for many of those to whom he claims kinship. It is only truthful to acknowledge that even among "existential phenomenologists"[5] his reputation, while considerable, falls short of acclamation. At meetings of the Society for Phenomenology and Existential Philosophy (SPEP), he is a maverick, too rationalistic and Spinozistic for its phenomenological wing, yet, because he persists in practicing what it preaches, too existential for its existentialist wing.

SPEP is a casting into taffy of the philosophical view of John Wild, among others, that phenomenology and existentialism are two aspects of a single philosophy called "existential phenomenology." Phenomenology, it is supposed, supplies the method; applying this method to the human subject reveals the structure of existence; the result is existentialism. The pretension is that while human existence, by virtue of its freedom, lies outside the purview of orthodox American social science, with its postulate of causal determinism, it nonetheless *has* a necessary structure which makes it a proper subject of a different, better, stricter science, phenomenology. Earle, on the other hand, in *Autobiographical Consciousness*, treats human existence as the *exception* to the necessities he examined in *Objectivity*, as something particular, free, unrepeatable and unpredictable. He thus departs from pure phenomenology not only in the direction of traditional rationalism by espousing the ontological argument, but also in the direction of individualism—in the guise of "existentialism."

Challenged with this apparent contradiction between his view and the phenomenological existentialists' commitment to strictly scientific examination of the necessary structures of human existence, Earle counters, of course, that freedom and uniqueness *are* the necessary structures of human existence, and that he, like them, arrives at this conclusion by phenomenological description.

When Earle takes as his subject some limited feature of consciousness, memory, for instance, his handling of it admittedly bears some resemblance to phenomenological description. To the extent that this is true, however, he fails, as do phenomenologists generally, to convince us that his is *the* "strictly scientific" description. When a phenomenologist's description of something is questioned, his method unfortunately allows him no recourse but to *repeat* the description. In oral discussion, where he *can* be questioned, I have found Earle no exception to this rule. What impresses me about his realistic view of memory is thus not the dubious claim that it is *the* description of an *evident* phenomenon, but the more traditional argument that, unless we *directly* knew something about the past, we should have no grounds for deciding whether something corresponded with it, just as what impresses me about his claim that a true idea is its own test is the consequences that he has shown that its denial entails.

When, on the other hand, Earle's subject is life itself—its freedom and uniqueness, its surrealistic juxtapositions, its loving communications—his method ceases even to *seem* "strictly scientific." He does not examine the universal structures of particularity or contingency; he finds contingent particulars lurking here, there, and the other place. The author of *Autobiographical Consciousness* is less a German professor than an English traveller, less a researcher than a curious observer, putting one in mind less of Husserl or Heidegger than of Montaigne and LaRochefoucauld.

In contrast to the methodological orthodoxy of existential phenomenology, Earle has consistently recognized both the limitations of any one philosophical medium and the coexistence of a plurality of media. Kierkegaard, he has said, is unteachable, but that has not led him, as it would lead a phenomenologist, to conclude that Kierkegaard is not a philosopher: the classroom and the lecture are not the only forms of philosophic expression. Except *possibly* for *Objectivity,* his books, while not as idiosyncratic in form as Nietzsche's, are more like collections of essays than like the systematic treatise which is alone acceptable at most graduate schools. (It is hard to think of any philosopher before the Enlightenment whose writings *would* be acceptable at those schools: Plato wrote dialogues, Aristotle jottings (?), Lucretius poetry, Augustine confessions, the Middle Ages questions and glosses, Pascal thoughts; even Descartes wrote meditations.) Earle has written stories, vignettes, travel tales, and memoirs, all of which seem to me, and I think to him, as "philosophical" as his more recognizably academic works. Nor is the word the only legitimate vehicle. He has had a go at painting, has always been seriously involved with, and knowledgeable about, music, has made several professional-class films, and is a fine photographer. And again, I have never heard him refer to those media as forms of extraphilosophical relaxation.

To build one's philosophy out of such varied twigs and grasses has the precedents of Kierkegaard and Nietzsche, whom existentialists claim as their sources, but it is too existential for those "existential phenomenologists" whose idea of radical innovation is to substitute one professional association for another and *Being and Time* for Spinoza's *Ethics.* Even science finds a place in Earle's grab-bag: his first passion was neither philosophy nor art, but chemistry. Earle's science, however, is not the "strict science" of existential phenomenology, nor is it the sovereign source of factual knowledge as it is for analysts. In fact, it does not yield *knowledge* at all, in the sense of the necessary, demonstrable truth of *Objectivity.* Chemistry belongs in *Autobiographical Consciousness*; it is a photograph; it is one more frame in which Earle catches the world, as the Elders caught Susanna, at an arbitrary point in its gratuitous life. *Autobiographical Consciousness* seems for the most part to reject the model of the transparent consciousness in favor of the view that each moment of living consciousness passes the world's light through its unique filter.

Ultimately the filter is the living person. Earle's most sweeping criticism of Sartre is that, claiming to describe the structure of consciousness, he in fact described only the structure of his *own* consciousness. And in *Public Sorrows, Private Pleasures*, a persistent theme is that political generalizations are often *private* anger disguised. In practice, Earle applies this view that thought is always some existing person's thought to his own thought: it is *his* thought, not necessarily our's or everyone's or the sole truth. Regardless of what is said in *Objectivity*, Earle in practice seldom, if ever, identifies *himself* as the omniscient observer, the subject who is transparent because transcendent, with no individualizing locus or refracting nature of its own. In philosophy, his attitude seems to say, the matter is not distinct from the form or the object from the subject: philosophy is human—not *too* human, but human—and that means it is irremediably personal. It is this existential humility, I think, (and it would make no sense to ask an existentialist whether the humility is personal or philosophical), which leads Earle, not to shun the society of his professional peers, but to hold aloof from professional*ism*, from the assumption that, unless it is universally agreed to, his view might be "only his view," from the assumption that "we" can arrive at "the truth" by an intensive twenty-minute discussion of the paper we have just heard.

To be sure, much of *Objectivity* explicitly repudiates this sort of individualistic, particularistic, "existentialist" pluralism. But even in the case of *Objectivity*, Earle never assumes that he has written the last, because uniquely true, book on the subject. I think he would counter that this is not because he recognizes, in the areas of *Objectivity*, the possibility of a plurality of truths, but because he is aware that his own views may be mistaken. Concretely, however, is there any difference between these two—between entertaining the possibility of a plurality of truths and remaining *forever* aware of one's fallibility? Did not Kierkegaard teach us something important about the perpetual suspense of decision?

As we move from *Objectivity* to later work, the existentialist element becomes plainer (although "strict science" is explicitly reaffirmed in the first chapter of *Mystical Reason*). *Autobiographical Consciousness* was originally called "Subjectivity," a title which made evident the parallel with Kant of which Earle is conscious and which he must have abandoned with regret, but which he did abandon in favor of a title which invites attention to the fact that the book's subject is individual, temporal, that is, existing, consciousness. He is now working on something he calls "Imaginary Memoirs." And then there is that curious title of the first chapter of *Mystical Reason*, "Ode to Phenomenology." "Ode"? "Ode"? "First Expectoration"? "The Gay Science"?

Analysts do not easily tolerate methodological non-conformity. Or rather, they do not easily tolerate offenses against their conception of what proper method is *not*, of what philosophy cannot and should not do. On substantive matters, on the other hand, analysts are more easy-going than phenomenologists. Perhaps analysts, having bound themselves within a severely restrictive methodology, feel safe from heresy, whereas phenomenologists, having been *liberated* by Husserl, are fearful of the uncharted vastness. Husserl assures us, indeed, that the phenomenological method is *strenge Wissenschaft*, but what most phenomenologists seem to have learned from him, what they run through in their prefaces as justification for speaking on matters which, but for Husserl, might be thought to require either logical or scientific expertise, is only the extremely general advice to *describe* what is *there* after *reduction*.

Possibly as a result of finding themselves thus abandoned, members of SPEP extol individualism and freedom but seem in fact to be dominated by a need for conformity. One seems expected to speak of "research," indeed, of "our research" and "our conclusions," as if philosophy were a cooperative, cumulative enterprise, like science. Having opened the meeting by chastising the analysts for dogmatism, SPEP proceeds to act out the strictest orthodoxy, half of the Society praising and glossing Husserl, the other half praising and glossing Heidegger. Discussions are often witch hunts into who has departed from the sacred text; meetings are dominated by the iteration of sacred words no less hypnotic, but less euphonious, than the chanting of *Om*.

Although his own words may be quoted against me, I think that Earle has never really been a part of the phenomenological church, and I think that the church, while not finding him sufficiently heretical to merit excommunication, has never felt entirely sure of him either. Earle is an authoritative scholar of both Husserl and Heidegger, but he does not really think it philosophally important that either of them did, or did not, believe something. The question is whether the something is *true*—and on that question Earle unhesitatingly practices the method of Descartes, the method of thinking hard about it, not the method of looking it up in a book. Knowing that Husserl is one of the philosophers from whom I have been able to learn very little, he seldom mentions Husserl to me when we talk philosophy, yet he seems not to feel, as so many of the members of

SPEP apparently do feel, that philosophy becomes thereby impossible. He tries to base his conclusions on reason, but they are *his* conclusions, not *ours:* philosophy as he practices it is not a group effort, and truth is not a social concept. Phenomenologists are as much "Technical Philosophers," in the pejorative sense Earle gave that term in "Notes on the Death of Culture," as the analysts and linguists he had explicitly in mind. While phenomenologists assiduously examine the finer points of human existence, Earle browses in its midst, blithely unconcerned with SPEP's sense of mission.

But while in style and substance Earle is more existential than phenomenological existentialism, while he is closer to Nietzsche and Kierkegaard than to Heidegger or Sartre, he has held back from the furthest reaches of subjectivism, individualism, and irrationalism, his existentialism restrained by a sense of the importance of universal law, by the sense that objectivity, even directed towards oneself, is not all bad, by the conviction that although reason is an existential act, it is not only that. In the same book in which he argues that political ideology is often only a disguise for private anger, he argues also that in politics private conscience must give way before larger, less personally "authentic," considerations. He stands somewhat aside from professionalism, yet he does not extol the "loneliness of the creative one"; on the contrary, he has said that when he writes philosophy, he always writes to *someone.* "Subjectivity" gave way to "Autobiographical Consciousness," but not to autobiography. He regards science as a human oddity, yet, in marked contrast to the metaphysical profundities which Sartre and others find in them, Earle has said that our good and bad moods, and presumably the valuations projected by them, "are all chemical."

The fact is that *Objectivity* and *Autobiographical Consciousness* gave us two different philosophies. The former portrayed us to ourselves as *man*—objective, transparent, impartial, untainted, the perfect window, the omniscient observer. The second portrayed man as *men,* each different, unpredictable, subjective, in a non-pejorative sense egocentric, a unique observer, more prism than window.[6] In *Objectivity,* Earle recognized and defended the inescapable cognitive claim that we know reality as it is in itself. In *Autobiographical Consciousness,* on the other hand, there is the same sort of meta-cognitive recognition which there is in Kant that cognition is itself human and that to think otherwise is not only personal vanity, but moral and religious error. In 1971, Earle edited an issue of *The Monist* in which he posed to the contributors, including myself, the question, "Is Philosophy Human or Transcendental?" Judging from *Objectivity* and *Autobiographical Consciousness,* Earle's answer to his own question would be, "Both." Reason and existence: instead of combining these in the gruel of existential phenomenology, Earle has clearly conceived them as antitheses at the same time that he has insisted that human consciousness is both.

But how is that possible? Clearly some sort of "synthesis" is indicated.

Several other things are clear. First, that Earle recognized the need to bring his first two books into relation and intended *Mystical Reason* to do just that. Secondly, while it sometimes seems, especially in practical areas, that what Earle leaves us with is a kind of Aristotelian mean, the final word of which is that a man of judgment is wary of extremes, he really envisions a tighter synthesis than that. Thirdly, however, the synthesis he envisions is not so close, so thoroughly a reconciliation and including-in of the antitheses, as that of Hegel, but a looser, more Kantian "synthesis," a matter less of dialectic than of analogies, reflections, and intimations. Fourthly, Earle's synthesis, again like Kant's, lies somewhere in religious territory.

Mystical Reason was intended to be, and was in fact, a "synthesis." The trouble is that it synthesized the wrong things. What was needed, what had been promised, and what we were awaiting was a synthesis of the universal with the unique, the necessary with the free. More particularly, we were expecting a synthesis of the subjective poles of those antitheses, a synthesis of objective cognition with existential individuality, of transcendental with human consciousness. We were awaiting Earle's solution to that most difficult of philosophical problems, that "world-knot," incarnation (or, on a different set of assumptions, emergence).[7] Instead, we were given a synthesis of two transcendental, universal, necessary, timeless things—two things from the sphere of *Objectivity*—the transcendent object, being, and the transcendent subject, the transcendental ego. *Those* antitheses Earle synthesized by asserting their identity. But what of existence? What of life? What, in short, of *Autobiographical Consciousness?*

Pending publication of the synthesis which I and others think is called for, let me speculate a bit about its likely character. In the Preface to *Autobiographical Consciousness*, Earle saw that the eternal and the historical, the transcendental and the human, connect in the idea of immortality, and he implied that he would address that problem at another time.[8] As far as I know, he has not done so.[9] I hope he does. *That* would provide the synthesis that is needed, a synthesis of eternal necessity with the limited duration of our lives. For by "immortality," Earle does not mean continued existence in time, an extension of our present life. That conception of immortality he expressed himself about long ago when, in a gathering of philosophers arguing bitterly over whether there is a life after death, Earle asked, "Would you really want there to be? Would you really want to live *forever?*" Of immortality in that sense, I am sure he would agree with Mark Twain that, "I have long ago lost my belief in immortality—also my interest in it." But Earle has also said, "There is one thing you don't have to be afraid of, and that is falling out of being." Immortality, to Earle, as to Spinoza, is *our* timelessness, timelessness ingredient in and constitutive of *life*. Immortality is our relation to the eternal, that "relation between the mind and the whole of nature," the knowledge of which is our salvation.

Spinoza's God is often called "the philosopher's god"—intellectually interesting, metaphysically useful, but religiously unavailable. To Earle, I think, Spinoza's God *is* religiously available. Quite recently, he wrote me that all his writing had been about God. I take that to include *Autobiographical Consciousness. Objectivity* is about the being of God; *Autobiographical Consciousness* is about creatures; the synthesis, when it comes, must be about the constitutive immanence of God in life.

Earle sometimes quotes what he says was Husserl's dying comment, *"Alles ist klar!"* If I were to choose one phrase which I think goes to the heart of William Earle, it would be, *"Alles ist klar!"*

To someone who accepts the ontological argument, *what* is clear is the existence of God and the necessary procession of all things from God. Clarity *is* the immanence of God in His creatures, the immanence of the eternal in the existential, the immanence of *Objectivity* in *Autobiographical Consciousness*. I think that the ontological argument (and the laws of thought and the rest of *Objectivity*) have, and always have had, for Earle, existential reality, personal religious meaning. What more religious, less "strictly scientific," affirmation can be imagined than Earle's "Metaphysics is nothing but the exclamation point after Wonder"?

If I am correct that *Mystical Reason* does not provide the synthesis which was needed in Earle's "third critique," then its title, which perfectly reflects its content, is similarly misdirected. Presumptuous as it may be, I will say that I think that, for Earle, mysticism, while it is something he has illuminated with his usual perceptiveness, is just another philosophical idea.[10] *Clarity*, on the other hand, is not just another idea; it is his existence. His book would have been better titled *Rational Religion* and addressed not to the identity of subject and object but to the ingredience of rational clarity, of the philosopher's god, into the heart of William Earle. I don't think Earle cares about mysticism. He cares infinitely about clarity. Like Spinoza, he *lives* by the idea—the clear idea, the test of its own truth—that the eternal possession of clarity is the highest blessedness. Since the day Socrates showed the world that he loved wisdom more than life because wisdom *was* his life, that has been the wisdom of philosophy.

Earle, "of all the men of his time whom I have known," best embodies it.

In my article, "Composition," I did the best I could to relate the transcendental to the human. "Philosophy," I wrote, "is an incoherence, an always strangled attempt to say something. Philosophy is the incoherence of 'transcendentalism' and 'humanism'."[11] Having had my own say, I have now speculated quite enough about the form of another man's say. "Strangled attempt," while part of the truth, is not a very satisfying "synthesis": it is too dominated by the "suffering of the negative." Hopefully, Earle can do better.

I must now acknowledge that Earle has twice told me that the synthesis which I miss in *Mystical Reason* is in fact there, in Chapter IV, the chapter on the true, the good, and the beautiful. Both times, I have looked; both times I have failed to find. I will try again. But if Earle will lay aside his *Imaginary Memoirs* long enough to explain the matter yet once again, perhaps at last I'll get it. Or perhaps, since I am not sure that in the end philosophy can wholly exclude autobiography, *Imaginary Memoirs* is itself the book I am missing.

ASHER MOORE: REASON AND EXISTENCE

1. Being an answer to a long-standing concern of Professor Earle's.

2. The disclaimer quotation marks, which will henceforth be omitted, proceed from my agreement with Earle that the philosophers in question have no special claim on these terms. Now, of course, many of *them* disavow these once-favored rubrics.

3. "Notes on the Death of Culture," *Noonday 1, 1958.*

4. The other, I think, is the idea of a subject who could have an autobiography.

5. *These* disclaimers (which will also be henceforth omitted) express my own conviction, which I am by no means sure that Earle shares, that existential phenomenology is miscegenetic, a conviction I defended in "Existential Phenomenology," *Philos. and Phenom. Research,* XXVII (3), 1967.

6. The two views are recognizably akin to the views Kant gives in the first and second Critiques, although Earle is more realistic than the first and less moralistic than the second.

7. In principle, of course, a synthesis of reason and existence in their *objective* aspects is also needed, a synthesis of necessity with contingency, of the universal with the particular. This is the traditional problem of creation, or, more profoundly, of providence (on different assumptions, it is the problem of order). But it would not be fair, I think, to claim that Earle promised us that synthesis or even that we were awaiting it with the same confidence as we awaited the subjective synthesis.

8. "And after death? Has the timeless ego any possibility of *recuperating* what it has all been? This chapter will have to wait." I am indebted to my colleague, Duane Whittier, for having singled out this short paragraph,

insisted upon its crucial importance, and kept it freshly in mind during the long wait for *Mystical Reason*.

9. This has now been accomplished—in *Evanescence* (Chicago: Regnery, 1984), which was published after the completion of the present essay.—Eds.

10. I mean "mysticism" in the sense in which it is an assertion of the identity of subject and object. On the other hand, there is an ineffability about the "ontological argument," and about self-evidence generally, which is temptingly similar to mystical ineffability.

11. *The Monist*, Vol. 55, No. 2, 1971, p. 179.

A Mess of Existentialist Pottage: The Existentialist Phenomenology of William Earle

1959 is a convenient date to use to mark the beginning of the impact of post-war existentialism and phenomenology on the consciousness of American philosophers. It was then a year since John Wild's famous "return from Europe" when he was converted to a version of existentialism, namely the realistic existentialism of Merleau-Ponty, which he felt he could incorporate into his own philosophical program. It was just after the publication of his Mahlon Powell Lectures, *The Challenge of Existentialism*, and it was the year in which he published his celebrated paper "Existentialism as a Philosophy."

There were also other events. In April 1959, the Western Division of the American Philosophical Association featured on its program a debate between Herbert Spiegelberg and William Earle on the relations between phenomenology and existentialism.[1]

It is here that we will begin our investigation of the "essence" of William Earle's existentialism by examining a number of its formulations from various stages in his philosophical development.

In the debate of 1959 Herbert Spiegelberg ended his attack on existentialism, which was no doubt addressed as much to Earle as to Scheler and Sartre, by stating that it is "a betrayal of the spirit of Husserl's philosophizing if phenomenology should sell its birthright for a mess of existentialist pottage."[2] This particular phrase was remembered by those who heard it long after the actual contents of the debate had evaporated from memory.

Is it possible to establish an essence of William Earle's existentialism? I am not so sure that it is. His thought is full of paradox,

19

tension, irony, exuberance, exaggeration, and "bright ideas." On the one hand he takes the stance of an Husserlian intellectualist and rationalist, on the other hand he advocates a solipsism of the present moment in which there is an experienced primacy of love over intellection. He denies that we have a concept of our existence and frequently states that the phenomenological method is inadequate to such an investigation, yet he continues repeatedly to make just such investigations even to the point of writing an "Ode to Phenomenology."[3] His relationship to phenomenology is a dialectical love-hate relationship.

Let us, however, begin with his *attack* on phenomenology. Earle begins by distinguishing contemporary existentialism which is "a mish-mash of phenomenology and an older and more authentic existentialism represented by Kierkegaard and Nietzsche" in order to come down solidly in favor of the older existentialism (and his own) which would purge itself of all aspirations to become a phenomenology of human existence. The true existentialists were "passionate" thinkers, whereas the phenomenological standpoint "is most definitely not itself a passion. . . ." Its presiding aim is clarity aiming at "rational intuition." Earle, like Kierkegaard and Nietzsche, holds that reflection is "a sickness" and says that we must distinguish thinking *about* existence from a thinking existence.

> Thought about passion and passionate thinking are not the same; the older existentialists argued for passionate thinking and existence; Husserl's phenomenology suspends these intentionalities which are then regarded as naive, in favor of a transcendental clarification of their structures; the contemporary existentialists are muddled precisely in their wish to do both, to be phenomenologists but of human existence in its most authentic moods; I find them, therefore, hanging like Mahomet's coffin between Heaven and earth.[4]

He argues that Heidegger's theory of *Dasein* or Sartre's formulations of existence in terms of *pour-soi* and *en-soi* do not succeed in exhibiting the essence of man because "there is no such essence." Nothing about human existence is necessary, not even the distinction between authentic and inauthentic acts. We are supremely free to give significance or insignificance even to existence itself; it is we who *choose* to make what we will in our lives essential or inessential. Freedom implies that there can be no determinate "essence or nature or character" of human existence. Therefore the only correct philosophical stance is to "turn away from the universal toward the individual and the concrete," and to realize that every philosophy, including those of Heidegger and Sartre—even when they attempt to define the essence of the human condition—are nothing more than "ontological confessions by their authors." They present certain possibilities which we may take or leave as we will, they are a form of ontological autobiography which shows forth possibilities that we may or may not find interesting but which have no coercive power or demonstrative force whatsoever. There is no touchstone to rule agreement or disagreement. There is no foundation for knowledge of human existence other than "the knowledge that we have no knowledge." In short: "If there is any phenomenology of human life, its first and last result is the simple insight that there is none."[5]

It is therefore not surprising that Earle should turn to his own immediate experience, his own autobiography, to determine what, if any, knowledge we can have of human reality. After 1959 he turned to "ontological autobiography." By "ontological" he seems to mean a life-experience which could have some universal significance, some typicality for other lives—something like, though he nowhere says this—Sartre's "existential psychoanalyses."

When Sartre's *Being and Nothingness* drew to a close he promised us an "ethic." This he decided not to publish for the simple reason that he could find no universal ethical principles. Earle would seem to be able to agree with this position easily. All universal ethical principles are either so empty ("do unto others as thou wouldst be done by", "never treat a human being as a means to an end") that they can give no specific guide to concrete human action, or so specific that they are tied to some small segment of human culture. Therefore, Sartre, who in this accepted Scheler's *Situationsethik*, wrote his "existential psychoanalyses," of Baudelaire, of Flaubert, of Tintoretto, of "the Jew," and his most successful analysis of Jean Genet. In each case he uses the picture drawn as a mirror to hold up to the human race in which to see themselves. In the absence of a generalized ethical theory we can only study some typical human choices of ways of being-in-the-world, those that are particularly illustrative for us at any particular moment in time. These are not *our* choices, they do not represent *our* lives, but they are possibilities for everyman. Though Earle's theory and thesis on "ontological autobiography" differs very specifically from Sartre's "existential psychoanalysis," since it does not study others but oneself, and was developed independently and without mention of Sartre, it seems to me to have very much the same ethical thrust. There is no universal norm for free choices; these are made concretely in individualized situations in which each free consciousness must assume, in isolation, full responsibility for his acts.

Let us look at Earle's definition of "autobiographical consciousness." The first step is a criticism of Husserl's phenomenology.

For all the distinctiveness of this approach, its aims were not
far distant from those of Plato or Kant: the effort to
understand the *a priori* eternal connections that existent
persons only enact, and which they must know on pain of
being ignorant or naive. With Husserl the aspiration to a
universal science of consciousness and its object is explicit; the
factual is disregarded at the start as accidental to the essential;
the factual is what *could* be otherwise, and thus is of no
interest to phenomenology, which looks for what could not be
otherwise.

Earle's approach will be "fundamentally *negative*," to the effect
that human beings must necessarily escape any "eidetic" or "essential" analysis; in effect that there can be no "theory" of human life,
no "essence" to it, and no "insight" into it.[6]

In his defence of ontological autobiography, Earle allies himself
with Aristotle: there is no science of the accidental, there is no science
of the particular, there is no science of contingent facts *(de contingentiis
non est scientia).* But the domain of existence

is precisely the domain of the accidental and the contingent.
That is precisely the reason why all questions of fact were
bracketed by Husserl in favor of an inquiry into essences and
meanings. A fact is but a contingent illustration of an essential
meaning, hence phenomenology can employ imaginative
variation more profitably than factual observation.[7]

In fact, to speak of a "phenomenological existentialism" is a contradiction in terms; the adjective contradicts the noun. Phenomenology wants an eidetic science of essential structures; existentialism
is a living and a thinking in the present. It is exclusively particular.
There is no essential meaning in either my life or my death.

On the other hand, *my* possible death, while it could certainly
bear some such meaning, is mine, and I in my contingency
am not, as Kierkegaard said with reference to Hegel, a
paragraph in the system. I am, in fact, only of
"autobiographical significance" to strict science. . . . what is
bracketed by phenomenology is of merely autobiographical
significance; it would be absurd for any existing man to
bracket his own existence with its singularity and contingency
as of "merely" autobiographical significance to him.[8]

And again:

For if the sense and meaning of my present life were
accessible to *Husserl,* for example, what point would I now

have in living it? My life would by that stroke be converted into a somewhat badly edited slow motion movie whose essential plot and theme had already been grasped timelessly in a scenario, by others, and which, therefore was pointless in itself, already having been grasped long ago. Could anything be more discouraging than any such view? And would not *any* such view be the one which made *every* human existence senseless precisely by having insight into its sense in advance? Traditionally, it amounts to fatalism.[9]

Because phenomenology wants to talk universally about what is inherently singular, it loses existence. Our singular and accidental lives are not proper themes for eidetic analysis. But, on the other hand, they are not unknown to us in living our lives. We do not have a concept of our own individual existence, but our own existence is accessible to us; I learn what it is to exist by existing, not by "watching others."

And then Earle draws a striking and puzzling conclusion, making a universal claim. It is not, he says, only phenomenology but the whole of philosophy which is "highly delusive." All philosophy, he writes, is nothing other than a set of "highly instructive examples of ontological autobiography."[10]

> It is by no means certain that there is a universally formulable sense to life. . . . If ontology wishes to complete itself it must direct itself to the autobiographical. . . . Since no human existence can pretend to be exemplary for all, we are not "reduced" to pure autobiography but elevated to it in its search for its proper form of expression. And here each must accomplish the elucidation of his own life by himself without rules.[11]

But, and now a paradox, Earle has not always been against general principles or eidetic conclusions. In his first book, *Objectivity*, he gives an indication of a method in philosophy of which he approves. He discusses the process of rendering explicit what is implicit in experience. He asks: how are the implicit and the explicit related?

> . . . they are both *phenomena*, that is, they are both appearances to the subject, and not something hidden from experience altogether; and secondly, they are in fact *identical in content*. An explicit phenomenon is not different in content from an implicit one; the explicitation or clarification is simply a rendering here of what was already given, and not of something else altogether. The clarified experience is the same

experience as the implicit and inarticulated experience. There is only one content. . . .

Since the difference is not in the content of the phenomenon, it must be in the subject or the subject's mode of apprehending the content, a difference within phenomenality. Let us recall it in our initial formulation: a difference between experiencing and knowing *what it is* that is experienced. The implicit was experienced; the explicit was knowing what it was that was implicitly experienced.[12]

This distinction is clearly based on the analysis of a universal structure of consciousness, namely, our ability in any particular experience to be able to distinguish the fact *that* we are experiencing from *what* it is we experience.

The truth is that I didn't explicitly see what he saw until he spoke; and after he spoke then what he said seemed to me evident enough because it characterizes my experience, and I can "verify" it directly. He did inform me of something, namely, what it was I had experienced. But he must first have rendered the experience explicit to himself in order to be able to name it. His words bear more than a chance connection with the matter being described. he says what he has seen.[13]

As a matter of fact, Earle uses just such a method in his own phenomenological analyses, the most extended and repeated of which concerns the phenomenon of love which, in some of his writings, he finds to be a more nutritious object for reflection than the bare transcendental ego. Indeed, he is analyzing a particular, individual experience, but he draws general (even universal) conclusions. Lovers prefer poetry to prose because it does not assert anything but rather expresses and articulates its own content.[14]

Love is passionate; it is "created in heaven"; lovers have always known one another; their love is eternal; it gives the meaning of life; it makes the two lovers one whole.

. . . when lovers say they exist in eternity, they do not mean that they find their love in unchanging or static boredom. . . . "Eternity" has many meanings and it could not have the same sense in the categorical structure of the world of love as it has for either the common world of daily life or the abstract world of mathematics. Its sense is equivalent to what Kierkegaard and Jaspers call the "fulfilled moment" and Nietzsche, the "great noontide". . . . The knowledge of lovers, then, is identical with their own unique union. . . .

Communication now reverts back to its primordial sense of
community. . . . Lovers within their universes declare that
they have always known one another . . . even though they
met only the day before yesterday. . . . Each lover knows the
other in the very depth of their intimacy. No generalization
follows. No prediction is possible. . . . Ethical laws are
suspended. . . . all love is in principle immoral.[15]

There is, therefore, a "categorical structure" to at least this important phenomenon. It is given implicitly in the immediate, romantic
encounter, and explicitated endlessly in language.

"Love," Earle writes, "is not an emotion, but an ontological event."
It belongs more to ontology than to psychology. "The world of love
absorbs the other worlds. . . ."[16]

But, at the same time, against this extraordinarily romantic description of love, there is the inexorable fact that lovers fall out of
love, that love comes and goes. From this point of view, having
given love over to ontology, Earle paradoxically discovers that it has
nothing to do with "metaphysics":

. . . there is nothing metaphysical involved in the matter at
all. The lovers are not gods, but very peculiar people, with
distinctive ears, warts, sizes, and shapes. They were born at
assignable places and times. They met in a certain cafe on a
certain date. They have definite ages and sexes. They must
eat, sleep, work, and all this follows the clock ticking on the
wall, not eternity. They fall ill from discoverable causes, and
are cured by specific remedies. Further, they fall out of love,
and eventually they die. Where is the divinity or the absolute
in all of this?[17]

Nothing more clearly reveals the paradox between psychologism
and ontologism in Earle's thought than his writings on love. It seems
to me that the root of both the theory of investigation he proposed
in *Objectivity*, and the concrete analyses of *The Autobiographical
Consciousness*, lies in his early reading of Karl Jaspers. According to
Jaspers man is always more and other than he can know himself to
be; his life can never be exhausted by conceptual or scientific knowledge. He is a unique, historical self, an *Existenz*. At the same time
an *Existenz* cannot be thought, but only lived; it does not provide a
definition of man or state a property of his nature; in his experience
it is always beyond words, always *implicit*. In attempting to explicitate
what it is *to be*, Jaspers discovers (in the words of Earle) that "the
most essential thing men have to say to one another cannot quite
be said."[18]

The final theme I wish to touch upon in the opus of William Earle is his doctrine concerning the "transcendental ego," which, autobiographically, neither he nor we can fully distinguish from himself. It seems to me that in an early review of *The Autobiographical Consciousness* Donald Morano gave an extremely accurate and pungent summary of all Earle has written on the subject. He writes:

> . . . Earle . . . searches for that singular source of subjectivity which makes me and you and each human being a unique existent with an autobiography; he invites each of us to divest ourselves of all which is not we. The philosopher here, in his search for his true self, becomes a novice, systematically subjecting to doubt all that he has taken for granted, bracketing the entire universe of objective and universal categories and meanings. As he strips himself of everything not the self, he discovers one absolute, irrefrangible source of meaning which is implicit in all of his disparate activities and undertakings, one transtemporal foundation for all of the diverse modes of his consciousness: an I, a transcendental ego.[19]

It seems to me that Morano, in what follows, correctly pinpoints the mystical and religious implications of his quest. His transcendental ego is a divinized self: "The self . . . can find within it nothing but itself, no God or superior subjectivity, no external nature, no world, and no other selves."[20]

From *The Autobiographical Consciousness* Earle went on to write, only a few years later, *Mystical Reason*. There he discovers that ". . . the transcendental ego itself is inherently the truth of God considered as absolute reality."[21] The transcendental ego, like God and "the absolute," escapes all logical and formal ontological constraints. Truth is to be defined not as the correctness of judgments the self makes about the self, but as the sense of wonder, loyalty, and truth the transcendental ego finds within itself.

> The joy of the contradictory, the *coincidentia oppositorium*, which is the very life of the transcendental ego or self, and of God himself, puts to shame the finite precisions of formal logic, and indeed opens the soul up to itself.[22]

It is by turning within, to the isolated and individual self, that we find "the absolute" which is inseparable from ourselves. We may begin from the fact that the self is conscious of a world, is "in the world," but this very structure of consciousness reveals itself as the absolute source of the world.

. . . This first glance of what Heidegger calls, with his usual elegance, *durchschnittliche Alltäglichkeit*, itself begins to disclose more mysterious sides, upon even the least reflection. The daylight world of human beings, the world of activity within culture and civilization, the more explicitly human world, itself has some aspects which at first may be disturbing for any empiricist or any man of affairs but perhaps, when plumbed, may disclose that not merely do the heavens disclose the glory of God, but that glory also glares in the daytime. . . . And so we are led dialectically to examine the absolutely central and originating role of the mystical idea of absolute reality which is one with each man in the structuring and constitution of the social and cultural world in which we find ourselves. Our present theme, then, is the derivation of every ethical idea from the transcendental idea of the *absolute*, or, what is the same, *the Holy*.[23]

Therefore, literally everything flows from the transcendental ego: knowledge of the social and cultural world, the experience of "the Holy" and of "God," also "the ethical," which, as in any mystical philosophy, is subordinated to something higher. All this could remind us of Saint Augustine except for the fact that by "turning within" Augustine found traces of something objectively independent and "higher" than that which is highest in us, the mind.

In conclusion, have we disclosed the "essence" of William Earle's existentialism? We have touched on his objections to phenomenology and on his own method; we have located the roots of his theory of ontological autobiography and its centrality for his method; we have taken his analysis of love, which he would not call "eidetic," but which nevertheless makes universal claims, as an example, and we have concluded with his theory of the transcendental ego which also at least seems to make universal and absolute claims about the structure of all human experience. Thus, it is difficult to escape the conclusion that there is a deep tension working throughout all of Earle's writings between a rationalist demand for analysis and the conviction that this demand will be forever and in principle frustrated. In spite of himself, and against his advice to Spiegelberg in 1959, he has attempted to wed existentialism to phenomenology.

JAMES M. EDIE: A MESS OF EXISTENTIALIST POTTAGE

1. *The Journal of Philosophy*, Vol. 57, January 21, 1960, pp. 62 ff. It is interesting that this same number of *The Journal of Philosophy* carried John Wild's essay "Existentialism as a Philosophy." It is noted that Maurice

Natanson also engaged in the debate with Spiegelberg, but his paper was not published in this issue.

2. Ibid., p. 74.
3. The first chapter of *Mystical Reason*. Chicago, Regnery, 1980.
4. *The Journal of Philosophy*, loc. cit., p. 77.
5. Ibid., pp. 81–84.
6. *The Autobiographical Consciousness*, Chicago, Quadrangle, 1972, pp. 44–45.
7. "Ontological Autobiography," *Phenomenology in America*, ed. James M. Edie, Chicago, Quadrangle, 1967, p. 72.
8. Ibid., p. 73.
9. Ibid., p. 74.
10. Ibid., p. 77.
11. Ibid., p. 79.
12. *Objectivity*, 2nd ed., Chicago, Quadrangle, 1968, p. 37.
13. Ibid., p. 36. See also "Implicit and Explicit Phenomena," *Review of Metaphysics*, vol. VIII (1954), pp. 211–224.
14. *The Autobiographical Consciousness*, op. cit., p. 103.
15. Ibid., p. 115.
16. Ibid., p. 120.
17. Ibid., p. 119.
18. "Introduction," Karl Jaspers, *Reason and Existenz*, New York, Noonday, 1955, p. 13.
19. Donald V. Morano, Review of *The Autobiographical Consciousness*, *Journal of the British Society for Phenomenology*, 1974, p. 176.
20. *The Autobiographical Consciousness*, op. cit., p. 67.
21. *Mystical Reason*, op. cit., p. 101.
22. Ibid., p. 106.
23. Ibid., p. 77.

The Not-So-Private Pleasures of William Earle

ROBERT C. SCHARFF

Mavericks—philosophical, political, or otherwise—are among the world's originals. That they are in the first place originals at all is not a matter of conscious choice. They cannot help the souls they have. Like the rest of us they can at best, in Nietzsche's phrase, "Become what they are." It is the way they do this that makes them mavericks. Their special inclination is to be willful about it. Like all originals, they are by instinct resistant to the appeal of the familiar, the normal, and the consensual. But mavericks seem somehow especially proud of that. Of course, they cannot join, follow, or agree. But above all, they want you to know how very much it is a first-person matter that they did not do so. Such assertive *Jemeinigkeit* makes mavericks fascinating, enormously stimulating, and often provocative—but perhaps also less frequently able to alter deeply the course of other lives. Hard as it is in any case to be receptive to what original spirits give us, too much ado about the act of giving may overshadow the gift, and then we cannot really learn from it. But my experience has been happier than this. I have been fortunate in knowing a genuine philosophical maverick—but more fortunate still in also having somehow been taught by one.

Everyone who knows the philosophy of William Earle knows his indebtedness to phenomenology, both newer and older. He speaks from the standpoint of a self which, in its reflexively recovered presence to itself and in its intentional relations to everything else, is as "transcendental" as Husserl's consciousness and as "absolute" as Hegel's spirit. Yet what a singular (in both senses) transcendental consciousness this one turns out to be. "I am I," it says; and in this

29

moment of absolute reflexivity, its essential being stands out from
its accidental existence.

> It can be lost in its projects, intoxicated with love, maddened
> with pain, or dreaming away its life; and yet all these
> activities are but so many acts in existence and in time of an
> ego that in itself eternally is, and in that capacity is
> independent of existence and of time.[1]

Other voices than Husserl's and Hegel's echo in these descriptions.
No worker in the field of essence or apologist for System, Earle is
interested in what happens when "the absolute falls into existence."

> . . . [T]he way in which the absolute ego engrosses itself in
> the general domain of existence, or the conditions under
> which it does so, mark that strange point where the ego
> transcendentally affirms itself by "choosing" to engross itself.
> . . . This choice always manifests a style or horizon within
> which further choices are indeed only specifications.[2]

So it is that Earle speaks to us in the name of an absolute and
singular subjectivity for which the very possibility of life, let alone
its "specifications," is a matter of choice. One would be hard pressed
to imagine a standpoint better suited to the uses of a philosophical
maverick.

How does one respond to the claims of so self-possessed a consciousness? Too easily, I think, one tends to hear only the pure
maverick; but in part that is because sometimes only the pure
maverick speaks. There is, for example, Earle's transcendental evaluation of the rational and objective philosophizing of the Ancients
as just another choice, or "option," among "an indefinite number of
spiritual alternatives open to the mind."[3] There is, too, his claim
that

> the history of philosophy is the history . . . of the most
> profound choices men have made. If they *talk* as if a single,
> literal truth were at stake, were statable, that some approached
> it and others receded from it, . . . it may be possible to
> understand these naive claims with some charity.[4]

Questions of charity aside, these are not exactly modest claims. They
have the effect of turning Earle's own spiritual alternative into something more than just one among the options. First-person philosophizing, because it remains transcendentally aware of itself as chosen,
appears to be the only option that is truly candid about its beginnings.
The implication is not surprising. How else could its own chosen
option appear to a transcendental ego which is "rooted in itself and

nothing beyond," knows itself to be "the origin of choices and decisions, as well as cognition," glories in its singularity and unrepeatability, and has radical freedom as its very mode of being? "All existing men in their subjective liberty," says the pure maverick, "are like so many gods."[5]

Yet when the issue of philosophical options arises, Earle is not always so intent on giving high Cartesian praise to choice itself. Especially when he speaks of his own autobiographical choice, frequently what he emphasizes is not that it is but one more "fundamental choice" for which there is never "any compelling reason," but rather that it is deliberately selected as "an alternative to rational, objective philosophizing."

> If rational thought aims at the one, the concept, and implicit in that, the necessary, timeless truth of universal scope aiming at "objectivity," one need only note here what is *omitted* or reduced to a derived and secondary place, of course the exact opposite: the subjective in its subjectivity, the manifold, the unnecessary or accidental, the nonuniversal or the singular, the irreplaceable, unique, and historical.[6]

Granted that a maverick is still speaking here, it is one who now seems at least as interested in our attending to the "subjective" phenomena he chooses to discuss as in our acknowledging that he chose them. This is the Earle who tells us his "public sorrows" and "private pleasures." When, on the one hand, he laments the ideological madness and sentimentality he sees in political and social radicalism, the degeneration of culture into technique-happy professions, and the alienating effect of civilized self-consciousness, it is because they seem to be *bad choices*—choices animated by some misguided species of abstract rationality. Earle is right to call these "bitter reflections" rather than transcendental ones. They show little regard for the wonder of choice itself but address instead the question of what options are *now worth choosing.* When Earle confesses that he can find "little or nothing in the contemporary scene worth imitating or continuing," that is because the currently familiar possibilities seem to him completely drained of whatever subjective richness and vitality they may once have offered to those who originally chose them.[7] On the other hand, the options his "weary but transcendental mind" finally turns to instead he calls his "private pleasures." But in point of fact, these options are commended to other contemporary consciousnesses equally concerned with working out a life subjectively worth living. For this reason, these options might better be called something like "genuinely individualizing" rather than "private."

With this suggestion, I come to the point of my title. I think that if one really listens to some of Earle's descriptions of his chosen pleasures, one can learn of possibilities which, if they must be called "private" at all, are not private so much because they are bitterly nonpublic or because they are one maverick's fascinating choices, but because they are *subjectively promising* to any current listeners who want to take responsibility for the course of their "own" lives.

The problem is, one hears little of such genuinely individualizing possibilities when Earle speaks as pure maverick. A fully reflexive transcendental ego, proud of its achievement, is looking in another direction. Above all, it is preoccupied with the phenomenon of choice as such, and with the implications for choice of having arrived at a standpoint which perpetually informs it that

> two things have happened: the very ego that lives emerges for itself as the unshakable center of its own life, but then the ego turns its attention not to the eternal and timeless, but to its own unique existence here and now in order to see what it is and how it is.[8]

Once this ego is, so to speak, transcendentally poised here in triumph, its attention is easily diverted toward a whole cluster of special problems: as transcendental, can I experience my immortality, or perhaps even my identity with the Absolute? Must I choose life, since indeed I can? Is there any hope of "dialectically considering" the condition of an ego which, "as absolute, . . . does not live, and as alive, . . . is not absolute"?[9]

Now these are fascinating questions, all right, but only when the focus is more on being absolute than on being alive. The fact is, when the ego's attention shifts to its existential itinerary, these questions are left behind. As reflexively recovered ego, then, we might say that Earle speaks on occasion somewhat "abstractly" himself. Even if it is true *that* an autobiographical consciousness is "at one and the same time transcendental and existential," this is evidently not true *for* it. We should therefore not be surprised that when this consciousness begins to monitor its own choices, we start to hear another voice—more interesting for my present purposes, less transcendental, no longer pure maverick, suspicious of objectivity—in a word, a voice urging us to "See *what* I've chosen" rather than "See what *I've* chosen."

What, then, does Earle tell us about the life that is subjectively worth living when he begins to describe what pleases him? Take, for example, his discussion of artistic intuition in *Public Sorrows and Private Pleasures*. The first thing to notice is that artistic intuition itself, as a topic, is more strongly present in the discussion than its investigator. Such intuition has frequently been thought unilluminating, even "blind," says Earle; but that is only because it has traditionally been measured by "fundamentally abstract minds confronting the dismayingly concrete and singular." Judged on its merits, artistic intuition has an unsurpassable power to "show" us how it actually is with

> man, his language, his ethical and political concerns, his birth and death. . . . The curtain goes up, and we are invited to a spectacle not of Being, Man, Nature, and whatnot, but what all these concretely culminate in, individuals in action.

Artistic intuition has direct access to precisely that stratum of experiencing from which traditional philosophy continually flees and about which it is thereafter haunted (as evidenced by its unending quest for the "grounds" of its first principles). Perhaps it is true, Earle concedes, that philosophy's ultimate aim has always been "to see what *is* from a transcendental standpoint, but that means *seeing*, and for that purpose I believe the arts win the day."[10]

This is thin summary of Earle's richer descriptions; but it should already be evident that while they are of course products of reflection, they carry no special stamp of legitimacy from any prior recovery of absolute solitude. Artistic intuition is presented not as something chosen and autobiographically agreeable, but straightforwardly as something human to be given its due in accordance with its own character. If there is anything "singular" about Earle's analysis, it lies in his eagerness to "own up" to the fact that what he says runs counter to a good deal of previous talk about artistic intuition. However, the justification for this contrariness is traced to the conditions under which the phenomenon is currently experienced, not to one ego's transcendental predilections: something is going to remain powerless to fulfill its vital promise unless someone brings it out from under traditional misinterpretations. Without preliminary transcendental fanfare and without stressing the pleasure it may afford him privately, Earle proceeds directly to a currently elusive element in human life which he seems clearly to recognize as both significant in its own right and of interest to others who inherit the same tradition as he does.

My point, then, is that some of Earle's "choices" deserve to be taken more seriously than any radically free and ontologically solitary consciousness can. "He" may indeed experience originally and unrepeatably the way certain Western forms of rationality misunderstand artistic intuition and obscure their own foundations in the process. The uniqueness of his experience may even have something to do with his being a good phenomenologist here in the first place. But "we" whose struggles to be ourselves emerge from an historical situation we share with him are already closer to his thoughts and recommendations than any transcendental ego in its full self-presence could ever choose to be.

This same point can be made from another direction, by considering further what Earle says about philosophy proper. As above, traditional philosophy usually comes off badly. Given its origins in Greek rationalism,

> there has always been a degenerative tendency in philosophy to ape the mathematical or natural sciences. In its preoccupation with the universal, it begins to take on the character of a system of logic or mathematics, and thereby turns the singular, existent, and historical into the illustrative; in its preoccupation with the objective, the not-me, it looks like some generalized natural science. . . . The net result is that each ego, as it is for itself first-personally, becomes invisible to philosophy.[11]

So it is that when, as here, "philosophy" is being transcendentally evaluated, the discussion soon reverses its direction in order to recover and praise precisely what was previously invisible or merely illustrative. But sometimes traditional philosophy receives better treatment. In one place, it is even defended as a repository of wisdom against the logical "analyses" of contemporary Technical Philosophers who see only muddled doctrines and therefore fail to understand how, more basically, "philosophizing implies as its necessary precondition, as well as its aim, an alteration of *attitude* toward life."[12]

We should pause here to ask, specifically, what "alteration of attitude" does Earle have in mind? Surely he is right that, at this late date, we know too much about classical "rationality" and its treatment of "life" to generate much enthusiasm for turning the soul around. Yet why revert to ontological autobiography instead? In "some dreams," first published a quarter-century ago, Earle tells us how he envisages the rise of a genuinely human culture (in something like the Hegelian sense) which would really "attempt to make *sense* out of its concrete historical life, a sense that is lucid, ultimate, and expressed." In such a culture, he says, philosophy would once again have the job of seeking to "clarify" a new "living substance" of the human spirit. But at this point, he claims,

> we must stop; for it is precisely the *content* of this new substance that cannot be anticipated. It is exactly this future sense of reality that must be created, and created from deeper

dimensions of the spirit than the current professionalized activities now envisage.[13]

For my part, however, I do not think it is necessary to stop here; nor do I think Earle himself always does so. Certainly he is right to say that the living substance of the human spirit cannot be "anticipated"—say, by experimental science, or by Nietzsche's superhistorian, or even by a transcendentally recovered ego. But to say further that this living substance must be "created" is overstated and misleading. That substance, and the "future sense of reality" which it carries, is always in an extremely important sense *already here*— though not, of course, "clearly and ultimately expressed." Currently, it is "in," among other things, the responses of Earle's fallen absolute to the "concrete historical life" it experiences and is angry, or bitter, or pleased enough to tell us about. And clearly, these reports are recommendatory. Like those of any original mind, they struggle to reveal to the rest of us what is already possible and subjectively promising that we do not yet see ourselves.

Perhaps it is true that a transcendentally recovered ego must in principle hold back from such recommendations. But it seems to me that in his less transcendentally and more passionately phenomenological mood (= attitude), Earle's philosophical vision—like the artistic intuition he praises—has allowed him, in his works of words, to accomplish a little "showing" of his own. Why should one not defend such philosophical seeing?

Earle himself, of course, is worried that such talk leads straight back to metaphysical and moral essentialism. But in this, it seems to me, he underestimates the effect a turn toward existence has upon his own standpoint. An ego divested of everything except its own self-presence and poised on the brink of choice may very well understand the living future as what has not yet been created. But an ego now monitoring its existential involvements is in a very different position. It is already straddling past and future in reporting on its present struggles to do something "substantial" in an inhospitable atmosphere. This, I think, is what Earle's recommendations can teach us. If they only summarized, in doctrine-like fashion, *what* he recommends, then he would be right in urging us to regard them as merely "clarifying alternatives." But his recommendations do not do this. Instead, in reporting his struggles as well as his results, they tell us *how to get to* what he wants to show us. They teach us that the genuinely "substantial" and individualizing is precisely not yet obvious and therefore not easily "chosen," because in various ways we all have "older" tendencies which obscure, distort, or otherwise divert us from it.[14] The lesson, of course, is that the only way to "follow" Earle's recommendations is to relive his struggles (and those of other contemporary seers who strike responsive chords), each for "oneself."

Hence, the forced option between the merely rational intersubjectivity of traditional *Bewusstseins überhaupt* and the absolutely solitary subjectivity of the maverick's autobiographical consciousness is avoidable—provided we neither forget the "concrete historical life" we already share and so fall back into the old assumption that only the objectively known is sharable, nor follow *Public Sorrows and Private Pleasures* to its bitter end and first try to "divest" ourselves of everything.

How deeply promising Earle's attitude of philosophical seeing is may also be represented a bit more dramatically by contrasting it with the most extreme cases where a recovered transcendental ego overshadows what it discusses, namely, the sorrowful reports on radicalism, pacifism, and civil disobedience. The essay on pacifism, for example, though allegedly occasioned by the Vietnam war, turns out to be a condemnation of the "principled opposition to all war." It thereby ignores entirely the problem of "selective" refusals to fight which was precisely the discomforting new essential for pacifism in its most recent dress. Earle is here so bitterly self-possessed, so sure of the right choices, that he cannot "see" to "show" us anything about what is, after all, something undigested and discomforting about our situation, too. We will have to look elsewhere to discover if the struggles of those troubled children, whose parents' model of battle is World War II, have anything to "recommend" about what those now self-evident (objective?) truths we "already have" about war might still (subjectively) mean.[15]

Thus, too, what is supposed to be a dialectical critique of "radical madness" in principle, is pursued by an author "who is not in the least a friend of the Movement or of radical ideas" and who attacks primarily "hysterically alienated moralists" themselves. Not surprisingly for an author so offended, there is finally nothing left but "the somewhat sour pleasure of a minor alienation . . . from those who have alienated themselves." Especially when political phenomena are at stake, too many choices have already been made by too solitary a self.[16]

However, this is emphatically not the proper note on which to end. If Earle's transcendentalism sometimes serves him badly, and sometimes even allows him the luxury of a moralistic refusal to struggle with human things themselves, that should only help us appreciate how easy it is to turn a fragile but infinitely more promising activity I have been calling here "recommendatory seeing" into its opposite. It has been during episodes of such seeing, both in Earle's writings and in his classes, that I have been most deeply affected.

Some readers may be ready to accuse me of trying to drag a reluctant transcendental thinker closer to other contemporaries who might recognize something of their own "hermeneutical" reflection in his recommendatory seeing. I plead guilty. I favor those moods when Earle's transcendental ego is subdued enough to allow his existential choices to speak for themselves; then, I think, one finds a "situated" consciousness which is just as centrally concerned with the interpretive enactment of vital but now still hidden possibilities as any of that broad range of recent thinkers which includes not only those influenced by Heidegger and Gadamer but certain neo-Marxists and critical theorists as well. However, this suggestion should be kept a secret, lest it arouse the pure maverick; and it is in any case really quite misleading. For to this erstwhile student, at least, the special attraction of William Earle's original philosophizing lies in the fact that, through it, one repeatedly encounters someone who does indeed belong in the company of these other thinkers—but keeps refusing to believe it.

ROBERT C. SCHARFF: THE NOT-SO-PRIVATE PLEASURES OF WILLIAM EARLE

1. *The Autobiographical Consciousness* (Chicago: Quadrangle Books, 1972), p. 65. Hereafter, *AC*.

2. *AC*, p. 74.

3. *Public Sorrows and Private Pleasures* (Bloomington: Indiana University Press, 1976), p. 165. Hereafter, *PS*.

4. *PS*, 174.

5. *PS*, p. 159. Cf., "The Phenomenology of Mysticism," *The Monist*, 59(1976), 526, where transcendentally considered freedom helps illuminate the ego in its "identity with Absolute Reality."

6. *PS*, pp. 165–166. Cf., "Preface" to *AC*, p. xi, where various existential phenomena which are "inaccessible to any objective mode of thought" but which become transparent in their transcendental significance "through a conscious adoption [=chosen] of the fully subjective point of view [=opposing objectivity]" are announced as topics for the latter two-thirds of the book.

7. *PS*, p. 77. See also, pp. vii, 117–118.

8. *PS*, p. 168.

9. *AC*, pp. 68ff.; also *PS*, pp. 169ff.

10. *PS*, pp. 137–138.

11. *AC*, p. 33. Socrates alone is exempted here, as the one for whom "wisdom" was precisely not objective knowledge but knowledge of "self." *PS*, pp. 120–121, 162–165.

12. *PS*, pp. 85f. The fact that "for the longest stretch of its history, philosophy was, embarrassing as it is to Technical Philosophy, concerned precisely with large visions and the edifying," is elsewhere linked to the observation that " 'truth' comes from 'troth,' which means loyalty and not propositional correctness." Its opposite is therefore an existential state (e.g., disloyalty, cheating, lying) not intellectual error. (Cf. pp. 104–105.)

13. *PS*, pp. 94–95, as part of an article published originally in *Noonday*, I(1958), pp. 24–26, and reprinted (where I first found it) in *Identity and Anxiety: Survival of the Person in Mass Society*, ed. by Maurice R. Stein, et al. (Glencoe: Free Press, 1960), pp. 382–383.

14. This is demonstrated repeatedly, I think, in "what" Earle "chooses" to stress, e.g., in general, anything that modern science cannot see (*AC*, pp. 83ff.), the particular strangeness for our age of any suggestion that the self can directly experience its immortality (the writings on mysticism), the surrealists' fondness for artistically dismantling whatever is usually taken seriously as real or moral (*PS*, pp. 142ff.), and the degree to which being moral has nothing to do with following rules (*AC*, pp. 184ff.).

15. *PS*, pp. 52–73; esp. pp. 53, 68, 71.

16. *PS*, pp. 3–29; esp. pp. 27–29.

II

Philosophical Vision, the Transcendental, and the Mystical

On Clarity, Integrity, and Philosophical Vision

PHILIP GRIER

In his recently published work *Mystical Reason* William Earle has provided us with an adventurous inquiry into territory where reason might be supposed at first glance an incompetent guide—namely mysticism.[1] He has attempted to show that the central intuitions which provide the content of rationalist metaphysics may be interpreted as identical with the essential content of the mystic's religious vision. Far from appearing strange, however, the features of this territory to which Earle initially directs our attention are as familiar as the central claims of seventeenth century metaphysics, here distilled in an extraordinarily lucid, economical way and presented as an outcome of phenomenological reflection.

The inquiry which Earle undertakes requires the investigation of two seemingly distinct claims of vision. Most obviously, there is the claim of a certain kind of "vision" by the mystic, of the presence of the divine, or of union with God. As Earle points out, the experience of the mystic "may acquire the barnacles of imagination and desire and deteriorate into rank superstition"; however, its central claim of an immediate apprehension of absolute reality, if credited, could not be an affair of the imagination, since absolute reality is not a possible object of imagination (pp. 27–28). It remains to be seen if the "vision" of the mystic may be comprehended in terms of another kind of vision, which we might call, perhaps archaically, philosophical vision.

The notion of "philosophical vision" as a special kind of "seeing" has persisted in the Western philosophical tradition since Plato made use of a "spectator" model to describe our knowledge of the Forms. Of course Plato also made use of the discursive model of dialectic to represent the nature of our knowledge of the Forms, and the two models of knowing seem incompatible in some respects. (Moreover, as Henry Teloh has recently argued, these two models of knowledge presuppose mutually inconsistent conceptions of the Forms, and it is not clear that Plato ever repudiated the spectator model or fully realized the differing implications of it and the discursive model).[2] The spectator model and its influence upon the subsequent development of Western philosophy have of course received much critical discussion recently along the lines suggested by Michael Oakeshott and Richard Rorty.[3] Whether or not one is inclined to count the influence of Plato's spectator model of knowledge as one of the Great Mistakes in the subsequent history of philosophy, it is clear that Plato's model is by no means the only conception one might designate by the phrase "philosophical vision." An alternative, and much more apposite conception has recently been explored in Quentin Lauer's work *Hegel's Concept of God*.[4] Lauer there discusses Hegel's conception of "speculative reason" in its connection with dialectical thinking, implying that the issue needn't be framed as *either* the spectator model *or* the discursive model of knowledge, but rather that there is a special kind of (philosophical) "seeing" in thought (*speculare*) the God or objectivity who is there present, which is not to be confused with framing thought *about* the God who is only *represented* by these thoughts.[5] In any event, whatever else one may understand by the notion of philosophical vision, Professor Earle is well able to give a clear account of his preferred term—"intuitive reason"—and he does so in phenomenological terms.

Phenomenological reflection, according to Earle, is "an open reflection upon consciousness and what consciousness is conscious of, the *ego-cogito-cogitatum*." What shows itself to such reflection is not only objectivities in their "world" but correlatively, my consciousness of those things. The phenomenon thus apprehended in its entirety consists of both object and subject, "and the point of view from which this whole phenomenological field is visible is that of radical reflection." (p. 3)

The "intuiting" in question is of course not a matter of simply "opening the mind's eye and taking in something which discloses itself completely at a glance," as Professor Earle remarks. It is rather a hoped-for achievement, a result of "intentional analysis", or as he also terms it, "dialectical phenomenology." The inquiry which seeks as an outcome the clear intuition of determinate essences or objectivities must commence in the "pre-theoretical" realm of vague or confused meanings, there selecting a meaning which may become, if the analysis succeeds, a determinate structure all of whose discriminable parts can be grasped as bound together in a dialectical whole in which the parts are what they are only in relation to the whole, and the whole is thinkable only in terms of the unity of those parts, and in which the whole moreover constitutes a self-supporting objectivity dependent on nothing else for its determinate being save its necessary implication in the structure of the *ego-cogito-cogitatum*.

The only appropriate mark of success in this matter of achieving an intuition of some determinate essence is of course the clarity of that intuited essence itself. Earle invokes Spinoza's dictum that an adequate or true idea is the measure of both itself as adequate and of the false, as the only possible criterion of truth in this endeavor.

Mystical Reason is thus, among other things, a carefully argued essay on the nature of philosophical intuition, on the clarity which is the mark of success in such intuiting, and is itself an extraordinarily lucid model of dialectical inquiry culminating in such intuition.

ABSOLUTE REALITY AND ABSOLUTE MIND

In this and the following section I will attempt to summarize part of the argument of *Mystical Reason*. To the extent I succeed, of course, the thought is not mine but Professor Earle's. In the final section I attempt to expand one aspect of the argument which he has supplied.

The notion of reason as intuitive is grounded by, and in a sense also revealed in, the ontological argument. That "argument," being neither discursive nor inferential in form, according to Earle, serves in effect to *identify* an intuition. "In any version, the argument, to whatever extent it is an argument, merely denies an absurdity: that my idea of an infinite being is not true of that being, that is, is indeed not an idea of it, but of something else." (p. 23) The possibility of this intuition, that is to say, the fact that the idea of infinite being is innate to rational consciousness, "is constitutive of reason's very essence. The essence of reason implicates perfect being as its intentional object. The essentiality of this relation makes rational intuition possible." (p. 24) The first "objectivity" identified in radical reflection thus provides a grounding for this enterprise of reasoning, and at once invites further inquiry into the nature of the subject for which this previously intuited object, infinite being, could be objective.

Descartes' *Meditations* supplies perhaps the most appropriate guide to reflection on the problem of this subject in the form of his *cogito*. Like the ontological argument, the *cogito* does not confront us with an inferential structure of reasoning, rather directs our attention by clearing away distractions and apparent obstacles which might hinder our grasp of a truth which, once seen, is seen to be undeniable: that the subject for which infinite being can be objective is myself as thinking thing, an ego which is distinguishable and hence distinct from any of its own acts of thought, as well as from any world which is presented to itself in those acts of thought, and hence transcendent to any such world.

This transcendental ego may be said to be identical with itself; in that case, however, Professor Earle observes,

> The term *identity*, then, has a strictly negative force, denying difference of any sort whatsoever within the transcendental ego. The ego, then, is internally reflexive, and its so-called relation to itself is nothing but an expression of the fact that the self in question exists wholly on the level of consciousness or awareness or knowledge; therefore it is not exclusively knowledge of something else but inherently *self*-consciousness. Its being is its awareness, and that is what a self is. (pp. 46–47)

Such a self does not of course have a *concept* of itself, if by "concept" we mean anything like what Kant meant. Such a knowledge of self would be conceptual rather than intuitive and immediate. The self's awareness of itself is not in terms of any universal, but is a direct and immediate apprehension of itself as actuality. "Indeed, in and of itself, each I is pure actuality." (p. 51)

It is participatory knowledge of one's own self as a singular actuality, a knowledge which is clear and distinct as Descartes argued, which serves to give sense to the attribution of existence to any object whatever in a world other than myself. ("The sober truth is that I *am* is inherently and absolutely clear to the I which meditates or reflexively grasps itself, whereas the existence of nothing objective whatsoever has any but a derived, provisional, and, at bottom, unintelligible sense. This reversal of the standard of clarity and intelligibility occurs analogously in every thorough metaphysical system.") (p. 53) Thus, as Earle remarks, "the transcendental ego is not merely intelligible to itself but . . . it is the radical source of intelligibility of whatever presents itself to it as objective." (p. 59)

A central fact about much of that which presents itself to the transcendental ego as objective is its ordering as a "world." "World" may have a number of senses in this context, but one of the most important would be the "human world," a world which is the correlate not simply of reason, but of "our hopes, ambitions, actions and defeats, our parents, lovers, friends, and enemies." (p. 63) "The human world disclosed to action and perception, the world within which such activities take place and which they presuppose, is then an objective correlate of the embodied transcendental ego, the ego insofar as it animates its own living body." (p. 63)

The argument thus far summarized has explored the two poles of absolute object and absolute subject, God and the transcendental ego, as grasped by rational intuition, phenomenological reflection, or (more quaintly) philosophical vision. The outcome of these reflections has been readily recognizable to students of Descartes, Spinoza, or Husserl. Professor Earle has directed our attention to certain inescapable truths which express the content of the intuition of infinite being as absolute object, which is absolute other for the transcendental ego or absolute subject. The capstone of his argument occurs in the form of one further intuition concerning the relation of absolute object and absolute subject, or of God and transcendental ego. It is this step which realizes the central thesis of the work concerning the identity of the core of mystic vision and rational intuition, namely the intuition that the inner being of the transcendental self is one and the same as God, that the transcendental ego is God thinking Himself, the self-awareness of absolute reality. (p. 71) The central burden of this intuition consists of a denial of the claim that God as absolute other for the transcendental ego could be *unqualifiably* other. God as absolute object cannot be unqualifiably objective in the sense of having no connection to absolute subject. " 'Objective' must imply objective-to, or, if taken as 'independent,' then independent of; . . . Both phrases explicitly relate that absolute reality to something else, namely ourselves, by way of declaring that reality to be objective to us, or independent of us." (p. 70) Earle elaborates this claim in a helpful way by reference to Rudolf Otto's *Idea of the Holy*, in which Otto provides a thorough phenomenological exploration of the encounter with God as *absolutely other*. Undoubtedly the experience of the *mysterium tremendum* makes sense only on the supposition that the occasion of the experience is the recognition of God's absolute otherness. But, Earle observes,

> If there is shuddering and awe before the *mysterium tremendum*, that shuddering and awe draw their sense from the transcendental ego, as their intentional source. And so the transcendental ego does know that before which it lays down its finite conceptual tools. It knows it sufficiently well to know that its finite tools are wholly inapplicable. But then its whole resources are hardly exhausted by finite concepts and representations. If they were, there would be no shuddering and awe, no capitulation before the absolute, no insistence upon learned ignorance. In fact there would be no problem for it at all; its problems would be strictly practical or finite, and running along its merry way, it would never find—in the indefinite series of events and things—anything whatsoever to give it pause, except those finite problems which envisage nothing but finite solutions, whether yet found or not. In a

word, the absolute diremption between the transcendental ego
and God cannot, in the last analysis, be absolute; for if it
were it could never be known, felt or even retain the slightest
sense. (p. 69)

Thus what was intuited as absolute reality, absolute object, must
"be intuited as for itself, and not as it is for us exclusively, or even
in part." (p. 71) That which is absolutely for-itself must then be the
transcendental ego itself as it is for itself. "Does it not immediately
follow that the transcendental ego is God thinking Himself, the self-
awareness of absolute reality?" (p. 71) Earle reminds us of Spinoza's
claim that our idea of God is identical with God's idea of Himself,
and of Meister Eckhardt's claim that "I am God." That there is a
sense in which each of these claims can be accepted literally; that
the two claims can be seen at bottom to be identical; and that reason
as intuitive is therefore also mystical—these are the central conclusions of Earle's argument concerning absolute object and absolute
subject, his radical reflection on the intersection of the ontological
argument and Descartes' *cogito ergo sum*.

The Transcendental Ego and the Ethical

In the discussion which follows this culminating insight into the
identity of the transcendental ego and absolute being *thinking* Earle
turns to an exploration of some consequences of this insight for three
areas of experience: the ethical, the aesthetic, and the logical. Each
of these explorations begins with the recognition that the transcendental ego is not simply identical with the absolute and hence eternal,
but as eternal actuality also lives "while it does so" *temporally*, that
is, *situated* in a world. The transcendental ego as eternal actuality,
or eternal act, appears in the world as a striving to enact itself, hence
a striving for the excellence of the divine, a realization of the Good,
the Beautiful, and the True.

In a criticism of most of the familiar philosophical efforts to ground
the demands of the ethical, or to give an account of the constitution
of the good by referring it to facts about human nature comprehended
naturalistically, or to a faculty of reason understood not to be intuitive
but merely instrumental, Earle argues that the true constitution of
the ethical can only be understood by reference to the human
conceived as an identity of transcendental ego with God, or rather
with God's consciousness of Himself.

The transcendental ego as *situated*, that is as a person participating
in a social world or a particular human community finds the sense
of that life *already constituted as ethical*. The content of what is

morally demanded may vary in some respects from community to community, but what does not vary in the case of what is genuinely required as ethical is the fact that the individual is not the author of that requirement; rather, what is morally required is present as constituitive of the human world, and the refusal by the individual to respect it brings about the destruction of that world, a moral chaos. (p. 80)

Earle's account of the origin of the ethical rejects all of the usual philosophical accounts of the grounding of the ethical either naturalistic or rationalistic, and instead invokes the idea of the transcendental freedom of the ego as the only possible means of discovering an adequate solution to this problem.

> . . . the transcendental ego is transcendentally free to act as it wills; it is, as Descartes shows, absolutely free, and in this respect shares the absolute freedom of God. For Descartes, our will is as free as the will of God, although obviously the range of its possible effectivity is limited to its body and the world interpreted by it. It is therefore a situated absolute. And so there always remains within the transcendental ego the possibility of affirming or consenting to its effectivity or life in the world, or withholding it altogether. Of course these are extreme boundaries, but nevertheless that infinite freedom of the transcendental ego can never be wholly ignored; there are indeed occasions when it is exercised, as in absolute Zen withdrawal—absolute indifference to the choice of either life or death—or in suicide, or cases of final pathological withdrawal, and pessimism. (p. 87)

It is usually the case when moral philosophers attempt to supply some account of the constitution of the ethical, of the non-optional character of moral requirements, that the account aims at some answer to the question 'Why be moral?' such that moral demands are seen to be inescapable in some sense, even when transgressed. Earle argues that, at a level more fundamental than is usually considered, the origin of the ethical must be discovered not in a condition of "inescapability," but rather in the free choice of the transcendental ego to submit itself to the horizon of moral right and wrong, of moral good and evil. Moreover, as he argues, it would be "a bad mistake to think of these ultimate choices as within the compass of ethical theory. The choice is not of a higher good, but of abandoning the horizon of good and evil altogether, . . ." (p. 88)

Assuming this is so, the question naturally arises, why should the transcendental ego in its inherent freedom will to submit itself to the category of the moral? Earle argues that only a single answer is possible at this level of inquiry: "the intentionality which is the origin of morality, then, is nothing other than the choice to worship God, not in his absolute being as such, but as manifest most explicitly in the living human person wherever that can be recognized. It is therefore the choice of the holy to love itself . . ." (p. 91) This follows from the intuition of identity of the transcendental ego with the consciousness of God of Himself, "in a word, that man is God, or more accurately, God in a living situation, but God, nonetheless." (p. 90) The sacredness and dignity of the person are thus not merely postulates as with Kant, but self-evident in the intuition of reason which Earle has articulated.

ON MORAL INTEGRITY[6]

These conclusions which Professor Earle has presented concerning the ultimate ground of morality in the intention of the transcendental ego to submit itself to the moral, an act which must itself be conceived as transcendent to the moral, provide the possibility for a brief reflection on the subject of moral integrity, a footnote merely, to what Earle has himself provided.

Earle's thesis that the transcendental ego, in choosing to submit itself to the horizon of the ethical, exercises its infinite freedom leads to an interesting series of contrasts with more familiar views of the relation between personhood and moral obligation.

For example, Thomas Nagel in his work *The Possibility of Altruism* draws a parallel between his own view and that of Kant regarding the "inescapability" of those moral requirements which are grounded in the agent's metaphysical conception of himself.[7] Says Nagel,

> On Kant's view the conception is that of freedom, whereas on my view it is the conception of oneself as merely a person among others equally real. However, different as they are, both are thought to be conceptions which we cannot escape, and are thought to provide that basis for ethical motivation which in other internalist theories is provided by various motives and desires. Because of the alleged inescapability of these [metaphysical] conceptions [of the self], a view of the Kantian type entails that we are not fully free to be amoral, or insusceptible to moral claims. That is what makes us men. (p. 14)

Earle has of course provided an account of the ethical in terms of which its demands upon the moral agent are treated as non-voluntary (surely a defining characteristic of the ethical). However, in Earle's conception of the moral agent as transcendental ego situated in a world, a dimension of freedom arises which transcends "the horizon of the ethical" but is nevertheless involved in the constitution of the moral agent. In the light of this conception of the moral subject as situated transcendental ego, some interesting reflections on the notion of moral integrity present themselves.

The notion of moral integrity does not figure prominently among the topics treated in the standard texts on ethical theory, nor does the subject arise under that name very conspicuously in the history of ethics in Western philosophy. This fact should occasion surprise when we consider that in forming an impression of someone's moral character, or in conveying such an impression to another, we are more apt to think and speak in terms of that person's *integrity* than perhaps of any other moral quality. Does the absence of such a term in the usual vocabulary of technical moral philosophy indicate that the notion of 'integrity' plays no fundamental theoretical role in our conception of moral conduct, or that 'moral integrity' is only a summary way of collecting a number of more specific moral predicates applicable to a person? I suspect the answer to both these questions is "no," and that some notion of moral integrity is quite fundamental among the presuppositions of moral conduct.

As a first step in elucidating the notion of moral integrity, there is a connection to be explored between moral integrity and personal identity. Some continuity of personal identity would seem to be a condition of anything we might wish to describe as moral integrity. For example, if one considers the institution of promising it is obvious that the institution presupposes a certain self-identity of the persons involved. Promising as an institution requires that the person who makes a promise at one point in time (that is, obligates himself to someone to undertake some future performance) admit to being the self-same person who made that promise when the time for fulfillment arrives, if not in all respects, at least in respect of the moral agency involved in the promise. We may recognize that changes of morally relevant circumstances might conceivably be such as to afford an excuse from the performance when the time arrives. But we would not normally consider an appropriate excuse the claim that "I'm just not the same moral agent who made that promise to you last month." It seems doubtful that any story could be supplied adequate to make this last claim (as opposed to a claim about changed circumstances) a morally acceptable excuse. A story concerning the psychopathology of an apparent breakdown of personal identity on some empirical, psychological level, or of a radical shift of personality might force us to abandon the moral claims derived from the original promise. But in such a case we would be inclined to say, more precisely, not that an acceptable moral excuse had been supplied, but rather that moral discourse had been rendered irrelevant by the breakdown of personal identity. The integrity presupposed in moral conduct clearly involves some continuity of personal identity on a psychological level, but is not identical with that personal identity.

But what is the relation between the moral integrity presupposed in moral conduct and personal identity on the psychological level? For example, from the fact that the notion of moral conduct pre-supposes some notion of moral integrity (or sameness of identity as a moral agent over time) does it then follow that among our moral obligations there is a fundamental obligation to remain the same person (moral agent) over time? In addition to being morally obligated to perform promises made, for example, am I also morally obligated to remain the person who made that promise? (As odd as this last formulation may sound, perhaps it is worth some thought in a society where one can find earnest recommendations in numerous monthly magazines on how to acquire a new, more successful, more alluring, or more aggressive self; how to keep up with the latest trends in selfhood; or, more simply, just how to be more self-centered!) The second "obligation" is surely specious; I am in fact always free from a moral point of view to change a great deal about myself in the interim—my likes, my loves, my projects, my sense of life; what I am not morally free to do is to unilaterally dispense with the undertaking I gave you. Thus it remains appropriate to speak of moral obligations to performances, but not of moral obligations to remain the same person. Personal identity and moral integrity cannot be co-terminous. Personal identity may be conceived as a necessary, but not sufficient condition of integrity in the moral sense.

As illustrated in the promising case the conceptual connection between moral integrity and personal identity is such that a failure of personal identity would obviate otherwise valid moral claims. This might, under the stress of extreme circumstances, be treated as an escape hatch of last resort from an intolerable moral dilemma, and be involved in the etiology of a psychological breakdown. However, under normal circumstances most of us would not be so crass as to boldly declare, at the opportune moment, non-identity with the moral subject (by all criteria of personal identity ourself) who sometime earlier issued the promise fulfillment of which is now due.

There is however a much more subtle variant of this move which one does encounter as a phenomenon of moral life, for example in the offices of bureaucrats or other persons charged with managerial responsibilities which threaten to outrun their moral resources. And the exploration of this example brings us closer to being able to explicate what we mean by 'moral integrity'.

In the everyday exchanges of views, requests, predictions, orders, commentaries, etc., which mark discussions between persons negotiating some common enterprise, there is a phenomenon which falls considerably short of the formal institution of promise-making, but which is nevertheless very much a part of our ordinary moral relations with each other. In the context of any face-to-face discussion one not only exchanges explicitly-labelled promises, orders, requests, etc., which might be recorded by a stenographer present. One also *intimates* a great deal by implication, by nuance, by facial expression, etc., much of which may amount to a minature self-portrait at that moment and under those circumstances. Such mini self-portraits might emerge in considerable detail without the speaker ever having to commit himself in forms of words which could be explicitly labelled as promises, orders, or the like. Nevertheless the speaker in effect would be sketching a persona for himself with respect to the issues under discussion which the hearer might then properly conclude he could depend upon with respect to the disposition of those issues in the future.

When that future arrives, the speaker may act in a way which disconcerts the hearer, seeming to repudiate the persona intimated in the original encounter and confounding the hearer's expectations derived from that persona. Setting aside the case of a genuine misunderstanding as morally uninteresting, we are left with two possibilities. When confronted by the hearer with the apparent discontinuity of attitude, or persona, the original speaker may point to what he claims are circumstances now sufficiently changed to justify a basically different approach to the matter. Or, more interestingly, the original speaker, relying on the oblique manner in which the original persona was intimated and the difficulty of quoting any very incriminating phrases from the first encounter, may with a cool demeanor repudiate any implication that a shift of persona has taken place, thereby implicitly denying that any legitimate moral expectations have been thwarted or that any exercise of excuse making would be appropriate.

One suspects that quite often essentially the same situation could be handled with either response. The simpler, more honest (naive!) response would be to tacitly confess one's change of persona by attempting to raise excuses (pointing to changed morally relevant circumstances). Ths response has the disadvantage of tacitly acknowledging the apparant shift of persona and opens one to charges of lack of moral integrity which may have to be answered. The more skilled (cynical) operator might handle the situation by relentlessly ignoring the hearer's surprise and making no effort to excuse himself, for the ostensibly decisive reason that no legitimate expectations previously licensed by him have been disappointed. Skillfully used under the right circumstances this maneuver can sow doubt, confusion, and a fatal hesitation in the victim at the crucial moment, thus freeing the manager for the continued pursuit of Larger Concerns unharrassed by the petty moralistic peckings of supplicants and subordinates.

Moral ambiguity such as this is perhaps inevitable in the managerial context; the example becomes more useful when generalized beyond the context of institutional roles and offices. The analogous phenomenon may arise in an indefinitely large number of informal contexts such as friendship, love, acquaintance, family relations, and so forth. Each of us in any of these contexts, without engaging in the sorts of pronouncements which might be interpreted as explicit acts of promising, in effect gives himself out to be a certain sort of person, that is, exhibits a persona to other persons which may give rise to certain expectations. These expectations may range from nothing more important than that we will normally strive to be amusing or in good spirits, to expectations about how we would respond under special circumstances of need to requests for assistance, support (moral or financial), honesty, and so forth. More realistically, each of us probably has more than one such persona—each, however, subtly distinct from the others—which we tend to exhibit consistently for particular sets of friends or aquaintances.

In these terms the problem of moral integrity can now be viewed, at least in part, as that of being sufficiently self-conscious about the variety of personae one exhibits in relations with others for there to be an aspect of the self which transcends the variety of personae, or perhaps runs through all of them in such a way as to provide for a constant readiness to recognize and acknowledge whatever moral claims may be apposite, and to respond to them appropriately. This is not to say that the choice to "lose oneself" for the moment in an identity with one persona to the exclusion of the others in a sense of play, irony, or whatever other motive must always be treated as a compromise of one's moral integrity. Obviously no such rules or allowances could be codified save at the cost of making us all stupifyingly dullwitted, or at least ridiculous. Rather, in this light, it appears that moral integrity should be conceived as a project, as a thing to be achieved amidst the play and interplay of personae which is one of the most important richnesses of human experience. When gracefully achieved, the project of moral integrity should prove compatible with this highest exercise of the dramatic art which is being a person, and not a constraint which closes the theatre!

So conceived the project of moral integrity amounts to the project of achieving a certain understanding of our selves as moral subjects or moral agents which is compatible with the complex situation of multiple personae, change of personae over time, as well as the more often noted problem of conflicting desires and inclinations to which we are subject under the constantly shifting circumstances of experience. The achievement of integrity must not threaten to obliterate the complexity of the self or of its experience, nor deny the sheer contingency of circumstances under which moral action must take place. Such an understanding of ourselves as moral subjects can reach its fullest development only when linked with a conception of its possibility or its ground such as that provided by Earle in his sketch of the transcendental ego situated in a human world, or such as the more familiar one presented by Kant.

Moral integrity, as a presupposition of moral conduct, does not then refer to sameness of person in the sense of personality, nor does it make sense to speak of moral obligations to remain the same person in this sense. Moral integrity refers to a more abstract and therefore partial feature of personhood, just that feature of personhood in respect of which I am capable of moral agency, capable of being "counted on" to conduct myself in relations with others in ways which reflect recognition of moral relations as well as relations of desire, competition, companionship, or whatever, and recognize as well that the order of moral relations may not always be entirely consonant with, nor subservient to, the other orders of inclination or desire. The feature of personhood in question would appear to be necessarily grounded in a metaphysical conception of myself, a conception which one might achieve with clarity, achieve only dimly, or fail to achieve at all. The Kantian conception of this feature of personhood, and that presented by Earle offer some interesting points of contrast and comparison.

Despite the obviously non-Kantian conception of the transcendental ego as a rationally intuitable reality, or absolute subject, it is interesting to note that Earle's conception of the self as transcendental ego when applied to his account of the ethical (at least as I have drawn it out here) does leave open the possibility of an account of moral agency similar to Kant's in one respect. In the Kantian conception the moral subject is the noumenal self which is free in the sense of being capable of being determined by the motive of duty for duty's sake and not merely determined heteronomously by inclination and desire as a creature only subordinate to the natural order. Similarly, in Earle's conception of the situated transcendental ego as moral subject, one conceives of the transcendental ego in itself as infinitely free (though precisely how one conceives of the passional nature of the situated transcendental ego is another question).

What clearly does not follow the lines of Kantian ethics in Earle's conception of the matter concerns the connection beween freedom and moral duty. In Kant's conception, the autonomy of the moral agent is viewed as a condition which makes it possible to act in accordance with the categorical imperative of practical reason, and precisely because that imperative is categorical, action in accord with it is morally necessary for the good will, that is, the will determined by respect for duty. As Nagel remarked in the quote given above, "a view of the Kantian type entails that we are not fully free to be amoral, or insusceptible to moral claims. That is what makes us men." In contrast, on Earle's view of the ethical implications of the freedom of transcendental ego, that freedom is precisely a freedom to submit or not submit to the horizon of the ethical. In choosing to submit to the horizon of the ethical, to live a life ordered among other things by its strictures, one exhibits that integrity in the absence of which the ethical cannot be achieved. And to be sure, that achievement is one of the more attractive features of what it is to be human. But does one then talk about an *obligation* to exhibit moral integrity? That merely involves us once again in the old conundrum about being morally obligated to be moral. On Earle's account of the motive for submitting to the ethical one sees the folly of trying to explain how it is rationally necessitated. Indeed, why not think of it as the choice of the Holy to love itself?

From this perspective one may assert more than a contingent connection between the achievement of philosophical clarity concerning the puzzles about the nature of the self, and the achievement of moral integrity. Moral integrity, as we have described it here, is among other things a special sort of exercise in self-consciousness, a consciousness of self as a morally responsible being possessed of an autonomy which transcends the merely causal order of events, and most fully actual when developed to the extent of a general conception of the possibility of such a dimension of the self. That possibility may be conceived as itself grounded in the more radical freedom of the transcendental ego as described in *Mystical Reason*.

In this connection I wish to pay tribute to the author of that work, William Earle, who seems to me an exemplar both of exceptional philosophical lucidity and of integrity as a colleague and friend, and whose lucidity and integrity have always seemed to me to be intrinsically linked as two facets of a single extraordinary person.

PHILIP GRIER: ON CLARITY, INTEGRITY AND PHILOSOPHICAL VISION

1. William Earle, *Mystical Reason* (Chicago: Regnery Gateway, Inc., 1980). Page references to this work will be given in parentheses in the text.

2. Henry Teloh, *The Development of Plato's Metaphysics* (University Park: The Pennsylvania State University Press, 1981). pp. 145–46.

3. Michael Oakeshott, "The Voice of Poetry in the Conversation of Mankind," in his *Rationalism and Politics* (New York, 1975); and Richard Rorty, *Philosophy and the Mirror of Nature* (Princeton: Princeton University Press, 1979).

4. Quentin Lauer, S.J., *Hegel's Concept of God* (Albany: SUNY Press, 1982), Chapter Two.

5. *Ibid.*, p. 58.

6. I wish to thank my colleague Professor Susan Feldman for her critical comments on this section. She helped me to clarify the argument in several respects.

7. Thomas Nagel, *The Possibility of Altruism* (Princeton: Princeton University Press, 1970). Cf. p. 14.

On the Possibility of
Transcendental Philosophy

J.N. MOHANTY

The best way to demonstrate the possibility of something is to show its actuality, for actuality implies possibility. At least since Kant, transcendental philosophies have been on the scene. However, such simple demonstration of the possibility of transcendental philosophy has not been effective and is not likely to be so—so strong is the presumption that transcendental philosophy just could not be possible, or if it *was* possible earlier it is not possible *now*. This last claim introduces a new point: namely, that certain types of thinking are just not possible today, either because they have been proved to be unworkable, invalid, false, misguided, or because the historical conditions of their possibility are no more there. I do not know of any such *proof* of the invalidity of transcendental philosophy. There is also no reason to begin by conceding the historicism that underlies the alternate claim that today such foundationalist thinking is not *possible* (or, is it meant 'not desirable'?)

In this essay I will consider some ways of showing that transcendental philosophy is possible. I will ask about its logical possibility, psychological possibility, subjective possibility and phenomenological possibility. Under the question of 'logical possibilty', I will take into account an argument by Donald Davidson which is taken to prove, by a sort of transcendental argument, the impossibility of transcendental philosophy.[1] By the question of 'psychological possibility' I mean the question about motivation: how is it possible for one, within the naive, natural attitude, to be motivated to take a 'transcendental turn'? Granted that logical impossibility is not demonstrated and that one can be motivated to take the turn, how can one have the proper *access* to the transcendental point of view? It is this question of access that I mean by 'subjective possibility'. Finally, is transcendental philosophy a matter of the right sort of *argument*, or is it possible, by the proper sort of *reflection*, to bring to intuitive evidence an entire domain of transcendental experience: this is what I want to discuss under the question of 'phenomenological possibilty'.

I. LOGICAL POSSIBILITY

If the transcendental philosopher wants to establish the necessary validity of our conceptual scheme (as against the skeptic), that enterprise presupposes that there are other alternative conceptual schemes, or at least that other conceptual schemes are conceivable. Now Davidson, as is well known, has argued that the very idea of alternate conceptual schemes is unintelligible. If Davidson's argument is valid, then he has succeeded in proving that the very idea of an alternate conceptual scheme makes no sense. If the idea of conceptual schemes alternate to ours makes no sense, it does not make any more sense to speak of a common conceptual scheme shared by all mankind. As a consequence, the very distinction between conceptual scheme and uninterpreted reality or data, must also be given up. To give up that distinction is to give up all transcendental arguments, and so all foundationalist transcendental philosophies. Consequently, Davidson may be looked upon as having given a transcendental argument to prove the pointlessness of all transcendental arguments. Let us see how that fateful demonstration proceeds.

Davidson distinguishes between two sorts of views (about many possible "worlds"). Some mean by "other possible worlds," what we would describe "by redistributing truth values over sentences in various systematic ways," which basically uses our present language and a fixed system of concepts. This is not what Davidson is out to criticize. He is concerned rather with those who envisage the possibility of describing one and the same world from "radically different" points of view (or, "conceptualize" one and the same "content" by "radically different" conceptual schemes). The contrast between these two views is thus succinctly put by Davidson: "Strawson's many imagined worlds are seen (or heard)—anyway described—from the same point of view; Kuhn's one world is seen from different points of view."[2] Davidson claims to prove that the second metaphor is unintelligible.

Underlying Davidson's critique are the following assumptions. It is assumed, first, that to speak of alternate conceptual schemes is to speak of *radically different* schemes in the sense that they must have to be mutually untranslatable; secondly, that a conceptual scheme must be "expressible" in a language (this one, in fact, is implied by the first); that a theory of meaning is reducible to a theory of truth (and that the latter theory is encapsulated in Taski's convention T). Given these three assumptions the putative alternate conceptual schemes, being mutually untranslatable and, in particular, being untranslatable to my (our) home language, would make no sense to me (us). From the third assumption it follows that the idea of an alternate conceptual scheme (in this radical sense), which could be true even if untranslatable, has to be rejected, for the notion of truth cannot be divorced from that of translation, if the convention T embodies our best intuitions about 'truth'. Now, how does this critique of the idea of 'alternate conceptual scheme' work against the idea of transcendental philosophy? This is how it works: if the very idea of alternate conceptual scheme makes no sense, the idea of conceptual scheme itself has to go. With it has to go the distinction between scheme and content. It would then be uncalled for, to legitimize the application of a conceptual scheme to given contents. The *quaestio juris* of the Kantian philosophy cannot even be meaningfully raised. We have here a fourth assumption, in addition to the three already mentioned, namely, that the task of a transcendental philosophy is to legitimize a conceptual framework.

In order to be able to show that Davidson's argument does not succeed in demonstrating the impossibility of transcendental philosophy in general, I will question some, if not all, of these assumptions. I will not question the second assumption. Although a conceptual scheme need not have to be a language, I will grant that it can be expressed in a language. I reject the third assumption, namely, that Tarski's convention T expresses our best intuitions about truth, and that a theory of meaning is reducible to a theory of truth (of the Tarskian or any other sort). The idea of 'alternate conceptual schemes' which Davidson criticizes is a red herring. There are no such untranslatable languages, nor is the idea of transcendental philosophy committed to this strong notion. It is not committed to such a strong notion, for in the first place, all transcendental thinking is not bound to deal with the question of legitimization; secondly, even when it does raise *quaestio juris*, as in Kant's case, it is not to justify one scheme as *against* other alternative schemes; and thirdly, a transcendental philosophy is possible which does not undertake to legitimize any particular conceptual scheme. All these points can be made even in connection with the Kantian project,[3] not to speak of other sorts of transcendental philosophies.

To the issue as between (i) conceiving of many possible worlds from the same point of view and (ii) seeing the same world from many different points of view, I will return later in this essay.

For the present, I will only insist on the need for admitting a minimal form-content distinction, even if not the full-fledged Kantian distinction. The 'content', then, like the Husserlian *hyle*, may be conceived as a "boundary-condition" for noematic discourse,[4] as the notion of the bare given that, without supporting any infallible epistemic claims, is satisfied with recognizing the passivity and receptivity of sensory experience. A more generalized version of this minimal concept (which is formulated in terms of sensory experience) would be one according to which within every level of discourse there would be appropriate distinction between the given and the scheme, but *no one that runs through all the levels of discourse*, a version that may have to be worked out along the lines of the Hegelian phenomenology.

II. TRANSCENDENTAL REFLECTION:[5] PHENOMENOLOGICAL POSSIBILITY OF TRANSCENDENTAL PHILOSOPHY

If transcendental philosophy has to uncover the way or ways consciousness or subjectivity constitutes objectivity, it in any case must involve consciousness's coming to reflect on its own operations. This explicit and methodical turning back of consciousness on itself is precisely what I mean here by 'reflection'. Reflection, in this sense, has to be distinguished, on the one hand, from that pre-reflective translucency or reflexivity which characterises all our conscious life, its basic *Bei-sich-sein*, and on the other hand, from what passes by the name of 'introspection' in older forms of empirical psychology. It is by appropriate reflection that the modes of object-constitution by subjectivity can be made available as phenomenological data rather than as hypothetical, theoretical posits.

I will not attempt, in this introductory essay, to sketch a *theory* of reflection; what I will give is rather a typology of it. Reflection may be either empirical or transcendental. I can do no better than quote the words of Schnädelbach to explain how Kant would have distinguished between these two kinds of reflection:[6]

> Sie [Transcendentale Reflexion] unterscheidet sich von der empiristischen Reflexion, die seit Locke als nach innen gewandte *intentio recta*, d.h. als Wahrnehmung des inneren Sinnes im Sinne psychischer Introspektion erscheint, zunächst dadurch, daß sie kein Verfahren gegenstandsbezogener Begriffsbildung ist, sondern eine Klärung der *Bedingungen* gegenstandsbezogener Begriffsbildung, die ihr voraus liegen.

Empirical, psychological reflection is directed towards the inner mental life in *intentio recta*, it is concerned with knowing a domain of objects (of 'inner sense', in Kant's conceptualization). Transcendental reflection is not itself an object-directed epistemic enterprise, but aims at explicating the conditions of the possibility of any and every object-directed cognitive achievement which happens to be at hand.

Transcendental reflection should also be distinguished from merely logical reflection. As Kant puts it, logical reflection is merely *comparative*. Given two or more objective representations at hand, logical reflection 'compares' them, that is, looks into whether relations such as inclusion or exclusion, compatibility or incompatibility obtain amongst them. Transcendental reflection would be concerned with the conditions of the possibility of such objective "comparison" of representations. Consequently, whereas logical reflection is a purely "analytic" procedure, transcendental reflection asks, how could given representations relate to whatever is their object or objects.

Now transcendental reflection, as reflection upon consciousness in its object-constituting role, may be either reflection on the noetic acts or reflection on their noematic contents. Thus it may be either noetic reflection or noematic reflection. Phenomenological reflection, that is, the reflection that is practised in transcendental phenomenology, begins with noematic reflection, and after delineating the structure of a noema moves on to reflecting upon the acts whose noema it happens to be. These acts and their correlative noemata may then be seen as belonging to the life of an ego. Although each of these steps *may be* regarded as a step in an *argument* (such as: a noema must be the noema of an act; an act must be someone's performance), a truly phenomenological reflection must be able to fill in these empty argumentative intentions with confirmatory intuitive evidence.

The noematic reflection on its part may be either phenomenological[7] or critical. Phenomenological noematic reflection is interested in the 'constitution' of noemata in their correlative acts; a critical noematic reflection is interested in laying bare the conditions under which a noema acquires 'validity', becomes 'true'—'truth' and 'falsity' being possible predicates of noemata (meanings, propositions, thoughts, theories). This latter sort is the neoKantian *Geltungstheoretische* reflection, or transcendental-logical reflection.

Another sort of reflection which may be either empirical or quasi-transcendental is historical reflection. It is empirical when one looks for the *actual* historical genesis of a real entity (a real belief or worldview, for example). It is quasi-transcendental when within the *noema* (or the sense that entity has for me), I proceed to unravel historical, sedimented layers of meanings or interpretations.

Different sorts of transcendental philosophies generally combine two or more of these sorts of reflection, one of them playing the dominant role, and they also make use of various forms of reasoning or arguments within the overall project.

III. Subjective Possibility: The Problem of Access

Granted that a transcendental philosophy is logically possible and also that there is a broad-spectrum method that opens up the transcendental domain of subjectivity for our inquiry, one may still want to know: how can we at all come to exercise this method? What I am raising is the problem of access. To say that it is transcendental reflection which establishes the access is precisely to beg the issue. If transcendental reflection is reflection on the transcendental, that is, the constituting subjectivity, how can I at all reflect on *that* if the only subjectivity I am familiar with is my everyday, empirical, conscious experience? This everyday empirical consciousness, far from being constituting, is a part of the world, causally connected with my body and its natural (and cultural) environment. How can I establish contact with *(my?)* transcendental subjectivity?

Hegel, more than any other philosopher, realized the force of this problem of access, and wrote his *Phenomenology* of 1807 as a response. The way he posed the question is: how can natural consciousness rise up to the level of philosophical consciousness? To put it in the present perspective, any reflection on consciousness, within the natural attitude, will be an empirical reflection and therefore cannot yield anything of transcendental significance. Hegel's plan was, as is well known, to lead natural consciousness along a pathway having several well defined stages or 'shapes of consciousness'—the journey culminating at a point where philosophy in the strict sense (that is, Hegel's *Science of Logic*) can begin. The account consists of description and critique, each 'shape' first tells its own story and is then subjected to a critique which leads beyond it. In this account, one is still faced with the question: who makes the critique, who examines the shapes of natural consciousness, what criterion is employed in this critique and what is the source of this criterion if not the natural consciousness itself? Are we not, in this account, already presupposing a standpoint that lies beyond the natural? And, yet, is it not precisely to such a standpoint that the story is intended to lead us?

Husserl is the other transcendental philosopher who seriously and incessantly thought about the problem of access, thus giving one the impression that he was a philosopher of perpetual 'beginning'. To cut a long story short, again we need to recall that it is the methods of *epoche* and reduction[8] that provided for Husserl the access to the transcendental domain. By bracketing existence so as to be left only with essence, then by bracketing all transcendence so that one is left with the purely immanent experience with its act-noema structure, and finally by suspending the natural world belief so that what is left over is the domain of consciousness within which the 'world' is intended as a noematic structure and the world-belief is recognized *as a belief,* the meditating philosopher finds himself *living* the life of a transcendental ego.

There are several questions that arise. As in the case of the Hegelian "access" one may ask: is it not the case that here too one is presupposing a conception of the transcendental to begin with? Why, otherwise, should one perform the reductions and the epoche? One may also ask, what could possibly motivate this radical "conversion"? A still more radical skeptical doubt would be: suppose someone, appropriately motivated, performs all the reductions, the eidetic, the phenomenological and the transcendental, but whatever changes, transformations or "conversions" occur, take place only in the interiority of that person's inner life as a result of his "voluntary" change of attitude. What light could, then, such an "inner" transformation throw upon the nature of consciousness—not to speak of the nature of the world? Postponing consideration of the question of motivation to the next section, I will briefly respond to the other two questions.

The first worry is unfounded. For, to talk of an access is also to talk of access to something. The query itself requires that we have a conception of where we want to go, the destination. Unless we have some idea of the destination, it would be pointless to talk of a path. One cannot begin doing transcendental philosophy unless one knows what to look for or, rather, the sort of thing that would satisfy the explanatory needs of that kind of philosophy.

The last of the three questions raised above suggests that the metaphor of path or access is misleading. That metaphor suggests that the transcendental is on the other side of the natural, as though we are talking of two totally disconnected domains and are wondering how to go from the one to the other. The Platonic two-world theory is a misleading conceptualization of the situation. To "purify" one's own conscious life by stripping it of naive interpretations, self-understandings and also of ontological commitments, is neither to transport oneself to another land nor to "transform' our everyday consciousness to something else. It is rather to exhibit its true nature, even in naiveté, in its role as interpreting both itself and the other, as constituting its, and a common (our) world. The transcendental role lies concealed "anonymously" within the empirical. Transcendental philosophy seeks to uncover this role.

IV. The Problem of Motivation: Psychological Possibility

What could motivate a philosopher, a mundane creature immersed in world-belief, to take the transcendental turn? As far as I can see, one or more from amongst several motives may motivate such radical turn, but, to be sure, all these are mundane motives. There can b no transcendental motivation for doing transcendental philosophy. From within mundane experience, there are occasions as well as needs—both theoretical and practical—which may motivate philosophizing in this manner. Consider Kant: his motives, in looking for the transcendental foundations of knowledge and morality, were as much historical (how to reconcile science with religion, for example) as epistemological (how is scientific knowledge as a body of synthetic yet *a priori* judgments possible?). Husserl's motive was, to start with, to clarify the basic concepts of logic and mathematics (which are historically accomplished disciplines) by looking for their "origin" in the eidetic structures of the mental life of the thinker, but—later on—to realize the immanent telos in the historically inherited idea of philosophy as the first philosophy. There may be many other possible motivations, which are effective within the naivity of world-belief, but which, when they are permitted to work out their goal, bring that very world-belief into the scope of critical reflection. Thus transcendental reflection must be motivated by mundane interests.

V. The World and Worlds

It is true that in the past the transcendental philosophies have had their starting points in a monistic conception of truth and so of *the* world. That monism has no future. The idea of pluralism of worlds has come to stay. A relativism that follows from the recognition of this pluralism is one of the desiderata of modern culture. The transcendental philosopher, therefore, cannot start with a preferred representation of the world, or with a preferred science or even a preferred ontology. He cannot any longer undertake to *justify* any one world picture or "version," to use Goodman's term, to the exclusion of other versions. If we are to find a way out of relativism, it can only be *after* the phenomenon of relativism has been granted its initial recognition. But where can we go from there? What path lies open for us?

Here phenomenology provides us with invaluable guidance. Each world, or rather each version, is to be viewed as a noematic structure. Just as the identity of an object is constituted by the system of noemata through which "one and the same" object is presented, so also in the case under consideration: the one world—not in the sense of the totality of all worlds, but in the sense of that whose versions they all are—may be looked upon as that *regulative* concept which not only orders the various quasi-incommensurable worlds, but also delineates the path that shall lead us out of a hopeless relativism towards communication and understanding. This last point entails that while we need to give modern relativism its due, it is no less important that we clearly see its limitations.

First of all, it needs to be emphasized that the different worlds, many of which are seemingly incommensurable, are not all totally disconnected from each other. On the contrary, many of them intersect and overlap, thereby constituting a common, shared domain. Secondly, be they incommensurables or not, once the naive ontological claim is bracketed, *a* world becomes *a* world-noema. The various world-noemata do not any longer have *the same sort of* conflict amongst each other, as the various worlds had. Thirdly, each world-noema may be correlated to—or constituted by—appropriate noetic acts (acts of interpretation, theory-construction, etc.). With this noesis-noema correlation, we gain a fresh ground that is not itself relativistic. The non-relativistic foundation that was initially lost with the demise of a monistic theory of world, is now recovered at the level of noesis-noema correlation. Finally, since it is always possible, in principle, to ascertain, and thereby to relive in its essential features the sorts of interpretive acts that go to constitute a world, however foreign, the correlation-structure with regard to any given world may be recovered as a structure within the subjective life of *any* thinking ego. The different worlds, then, find their "origin," or the origin of their senses as worlds, within the subjective life of a transcendental ego.

Underlying the possibility of any world whatever then, or of the sense "world," is the general structure of the transcendentally purified life of consciousness. This is the same as the ultimate, not further objectifiable, world-*horizon* which may be our only hope today in our search for *the* world. But this world-horizon cannot fill in the place vacated by the Absolute of metaphysics.[9] As Findlay has insisted, any particular world might not have existed and so is contingent, but the horizon as that which makes any world what-soever possible, the structure of transcendental subjectivity, cannot be meaningfully denied. As an *a priori* structure, this horizon is closed, but it is—again learning from Findlay—open-ended with regard to its contents.

Transcendental philosophy thus may—indeed must—begin with a pluralism of worlds, but would overcome this pluralism *from within*, rather than by opting arbitrarily for a preferred world-view.

I am now in a position to speak to the issue so forcefully formulated by Davidson. Are the different worlds all from the same point of view, or are they from different points of view? I do not think anyone would want to deny that there are different points of view from which one and the same thing can be seen, one and the same subject matter can be studied. But what needs to be denied is that there are *radically* different points of view, such that these points of view or the associated conceptual frameworks, or possibly even the perceptual views, are totally incommensurable and mutually untranslatable. I quite agree with Davidson that radical difference in this sense makes no sense. But between the view that there are such incommensurable worlds (or, mutually untranslatable languages, totally unintelligible alternate conceptual frameworks) and the view that all talk of possible nonactual worlds involves nothing more than "redistribution of truth-values" over sentences in our present language "in various systematic ways";[10] or, for that matter, between the conception of many imagined worlds all described from the same point of view, and the conception of many worlds as but different perspectives on the same content, there is an intermediate position which I want to adopt. For formulating this intermediate position, the idea of 'transcendental ego' is precisely what we need.

We have to distinguish between two levels of discourse: the internal and the external. At the internal level, there are radically different worlds, conceptual frameworks, languages—such that for the person who *naively lives within one,* the others are "bare others," at most "interesting," but "make no sense." Translatability and intelligibility are at most *ideals,* but never meant to work out. Translation, understanding and communication take place within a common, shared world. So far, this is a valid description of our experience of our own (shared) world and of the "bare other," the alien world that "makes no sense." At this level, there is a home language.

One requires, however, if I am to be able to speak of alternate conceptual schemes, that I must be able to translate the other's into my own; or mine into someone else's. This requirement has nothing to do with the primacy of the English language or, for that matter, of any other language. What it requires is that the languages must be mutually translatable. But when I assert this, I am not taking the "internal" standpoint, but rather the "external" standpoint of a transcendental ego, for whom any language is as good as any other, before whose gaze all possible worlds are spread out and none is more his own than any other. The transcendental ego's is no standpoint: all possible standpoints are arraigned before his gaze. The transcendental ego has no "home" language.

Thus, the (empirical) person living in his world, speaking his language, using his conceptual framework, is subject to a point of view of his own, shared by his community—*in different degrees* by his age. But he does not, in his pre-reflective naivity, know that he sees the world *from a standpoint*. He lives in, perceives, knows the world, the only world that is there. That, however, he is subject to a standpoint, a perspective, a conceptual framework is brought out by reflection. But to be able to survey all possible points of view, conceptual frameworks, languages objectively—as making sense to each other, therefore as commensurable (and mutually translatable) one needs to take up a stance, which is none other than that of a transcendental ego.

The thesis of relativity of worlds is an initial response of reflection. But this thesis of relativity has to be limited by the thesis of the common horizon within which these many standpoints are after all possible. The *one* world is not the common *content* to which the different worlds or versions provide or apply different conceptual schemes. The one world is rather the regulative ideal which is *being constituted* through the mutually overlapping, coinciding, conflicting plethora of world-noemata. The many worlds are then neither gotten by redistribution of truth values for sentences in the home language, nor are they different conceptualizations of one and the same pre-existent world. They are noemata *of* one world, but the one world is also *being* constituted through them.

J.N. MOHANTY: ON THE POSSIBILITY OF TRANSCENDENTAL PHILOSOPHY

1. D. Davidson, "On the Very Idea of a Conceptual Scheme," Proceedings of the American Philosophical Association, 17, 1973–74, pp. 5–20.

2. Ibid., p. 9.

3. Thus Dieter Henrich: "It is a mistake to describe the transcendental strategy as the defense of one conceptual framework against another." Henrich refers to "the unfortunate association," established by Strawson, between the problem of transcendental reasoning and the possibility of competing frameworks. "Getting rid of framework, however, does not make transcendentalism evaporate," or, again, "To justify a knowledge-claim is not necessarily to justify it against a competitor." ("Comment on Rorty," in: Bier, Horstmann and Krüger, *Transcendental Arguments and Science*, p. 115.) Although Kant characterizes the question of the Transcendental Deduction as a *questio juris*, it would be wrong to interpret a *questio juris* as one of settling from amongst conflicting claims. For more, see Henrich, p. 116f.

4. D. Føllesdal regards *hyle* as "the boundary conditions which limit the range of noemata." See his "Brentano and Husserl on Intentional Objects

and Perception" in: *Grazer philosophische Studien,* 5, 1978, pp. 83–94, esp. 93–4.

5. On 'reflection,' see H. Wagner, *Philosophie und Reflexion,* München/ Basel: Ernst Reinhardt, 1967 (2nd edition); H. Schnädelbach, *Reflexion und Diskurs,* Frankfurt am Main: Suhrkamp, 1977; R. Schaeffler, "Zum Verhältnis von transzendentaler und historischer Reflexion," in: H. Kohlenberger and W. Lütterfelds (eds), *Von der Norwendigkeit der Philosophie in der Gegenwart; Festschrift für Karl Ulmer zum 60 Geburtstag,* München: R. Oldenbourgh Verlag, 1976; J. Simon, "Satz, Text und Diskurs in transzendentalphilosophischer und sprachlogischer Reflexion," in: H. Röttges, B. Scheer and J. Simon (eds), *Sprache und Begriff Festschrift für Bruno Liebrucks,* Meisenheim am Glan: Verlag Anton Hain, 1974; Klaus Hartmann, "Analytische und Kategoriale Transzendentalphilosophie" in: G. Schmidt and G. Wolandt (eds), *Die Aktualität der Transzendentalphilosophie,* Bonn: Bouvier, 1977. Also see H. Krings, *Transcendental Logic,* München: Kosel Verlag, 1964.

6. H. Schnädelbach, loc. cit., p. 91; cp. Kant, *Critique of Pure Reason,* B 316f.

7. Schnädelbach's use of 'phenomenological reflection' which he finds paradigmatically exemplified in Locke is misleading. My use of it comes much closer to what he calls "Sinnexplicative Reflexion." The noemata are *Sinne,* and phenomenological reflection is directed towards laying bare the constitution of meanings.

8. For my present purpose I use these two terms for all three: eidetic, phenomenological and transcendental reductions.

9. J. N. Findlay, *Ascent to the Absolute,* pp. 204–205.

10. D. Davidson, loc. cit., p. 9.

The Life of Spirit

William J. Langan

The truest honor I can bestow upon a thinker of William Earle's caliber is to reflect upon his thought. Three of his works, *Objectivity*, *Autobiographical Consciousness* and *Mystical Reason* form a special kind of trilogy in my mind. Taken together they constitute an exploration of human reality from the perspective of what it is to be conscious, a systematic and fascinating philosophy about what it means to be human.[1] It is that philosophy I wish to develop in this essay.

Objectivity was written to counter a then-prevalent positivistic movement in Anglo-American philosophy that identified any kind of realism, be it Aristotelian or phenomenological, with nonsense or speculation. Epistemology dominated philosophical discourse, and epistemology meant linguistic analysis. Today philosophy has overcome that bias; but its underlying metaphysics has endured and even worked itself into common culture. We are all things or machines that function according to laws more or less known (unknown, for the most part) that boil down in the last (also yet unknown) analysis to mechanical equations. Sigmund Freud remains the paradigm of those who desire to treat spirit as fact. Part One of my essay uses *Objectivity* to expose the fallacy of such a reduction.

Naive enthusiasm might lead one to read *Autobiographical Consciousness* as a celebration of subjectivity, as if Kierkegaard's infamous slogan that "Truth Is Subjectivity" is the message of the book. Nothing could be further from the truth. Part Two of my essay explores the difference between a pathetic self crying out its absolute freedom and Earle's actual and true notion of an ego absolute to itself but choosing to live in the world. This develops what I consider to be the central idea of Earle's philosophy—the mystery of existence understood as the *life* of the transcendental ego.

In the works I am discussing, Earle does not consider *authenticity* in any formal sense, certainly not in the way Heidegger or Sartre did. But implicit in his analysis of the way a transcendental ego exists or lives its life, becomes *engrossed* in the world or aspects, regions or things in the world, and especially in the way an ego reveals itself to another ego in love, existence takes on something of the miraculous; this strikes at least this reviewer as the equivalent of authenticity—Part Three explores Earle's celebration of such moments.

Part Four examines Earle's analysis of the *ontological argument* given in *Mystical Reason,* which he claims is not an *argument* at all but only reason's discovery that absolute reality is its one and only *proper* object. The concluding Part Five reviews Earle's reflection on the *cogito* of Descartes that culminates in what must be his most controversial claim: the final intuition that the transcendental ego is one and the same as absolute reality!

PART ONE: CONSCIOUSNESS: WHAT IS IT?

> Psychoanalysis cannot situate the essence of the psychical in consciousness, but is obliged to regard consciousness as a quality of the psychical, which may be present in addition to other qualities or may be absent.[2]

Freud's last "major theoretical work" thus begins. *Being conscious* is not only *not* the being of thinking, as philosophy from Plato through Sartre has held, it is only an accidental property thoughts may or may not enjoy. Forget those thoughts we have forgotten or registered without notice—latent thoughts; Freud insists that thoughts exist in the mind which *never were conscious* and never will be so, save possibly through extensive psychoanalysis; they are *repressed* ideas energized by psychic energy seeking discharge thereby constituting the major source of *anxiety.* "Thus we obtain our concept of the unconscious from the theory of repression."[3]

Why is Freud's insistence that *consciousness* has nothing *in essence* to do with thinking important? Freudian and computerized motions of thought recognize the bi-polarity of thought: ideas consist of some quantum of energy directed towards or fixed on some object. But no sense of *intentionality* is involved. That so-called activity of thinking is *blind.* The computer screen reads out whatever it was pre-programmed to deliver—an electrical system wired to create images on a screen *we* read as a message. Freudian psychology sees psychic behavior in much the same way: energy programmed towards an

object. No psychic activity defines itself in essence through its object—
it is only an economic quantity of energy seeking release or discharge:

> From this we can easily go on to assume that this displacable
> libido is employed in the service of the pleasure principle to
> obviate blockages and to facilitate discharge. In this connection
> it is easy to observe a certain indifference as to the path along
> which the discharge takes place, so long as it takes place
> somehow.[4]

The object effecting discharge is really fortuitous or accidental, serving
only as an indifferent possible path of discharge. It is not meant or
intended any more than the computer means or intends (is conscious
of) what its screen displays.

Freud's notion of psychic activity clearly *reduces* thought to a
secondary phenomenon, despite protestations to the contrary. That
reductionism has put philosophy on the defensive. Areas of human
experience not yet subsumed physiologically through reduction to
brain-function, body chemistry, genetic disposition or some other
materialistic base are generally portrayed as analyzable statistically.
And human reality is envisioned as one complex machine—individual
or group—on the verge of being understood for the first time; with
philosophy or reason conceived as a relic, an archaic vestige whose
study held value only before the inner workings of the machine
were understood.

Philosophy itself has contributed to such reductionism—and continues to do so, albeit unwittingly. Logical positivism itself has
supposedly been adequately discredited. But language analysis in-
terprets meaning in terms of linguistic usage—a program all-too-
readily adaptable to the reduction of thought to a form of behavior.
And the so-called new methods coming from continental Europe,
structuralism and deconstructionism for example, often seem in search
of a method to decipher magically the complex programs governing
social development—thereby reducing thoughtful action to behavioral
analysis. The pursuit of wisdom has been displaced by the teaching
of logic and clear thinking. Training in philosophy has become an
exercise in argumentation—all in all a situation not dissimilar to the
sophism so strongly critiqued by Socrates in his trial. It almost seems
as if Kant's distinction between the noumenal and phenomenal, so
carefully drawn to ensure a place for philosophical reason, has
backfired. Philosophy as *love of wisdom* no longer exists.[5]

Against such reductionism Earlie's *Objectivity* looms like a breath
of fresh air penetrating the constricted monad that is philosophy.
He rightly insists upon the importance of the object about which

we think, attributing to it the reality that philosophy from Aristotle through Descartes has properly recognized:

> The centaur which I am imagining is not at all an idea, although, to be sure, I have an idea of it. Thus my thinking of the centaur is my awareness of the centaur. The centaur itself, not being an awareness of anything, is not therefore properly an idea, but rather the object of an idea.[6]

When we think or experience something, that something *is there*, given to our experience as real. And no questions about that experience, we shall see, are even intelligible, without recognizing the reality of the object experienced.

To say "I see the sunset" is already a reflection on my seeing the *sun set*. An obvious objection really proves the point. Imagine I am looking upon the sun as it sets, absorbed in its colors, its hue, its magic; and you ask me in a way that does not pull me out of my engagement with the sunset what it is I am doing, I will no doubt respond "looking at this beautiful sunset!" My immediate experience is simply one of apprehension, I am not even thinking "sun" and "setting", I am absorbed in the beauty before me. My answer to you is a prereflexive thought or report, a verbalized stream of consciousness. Of course, if your question jars me loose from the vision I might *use* the same words to tell you what I was formerly doing, and so reflect on a now-past experience.

Either way the immediate experience is a *sine qua non* that is indubitable—first, for even the question about what I am doing to make sense; and secondly, as the recourse to which any statement about my experience must be made, for its truthfulness to be evaluated. This holds true for any thought or experience. The experience itself is a given base; claims *about* it constitute reflection *on* it; and debate over truth of such claims constitutes yet another level of reflection and must, despite whatever system or theory in question, look to the primary experience for justification. For questions or claims about it to even make sense, the primary experience must be taken as indubitable.

Reductionistic notions of thought *fail* this simple phenomenological test. Freudian psychology supposedly begins with immediate experiences, but moves on to an interpretation of them—in terms of childhood traumas, repressed desires and the like. Its basic tenet, that the object dreamt or thought has nothing to do with the thought itself, directly contradicts one key element of the primary thought or experience being explained, to wit, its intentional meaning what it thinks. Almost every reader of this essay will understand that point, so I will not belabor it. Earle's *Objectivity* readily refutes all such psychologisms.

That criticism may seem abstract to readers unfamiliar with *Objectivity*. It amounts to a simple point: statements about experience must not contradict the experience they are about. Recall my looking at the sun setting. You ask me to describe it without breaking me from its enjoyment; I report it as reddish-orange in hue. Your questions begin to draw me out of my immediate experience. It is the sun setting. It casts that reddish-orange hue on the—what do poets call it, the horizon:—in and below the clouds and somehow through them; the beauty of it, the cloud-shapes, or is it the fog rolling in? A myriad of colors even paint-by-number could not produce, only Ansel Adams; rays of light; disappearing orb. Led to reflect on my experience, I notice *what* it is that I am experiencing, I eventually *take note* of it.

My experience is mine, private and no one else's, not even yours. But my halting and appreciative descriptions of it move the object into the public domain, begin to make it real for you.

What is happening is that the reality I was experiencing has now become or is beginning to become *explicit*, not only for you but for me as well. Earle calls this the "emergence of explicit objects."[7] I make explicit objects or aspects implicit in my experience of them.

A linguist or empiricist suddenly challenges my report, armed let us imagine with a spectrograph aimed in the same direction. It reads pinkish-red we are told, rather than the reddish-orange I reported. Assuming it is correct, what does that signify? Nothing more than that the *words* I used to describe my experience were defective in that they failed to match scientific or ordinary usage. For their defectiveness to be true, however—for the criticism, that is, of my description as inadequate to be true—my vision of the sunset is presupposed. What is *questioned* is only the way I make explicit what I experience. The experience itself must be consulted, to choose between the two conflicting accounts of it. It may turn out my color-designations vary from those standardized in the laboratory or by public-usage. That is a criticism of my reflections on my experience, not the experience itself. In fact for my description to even be put into question in any rational manner, the experience *of* which it is a description *must* be accepted at face value, so that the adequacy of the description of it can be evaluated.

Any attempt to reduce thought to a non-intentional entity must meet the same criterion. The *thinking* must be accepted *prima facie* for any reflections about it to be measurable as true or false. But thinking is, as phenomenology has so long demonstrated, intentional. The act of thinking means or intends its object, is *essentially* determined as much through the object as through the act of thinking. When Freud asserts that consciousness is a quality which may be present in thought but more often is not, he is saying that intentionality is not essential to thinking. (The fixation of psychic libido on an object is not intentionality at all.) He is thus *formally* erring. His reflection on an immediate experience claims to be true about that experience, and yet denies an element of it.

A last example to illustrate the point. It is said that Sartre's analysis of Jean Gěnet profoundly affected the writer. If so, it could hardly be because Sartre had uncovered something essentially unconscious. How could such a fictional biography strike Gênet as *true* of him? He had to recognize in Sartre's account a truth about himself, he had to recognize his own experience in Sartre's analysis. Whether he reflectively realized it before, whether he admitted it to himself, denied it or tried to hide it from himself, or whther he was simply moved by the fact someone had so thoroughly understood him, none of that matters. His immediate self-experience is the given, the touchstone which is unquestioned, and by which we can recognize the truth of Sartre's account.

PART TWO: CONSCIOUSNESS: WHAT TO DO WITH IT?

My primary concern in arguing against reductionism is that it constitutes nothing less than an escape, a flight from the responsibility to be. If human experience is truly intelligible only in terms of an unconscious or some other physical process that functions the way energy functions in physics, then the Socratic dictum "know thyself!" is rendered meaningless. And so is all of philosophy that conceives of itself as the love of wisdom, "that form of knowledge which it is essential to the knower to know."[8] Inherent in wisdom lies the notion that I am responsible for becoming the person I am becoming, for being who I am. Even Freud's own writings exhibit a passion for self-understanding, a sense of authenticity stemming from self-discovery that could make no sense were it physical matter such as brain cells, neurons, synapses or libidinal instincts we were discovering. Those are *things*, not ourselves, and we in no wise become authentic in knowing them. Socratic self-knowledge is quite different, a way of being or a form of consciousness as Earle calls it in *The Autobiographical Consciousness*.[9] The key to understanding this is responsibility, the sense of myself as a task, a project, a being which has itself to be.

Speaking of the self this way is not easy. We constantly slip into one of two erroneous modes of thinking about the self. Either we *reduce* the self to an object, or the result of some objective process—

the tendency dominant today, certainly in psychology but also in philosophy; or shunning that we commit an opposite blunder, we reduce the self to *mere subjectivity*. Part One attempted to ward off the former danger by insisting that experience or thought cannot be reduced to something happening inside one's head, so to speak, some inner process essentially explainable through empirical research rather than philosophical reflection. *Autobiographical Consciousness*, among other things, warns aginst the second error by emphasizing the dialectical interplay between the transcendental and existential that comprises human subjectivity in its self-experience.

Consider Socrates' last discussion, at least as Plato depicts it in the *Phaedo*. Man is a composition or synthesis of two "things" if you will, the mind or soul and the body. But he is not essentially that snythesis; he is essentially a soul imprisoned in the body. Socrates' arguments for the immortality of the soul are well-known so need no repetition here. But they turn on his argument that man is essentially soul, whose function is to reason; that and his definition of death as separation of soul from body. Subjectivist views of the self have not really gone beyond that presented by Socrates in the *Phaedo*. They do tend to emphasize freedom, in the sense of one's being free to constitute himself, at least contemporary versions do. But that is deceptive, as I will try to show below. First, though, let us continue with Socrates for a moment. The point of his argument is, of course, that death is not decisive, it is only a transition from one state to another. He even chides Crito who, despite all arguments, speaks of Socrates' corpse as the real Socrates.[10] Both men conceive of human reality as a synthesis of soul and body; but Crito takes the visible object for the essence—when it is no longer living, Socrates is no longer living. Socrates takes himself as subject, a self whose essence lies in reason; the life of the body has nothing essential to do with him.

Could there be on either view a knowledge which is essential to the knower to know? Certainly not for Crito. Assuming Crito right, the only conclusion to be drawn is that Socrates lived his life in a misunderstanding of himself. Could one argue that he is therefore inferior to Crito in some fundamental way? Hardly. He still has attained world-historical status. But now suppose Socrates' view is correct. Is Crito inherently inferior? Hardly. He may have to undergo reincarnation some more, but (still assuming the Socratic perspective) he too will eventually overcome his ignorance. Since man is essentially soul, and soul is eternal, no knowledge in any life is essential to the knower to know. From the eternal perspective what does the delay of several lifetimes really matter?

The Christian perspective is basically that of Socrates in the *Phaedo*, though a new wrinkle is introduced with the notion of *faith*. One can be eternally damned if one does not have faith. Assuming the Christian-Socratic perspective for a moment, we can certainly say that such faith *would* constitute a knowledge essential for the knower to know. But if faith is something reason leads us to, as Dante and Thomas Aquinas would have it, then we are right back in the Socratic perspective. It is true Dante denied him the joy of salvation, not through any fault of Socrates but only because he lived before Jesus. Later theologians have recognized the moral inequity that involves, finding in the Socratic attitude (or Socratic faith) something salvific.[11] But that makes those of us who lack such faith into so many Crito's. Our unbelief can not condemn us to eternal damnation any more than the accident of his birth can condemn Socrates. On the other hand, if faith is entirely gratuitous, a free act on a loving-God's side, as Paul and Luther would have it, then nothing *we* do on our own is essential to salvation, and so no *knowing* can be considered essential to the knower to know. Either way, faith does not, it turns out, constitute a knowledge essential to the knower to know.

Both the Socratic and Christian perspectives take man as pure subject, call it mind or soul or whatever. But taking man as so radically subjective turns the subject or true self into another *object*, defined through its essential opposition to the body. All philosophies of radical subjectivity commit the same error. Nietzsche's metaphor of the lion who roars out that he is free symbolizes the mistake: vacuous freedom is just another *thing*, a fact; by itself it really means nothing. Total freedom is empty freedom. What one *does* with one's freedom simply does not matter, any more than it matters what one reasons, if one's *essence* lies in reason alone. No knowledge essential to the knower to know exists for either case.

What is missing in all these cases is a sense of *responsibility for being* who one is. If one is not responsible for oneself, then no knowing essential to the knower to know can exist.

Responsibility for being is not the same as legal or moral responsibility, though the latter may well be rooted ontologically in the former. It is rather that ontological self-determination Kierkegaard intends in his cryptic definition of the self as spirit commencing *Sickness Unto Death*:

> Man is spirit. But what is spirit? Spirit is the self. But what is the self? The self is a relation which relates itself to its own self, or is that in the relation (which accounts for it) that the relation relates itself to its own self; the self is not the relation

> but (consists in the fact) that the relation relates itself to its own self.[12]

Kierkegaard, following Plato and the whole philosophical tradition in general, identifies the end terms of the relation as body and soul. The key point, though, is that man is not some synthesis or joining together of two opposites, two different *things* somehow united— which could only be by a union determined through dominance of one *thing* over the other, that term which establishes the union.

But if neither term of the relation is responsible for the relation, does that not make spirit—or the relation—some *third thing* establishing the union among the three? Language seems to compel us to agree. And yet it is precisely that which Kierkegaard, and Earle, if I understand his *Autobiographical Consciousness*, seek to avoid asserting.

Sickness Unto Death does so rather obliquely, by raising a question that I believe aims at disclosing that dialectic between transcendental and existential life that forms the theme of *Autobiographical Consciousness*.

> Such a relation which relates itself to its own self (that is to say, a self) must either have constituted itself or have been constituted by another.[13]

To avoid confusion, some terminological clarification is needed. When Kierkegaard dismisses, as he does, the possibility of the self relating itself to itself without being constituted by another, he is dismissing (as Earle also does) the possibility of the self *existing as* pure transcendental ego. The self may *be* transcendental ego, as Earle argues, when it divests itself of its existence. But the resultant transcendental ego is incapable of life, divested as it is of the joys and sorrows, pleasures and pains, achievements and failures of existence. The self Kierkegaard speaks to is an existent self, a self which lives, has projects, and can *despair*.

Being ostensibly a study of despair, it is hardly surprising that *Sickness Unto Death* couches its argument in terms of despair. What Kierkegaard says, in fact, is that a self which constituted itself as self-relation (in no relation to another) could only despair over being, could only will not to be (which is, in Earle's terminology, not existing.) Such a self would be self-constituting; and would constitute itself *as* despair. But such a self could not possibly *live in* despair! For the simple reason that *its being* the Unhappy Ego would be a free choice or act on its own part: no real sense of despair, no *living anguish* would be possible.

His argument is logically sound. Despair as the will not to be could only *be* a refusal to exist: a transcendental ego divested of its entire existence that simply holds itself in its refusal to live. Not even suicide fits that description, for suicide would be an existential act, a refusal to live no longer, commited *in time*, by an existing ego. Transcendental despair simply names an absolute ego freely refusing to exist. It is self-constituting, for nothing could *make* it exist. Such a thing is not possible, and Kierkegaard knows it, and so insists that it reduces, in the final analysis, to a form of despairingly willing to be oneself. Which is, in his terminology, a form of self relating itself to itself in relation to another (that is, in existence).[14]

Pure transcendental ego finds itself in existence, discovers itself through that radical reflection Earle calls divestment. I do relate myself to my own self, I am self or transcendental ego, and can recover myself as such in reflection. But that reflection, that self-recovery, is done by an already existing ego, a self in relation to another.

PART THREE: THE MIRACLE OF EXISTENCE

Our discussion so far has been abstract. What is imperative is that the sense of self as spirit—self determining itself in its very being, in its being a self-relation—receive full elucidation; without falling into the trap of asserting a radical free subjectivity. Were I to live or exist as absolute, as pure spirit constituting itself as self-relation *in no relation to another*, as philosophies of radical subjectivity maintain, I would be pure god in a worldless being. Nothing would interest me, nothing could surprise me, nothing could appear strange or miraculous or fascinating (as Earle puts it[15]) because all would constitute part of my absolute self-creation. Like a god before creation, every possible idea would already and eternally be known by me. Nothing could be strange or unfamiliar. I could not love, for love by definition is desire for an other which could not exist. I could not even despair, as Kierkegaard recognized, for despair demands a relation to another such a totally self-constituting being lacks. The only name suitable for such a being, quite frankly, would be *transcendental boredom*.

Yet I can and do experience myself as absolute, as totally responsible for being who I am. No matter what happens, it happens to *me*; no matter what I do, *I* do it. I am indeed the center of my life, and in my consciousness of what happens to me and what I do, and in my judgments upon the same, I assume full responsibility for being who I am. In no way can I honestly deny that responsibility, by reducing myself to some complex objectivity, some empirically-determined existence not ultimately responsible for itself, some product of other processes.

Earle's solution to this paradox is simple. The self is absolute, in its self-relating determination of itself. But it *exists* only in relation to others—other egos, other things, the world. That existence opens the self to others that constantly carry with them the sense of the strange and the miraculous, others who fascinate and frustrate it. The *life* of the absolute "I am" is not constituted by me but happens to me; yet I remain the absolute "I am" in that existence, always able (in theory if not practice) to recover myself as absolute. As Earle puts it:

> . . . if the *existence* of an eternal ego were not accidental to it
> but implied by its very nature, then indeed its *life* would be
> eternal, and each of us would be required upon pain of
> violating logic to live forever. Happily, this is neither possible
> nor necessary.[16]

It should be clear by now that the theme of *Autobiographical Consciousness* is the transcendental self *as existent*. Which makes it not dissimilar to Kierkegaard's notion of the self as spirit, as relating itself to itself *but constituted* in that self-relation by another. The problem with the Dane's analysis of self is that, undoubtedly due to his religious proclivity, he identified that *other* as a transcendent power, some being outside existence. In doing so he confused himself, he failed to understand his own insight. Yet it may not be without significance that he plunged himself into an analysis of despair; what would be more natural for a transcendental ego suddenly faced with its responsibility to be? As Earle observes:

> The life of the transcendental ego, therefore, is its plunge
> into chaos. Religiously and mythically, it is the "fall." Without
> that fall, the self would not exist at all; it would perpetually
> and eternally reside within itself.[17]

Faced with the chaos and strangeness, the *otherness* of existence, one might well despair of it. Kierkegaard was not alone in depicting modes of despair.

As Earle notes, the Schopenhauers of the world choose to exist in denunciation of others, of the world; it is evil or ugly or intolerable. But in doing so they determine themselves. And the Whitmans of the world choose to see everything as beautiful, to be celebrated and approved. Such totalizing attitudes or moods stem from the free self-determination of the ego passing judgment upon life as a whole . . .

> . . . an attitude or mood not in the least dictated by that
> existence or anything in it, but created freely within the self.

Euphoria and melancholy: neither can defend itself by
anything within life . . .[18]

Nor is such defense necessary. Still others, Earle goes on, *engross*
themselves in the world in particularities, choosing between the 'good'
and the 'evil', the 'beautiful' and the 'ugly' or whatever. Even these
discriminations are totalizing: ego is immersed in the world, but only
very generally. Its existence reflects more of itself, its mood, its
judgment—or better, itself as judge, yet still generally. The more
particular our engrossments become or are, the more of ourselves
we reflect. And indeed, the more we become.

This point in particular, it seems to me, needs special emphasis.

My life is in fact an ontological autobiography. It reflects the self
I have determined myself to be. If I choose to be a pessimist, my
life reflects that pessimism. To others, the procedure appears retro-
gressively. If I live pessimistically—my philosophy or religion emphasizes the other world or the horrors of this world or some other
form of escapism—then I am judged a pessimist. Assuming the
analysis (judgment) is adequate, it is not only a passing psychological
observation but an ontological recognition. The transcendental ego
does reveal itself (what it determines itself to be) in the life it leads,
in the way it takes up its life.

The mathematician or logician who cares only for his formulas
and problems, who is engrossed in the realm of ideal abstraction,
exists only as an abstract thinker. To the rest of existence he is, Earle
says, *absentminded.* He does not attend, does not present himself, to
the human world. Except of course insofar as he publishes. But
moralizing here is dangerous. We all immerse ourselves in different
ways, always particular ones, and thereby limit who we are, close
off to ourselves considerable domains of existence.

Autobiographical Consciousness contains much more on this and
other subjects. Along the way, as it were, it defines philosophy,
argues for the reality of love, articulates a theory of time rooted in
personal presence, examines the value of values and the necessarily
non-objective root of morality, ponders the paradox of our fascination
with that we most vehemently reject, horror itself; as well as the
ultimate paradox of an absolute *existing itself* as finite, limited, towards
death. Possibly uncharacteristic self-restraint prevented Earle's adding
a final, indeed the final, chapter:

And after death? Has the timeless ego any possibility of
recuperating what it has all been? This chapter will have to
wait.[19]

But as Nietzsche would observe, such humility is a self-nihilating virtue. We have been speaking of various modes of engrossment, various ways of constituting oneself in taking up existence, either as a whole or broken down into particularities. Let me quote what he says about the one mode of engrossment that permits one to exist one's absolute singularity in the world:

> Now it is a "person," personally existing with another person; and here, to "exist with" means that the person of each has become essential to the existence of the other. Hence when two persons become essential to each other's lives . . . in their reciprocal intersubjective relationship an ontological finality exists, which constitutes the world of both. Measured against this, all other modes of existence represent so many forms of abstraction, no matter how passionately they may be pursued. The universal name for this final, personal engrossment in which each subjectivity finds the other essential is, of course, love.[20]

Could Earle be suggesting that one ultimate solution of the paradox that "as absolute, the ego does not live, and as alive, it is not absolute"[21] is to be found in love?

PART FOUR: THE ONTOLOGICAL ARGUMENT

Objectivity argued that thinking enjoys a mode of being irreducible to anything else, be it body or brain or energy of any kind. The *self* thinking therefore constitutes a transcendental reality. It is an ego who, in reflection on itself, can only be taken as *sui generis*. But *Autobiographical Consciousness* has argued that the existent self is that self as it constitutes itself in relation to the world and others in the world it does not create. If the first functions the way I have used it, as an antidote to reductionism, does it not do so by absolutizing the self as pure subjectivity? Yet the latter work, while admitting the self can, in *divesting* itself of its existence, become purely subjective, absolute in that sense, also argues, at least as I interpret it, that such divestment is a self-reflection conducted by a self *already* immersed in the world, already existing and so *having to engross* itself in and amongst the things and ideas and persons of its world. Does this not de-absolutize the self?

It is time to turn our attention to the notion of the Absolute, and *Mystical Reason* does just that. While intended to encompass mystical experience in general—concluding as it does with some forty pages from the writings of the mystics—its basic argument concerns reason in the philosophical tradition. It starts off with a claim as simple as it is disarming: the ontological argument in its various formulations constitutes a simple and direct and adequate comprehension or intuition of the Absolute. Earle reduces the several versions of the ontological argument to three. "In one, we begin with the idea of an infinitely perfect being . . . In another version, we begin with the essence of an infinitely perfect being . . . recast in terms of language [we] define a perfect being . . ." the outcome of each of which is:

> three times over, there is an infinitely perfect reality, it must necessarily exist, and it is, formally considered, identical with that of which we have formed an idea or definition.

Or, stated more plainly, "the perfect being which forms the object of our idea is one and the same as the perfect being itself."[22]

Lest the full impact of this conclusion escape the reader, let me explain. Those who take the ontological argument as an attempt to prove something are wrong. Mind or reason *grasps* the Absolute in the simple act of thinking it. Earle goes on to add two *addenda:* the ontological argument is not really an argument at all, but instead the way reason must ground itself in reality; and the particular modes in which an individually existing mind might articulate its idea of the Absolute, to the extent they are particular and hence imperfect, reflect only imperfections of the mind as it exists—the Absolute itself is what reason intends, even in those errant formulations.[23]

Phenomenology of everyday experience discloses the various particular objects we experience as meaningful only in terms of the context in which we experience them. It is this or that something in the world I am intending, which draws my attention to it. But that *something-or-other* is, can only be intended, Earle claims, in reference to *other* somethings.[24] Each object we experience presents itself as a *relative* reality—relative in the sense it cannot *be* what it is in essential disconnection from other things. It is *real*, it is not a mere idea but the object intended by our experience, as *Objectivity* demonstrated, and so it *is*. But its being what it is for us is relative to the nexus of relations from which or rather through which we grasp it. No object thus experienced can be *perfect*. By "perfect" is only meant that the reality of the object experienced is independent of our experiencing it—from which it follows that it must be independent of our intending any other objects, regions or horizons of experience.

Yet the ontological argument shows reason can experience perfect reality. From whence does such an experience come? Not from everyday experience, but from an immediate apprehension of the Absolute.

What this means has to be turned about. Every object of everyday experience is fundamentally different from that of the Absolute (or perfect reality) insofar as its reality is relative, whereas the reality of the latter is not. Earle thinks the essential relativity of things is an *eidetic* truth clearly established by phenomenology. And so each particular object we experience refers us to that reality which is non-relative, or absolute.

> Consequently each relative reality, or particular object, declares of its own essence that there is an absolute reality, which in and of itself is not a particular object essentially contingent upon others.[25]

Every experience or, to phrase it scholastically, every idea, when we reflect upon the reality of the object of the idea, puts us in mind of the idea of perfect reality—which, as the ontological argument demonstrates, is not merely an idea but a direct apprehension of the object of which it is an idea. Reason is not *mystical*, Earle is arguing, only in those special moments celebrated by the mystics; it intends the Absolute in every experience, although that presence goes unnoticed for the most part, and that despite the fact simple metaphysical reflection readily discloses it. Reason essentially intends the Absolute.

Admittedly this notion of the Absolute appears so formal or abstract it is hard to see how it could relate to what the mystics speak of. Earle does work out some features of it, in particular through a consideration first of essence then of existence.

As for essence, common sense itself provides an intuitive notion of the Absolute. Inanimate objects, stones, rocks, and such are seen as possessing *less perfection* than plant or vegetative life for the simple reason they *lack life*. And life is only minimally present in plants; animals able to move, hunt, make love, play, remember and feel are perceived as higher or more perfect or more real. It is not mere anthropomorphism, Earle argues, that underlies these evaluations. There is something more *self-sufficient*, more real, closer in essence to the notion of the Absolute, about the higher stages than the lower ones. And mankind takes itself as still higher than the rest of the animal kingdom—because man is more himself, more sufficient to himself, more capable of being true to himself, he possesses more of an identity. And so man is closer to that being which is itself by itself.

Man as an individual conscious of himself, with a personal identity, is seen by common sense as higher than mere animal life simply because he is closer to that being which is sufficient-unto-itself. "Looked at objectively, are we not obviously the most alive, the most individual, the most free beings we can experience?"[26] No honest analysis of human culture can deny the fact we do find our *dignity* in just these dimensions of our existence. And dignity reflects *worth*. Man is worth more, he is higher on the chain of being, than other life forms. Those philosophies which deny this, in effect using a *lower* standard of worth (for example, mere life) strike me as in bad faith and certainly counter to common sense's intuitive notion of worth or reality. Earle calls them "a sacrilege of the almost highest order, a reversal of the hierarchy of being."[27] It is a sacrilege not because man has arbitrarily chosen himself to represent god, but because reason recognizes a hierarchy of being which places man higher than animal. Some beings are, that is to say possess an essence, superior or more important or higher than others.

In essence, then, inorganic life is lower than organic life; vegetative existence inferior to animal life; and animal life is lower than self-reflecting human life conscious of its personal identity. The latter is superior because spirit is more present. And pure spirit, pure mind would be still superior. That these are judgments of mind goes without question. They would not otherwise exist. We are mind exploring reality, and the truths we seek are about reality as given to mind. That fact does not denigrate their being true.

Earle goes on to fill in our sense of the Absolute from considerations of existence. While those considerations do show his notion of the Absolute to be closer to that of the mystics than might seem at first, their train of thought is involved and its relevance to mysticism requires a good deal of familiarity with the latter. Earle compares different modes of being. The impossible is that which *cannot* be. Thus reason is unable to apprehend it—the square-circle, for example. The merely possible is simply what is not impossible—it might or might not be. It *can* be apprehended by mind. The actual is the possible which exists—it *is* apprehended by mind. Actual being is therefore still contingent. It might not be dependent upon anything else, but it is still contingent upon apprehension by mind for its being to be not merely possible but actual. Absolute being is actual being which is not so contingent, which *commands* apprehension by mind. To grasp the import of this, one more piece of the puzzle is needed.

PART FIVE: THE FRACTURE MENDED

The final point of *Mystical Reason* is perhaps best expressed in the Introduction to that work:

> . . . mysticism deepens itself into an intuited identity of the self of the mystic and God, and reason plumbs itself into its

own rational intuition of the identity of the *transcendental ego* which exercises reason, and *absolute reality* of which the transcendental ego is the consciousness.[28]

Descartes hit the nail on the head, Earle somewhere observes, when he presented his deepest thinking in the form of *meditations*. For is that not what philosophy is, reason in dialogue with itself? And that dialogue, that self-reflection, Earle argues, ends in the discovery that the transcendental ego—the living ego divested of its existential regalia—is indeed identical to the Absolute of the mystics or the perfect reality of rationalism.

Personally I have considerable problems with Earle's dialectical phenomenology of divestment and engrossment. He makes the movement from transcendental ego to empirical ego and from empirical or living ego to transcendental appear far easier and more natural than I at least have found it. But I have no doubt that he recognizes and formulates a valuable insight into philosophical reason. I need only think back to that original enthusiasm for philosophy, that simple love of wisdom that enticed so many of us into philosophy. Too often the business of the profession obscures that passion, that love, that *sense of being*. Earle certainly succeeds in reawakening it in me, at least, in his insistence on a knowing that is essential to the knower to know, and the transcendental ego's self-mediating discovery of its own absolute identity.

If existentialism can be characterized as that philosophy which translates the metaphysical question, *What is Being?* into the individual problem, *Who am I?* then *Mystical Reason* can be said to discover in the Cartesian *cogito* the answer to that question. *I am I!* I know myself more directly, more intimately, than anything else. We become so distracted by the furniture of the universe that we see a problem where none exists. Because the other, the not-me, is *other*, knowing it is always problematical. And when I take myself *as* other, when I ask about my *real* motives or when I seek to *understand* my personality or when I measure myself against my peers or when I try to figure out how *I fit* into the scheme of things, then I become problematical to myself. So taking myself involves an assumption,

> an assumption that what is *not* I is clear to me. I then must try to find a category drawn from the not-I to answer the question as to what I am! Failing to find any such category, I then imagine that I am an enigma to myself, surely the maddest argument one could devise.[29]

I am I! Earle insists is the only and appropriate answer to the existential question. It expresses mot merely the tautalogical equation of an essence identical to itself—Sartre's *en soi* which is and is what it is—but also the actuality of that essential identity of myself with myself.[30] Tautologies express only an equivalence of meaning; that I am I expresses not only my self-identity but my being as well. It is no accident, Earle has said, that Yahweh reveals himself as: I am who am. The ego in the purity of its self-reflection *is* who is.

And the relative being of all other beings is relative, finally, to my being.

Descartes did not formulate the *cogito* in this way. But consider the *structure* of his *Mediations*. Descartes begins in reflection, the transcendental ego thinking about itself as *lived*. He immediately distinguishes himself as reflecting ego from himself as will, as ego living in the world. Pure ego is *reason*, the knowing ego, and this ego sees clearly and distinctly that it is, knows itself in its being with apodictic certitude. The lived ego *acts*, in a world peopled by things and events it may not see clearly, because they are given to it as other. Engrossed in the world, the empirical ego lives its life more through will than reason, forced to react to the world about and events that just happen without its complete understanding. But divested of the everyday world, within the bracket of transcendental doubt, the ego knows itself and knows itself with certitude.

Actually Descartes begins his reflections with the mind's search for truth. What he stipulates as being true *objectively*—which is to say transcendentally, for ego as reason, independent of will or the lived ego—is that which is so clear and distinct to reason or mind that one is unable to doubt it. The objectivity of truth, its *being true*, lies in its mode of presence to mind. He then goes on to discover first himself, as pure thinking subjectivity; and then perfect reality or God. Descartes presents mind's discovery of the Absolute in the form of a proof, the ontological argument discussed above.[31]

Earle's most controversial claim enters here. Deeper reflection on the *cogito* and on absolute reality reveals them to be one and the same. One can find insinuations of this in Spinoza, perhaps even in Liebniz, but not really in Descartes. Which is not to reject Earle as *wrong* for pushing his reflections beyond the limits of Descartes' own meditations but only to recognize them for what they are.

To follow Earle's thought, several points need to be developed. First, the *knowing* that constitutes the objectivity of truth just discussed needs clarification. (§1) Then it must be compared with the I which is known, pure subjectivity. (§2) Although our discussion occurs within the bracket of transcendental reflection, those terms and in particular their being held apart as opposite reflect the lived world in a very special and crucial sense that needs to be brought out. (§3) Then we shall be in position to consider Earle's final identification of pure subjectivity with pure objectivity, of absolute mind with absolute reality. (§4)

§1. *Knowing and objectivity.* The relative being of all other beings, I said earlier, is relative to *my* being. What that means can now be explained. Their being-true or being objective *is* their mode of being or presence to mind. Not only is the indubitability of the *cogito* the paradigm for the certitude that clear and distinct presence to mind brings; being present clearly and distinctly is what is meant by being objectively true. Mind or transcendental ego enjoys an absolute primacy: mind's immediate presence and translucency to itself is the indubitability of self-certain existence no less than essentiality. For me to be certain anything other exists or is what it is demands a comparable certitude. And if it achieves it, it is presence to mind that is achieved. No *other* shares the self-identity of mind's presence to itself, even should it acquire comparable (clear and distinct) presence to mind.

The objectivity of all other knowing is thus essentially different than that of the *cogito.* If all other knowledge is representational (Kant) or impressionistic (empiricism) then my knowing myself is intuitive and participatory. I *am* in the act of knowing; to be and to know are one and the same. All other knowing is to objectify, to make objective through the presence of the idea of the other in mind.

§2. *I am I. The Absolute Fracture.* When we attribute being to ourselves through use of the word "am," Earle observes, we are attributing a very different kind of being to ourselves than that we attribute to anything else of which we say it "is." To say "I is" would not only commit a grammatical blunder but an ontological absurdity as well.[32] Descartes indeed erred in the second mediation by attributing substance to the *cogito:* everything else might be a thing, but I am different. My *being* is unique. Its uniqueness lies in the self-identity of being and knowing (Sartre's *pour-soi,* whose being lies in awareness of being)—something untrue of any other: its being is not my knowing it. Objective being lies in a presence to mind radically different than mind's presence to itself.

Cast in Platonic terms, Earle argues, the opposition is even more evident. Being is not conceived as some sort of abstraction from becoming, the world as encountered in everyday experience. The latter may be immediate and tangible, but reason recognizes only being, not becoming. Kant's categories function much the same way; a particular object is known only as it is subsumed under the idea— indeed, objects are defined in terms of the concepts used to synthesize or order the manifold of sensation. Becoming is chaotic, unintelligible, *strange* precisely to the degree it is not pure thought clearly and distinctly present to mind. Earle is striking an analogy between being and becoming on the one hand, and my own being-for-myself and the being of an other on the other hand. Its point is simple: an absolute fracture exists between the former and the latter in both cases.

He finds the same fracture running through most metaphysical categories. Attributing *singularity* to a thing demands a certitude so infinite in task and impossible to conceive within the life of experience it can only be a projection of that immediate sense I enjoy of my own singularity. Even spatio-temporal uniqueness, bereft as it is of any sense of identity, is a function of *my* presence defining the here and now.

Substantiality, too, is fractured. The sense of a being that exists in itself comes from my sense of myself—only the for-itself knows that as in-itself. Any other object conceived as in-itself is that only for-me, hence not truly a substance in the same sense.

The fracture can be witnessed in the confusion in debate over whether or not man is *free*. I always experience myself as free, as engaged in a situation I must respond to. I may have chosen neither situation nor freedom, but I have them both. To even doubt that I am free is to take *myself* as other, to imagine myself subject to laws or forces that I understand constitute the reality of things, an application of the wrong categories, if you will.

Finally, Earle considers the category of property. What I take to be the property of a thing is quite like Aristotle's *accidents* of substance; external relations somehow not intrinsic and yet belonging to the thing. But *my properties*—even speaking this way reveals the problem—are intrinsic to me, are what I am. What I do is *properly me*, my manifestation or presence in the world. And that independent of the question—actually an illusory one—of whether I could have done otherwise.

§3. *The transcendental ego and its world.* Our reflections thus far have given a primacy to subjectivity over objectivity. The very objectivity of truth is rooted in the mode of presence to mind or the transcendental *subject* of the idea. But the transcendental ego discovers itself in that reflection Earle calls divestment, Husserl phenomenological reduction and Descartes radical doubt. The ego thus begins in the lived world, a world that carries with it its own sense of subjective intention and objective reality. Does not all we have said depend upon the lived ego's experiencing itself in the world? Does not the idea of truth itself arise from the ego's questioning its own actions and judgments in the world? And in that sense is there not a primacy of the lived ego over the transcendental ego?

I think so. The very idea of subjectivity as opposed to objectivity arises from the lived world. To put the problem another way, as lived or empirical ego I find myself situated in the world which I not only know in limited fashion but in which I must act. I only discover myself as transcendental ego in an act of metaphysical reflection or divestment. My situation is given to me as the objective or external reality facing me. The transcendental distinction between pure subjectivity and absolute reality thus *reflects* the distinction between subjectivity and objectivity already operative in the lived world.

Earle at least acknowledges this problem. Not only does having to exist distract pure thinking from absolute reality, the ego first finds itself having to exist and only then *recuperates* itself metaphysically. That would seem to imply a primacy to its having-to-exist. And so its distinction between itself as subjectivity and others or objective reality is given primordially. But Earle does not yield that point.

> Within these considerations, that which motivates the transcendental ego to recognize its own other I believe must be called an arbitrary fact. The ego associated with its living body finds itself confronted with its living other in experience: that general fact cannot be deduced from itself nor from reason. It simply is so. For some, it is a metaphysical irritant; for others, a source of awe, wonder and the singular delights and miseries of life. It is the world in which the transcendental ego has transcendentally chosen to live and in which it continues to live at its own option.[33]

I find an ambivalence in this passage. If it is just an *arbitrary fact* that the ego finds itself in the world confronted with its other; and if the transcendental ego recuperates itself from its engrossment in the world; then the transcendental distinction between subjectivity and objectivity does indeed reflect the lived or existential distinction between self and other which is just *given*. But if the transcendental ego has *transcendentally chosen* to live in a world in which it is confronted by its own other, then the idea of objectivity precedes the idea of the other as not-me.

In the second case the being or reality of others becomes a problem. Objective being is that which is clearly and distinctly present to mind. But projecting onto such objective being our own self-identical sense of being, we conceive objective reality as other than me, external to me, independent of me. And so objective reality comes to take on a second meaning—not only what is present to mind but what is presented to mind from the outside. This second sense of the objective can only be derivative. And yet, engrossed as we are in the world, it seems to be primary. Descartes himself clearly recognized the problem. For him it was the problem of the external world. His solution was simplistic. God exists, I exist. I know an objective reality which is clearly and distinctly present to me—objective in the transcendental sense. Does it enjoy existence outside the mind? Yes, because God makes it so. So objective reality is objective in the existential sense as well.

Few of us are happy with interactionism. But Earle's second position—that the transcendental ego has transcendentally chosen to live in a world wherein objective reality is *other* than it—seems little different. His first position, that my being faced with my other is an arbitrary fact not deducible from reason, leaves the issue unresolved. I believe this is one of the primordial dilemmas facing both metaphysics and mysticism from Parmenides onward.[34]

§4. *Absolute mind as absolute reality.* Given the course of the argument thus far, Earle's final and I believe most controversial claim—that the ego in radical reflection upon itself discovers itself to be identical with that absolute reality previously disclosed as the one and only appropriate object of transcendental thought—can now be examined. Having established objectivity as presence to mind, having established absolute reality at that which is solely present to mind, and having established mind as uniquely present to itself, does it not follow that absolute reality and absolute mind are not two different presences, but only the same presence conceived differently? Earle thinks so.

The ontological argument has established absolute reality as the *proper* object of thinking. All other objects are relative to it. But why should absolute reality be thought of as *object* of thought? That somehow makes it relative, not absolute. The absolute reality which thinking thinks must be stripped of its being an object of thought. It is simply thought itself.

> God, as objective, cannot be absolutely absolute. "Objective" must imply objective-to, or, if taken as "independent", then independent-of; and with these expansions, we can perhaps see that we have surreptitiously given a limitation to the absolute reality originally intuited. Both phrases explicitly relate that absolute reality to something else, namely ourselves, by way of declaring that reality to be objective to us, or independent of us.
>
> It is necessary, then, to remove this final limitation from what was intuited as absolute reality; it must, in other words,

be intuited as for-itself, and not as it is for us exclusively, or even in part.

And next, what is that which is absolutely for-itself, but the transcendental ego itself as it is for itself? Does it not immediately follow that the transcendental ego is God thinking Himself, the self-awareness of absolute reality?[35]

With this Earle concludes his argument or meditation. He has found a final intuition, one mystics also speak of: the presence of the Absolute deep within the self. And if he speaks of it with something of the same paradoxicality most mystics speak of it, that perhaps can be understood.

Meister Eckhardt said, "I am God." The mending of the fracture, then, is in one additional intuition, that the inner being of the transcendental self is one and the same as God. Or, put otherwise, absolute reality subjectivized.[36]

Most intriguing, of course, is the fact Earle discovers this last intuition at the heart of rationalism, not in the frenzy of ecstatic experience.

The paradox so often found in mysticism shows itself again, in the last sentence quoted. The self discovers itself to be God or absolute reality—but not quite. Only absolute reality *subjectivized*. What is the subjectivization of absolute reality? Perhaps only mind's realization that absolute reality is objective only in the sense of being present to it, and not in the sense of being present *as* other—mind's discovery of identity with the Absolute. Or is there here a hint of a qualification? A union in being which falls short of simple identity?

WILLIAM J. LAUGAN: THE LIFE OF SPIRIT

1. Earle even suggests these works can be so viewed, in his Retrospect to *Mystical Reason* (Regnery Gateway, Inc., Chicago, 1980), pp. 201–1. Hereafter *MR*.

2. Freud, *The Ego and the Id*, tr. Strachey (W. W. Norton & Co., Inc, N.Y., 1962), p. 3. Henerafter *EI*.

3. *EI*, p. 5.

4. *EI*, p. 35. Speaking of unconscious energy in the ego, Freud goes on to observe: "We know this trait; it is characteristic of cathectic processes in the id."

5. Certainly some think so. Witness R. Rorty's obituary on such philosophy in the *New Republic*, Oct. 18, 1982, pp. 28–34.

6. *Objectivity*, (Quadrangle Books, Chicago, 1968), p. 19. Hereafter *OBJ*.

7. *OBJ*, pp. 33ff.

8. *The Autobiographical Consciousness* (Quadrangle Books, Chicago, 1972), p. ix. Hereafter, *AC*.

9. *AC,* p. 10.

10. *Phaedo* in *The Last Days of Socrates,* tr. Tredernick (Penguin Books, Baltimore, 1967), p. 179.

11. John S. Dunne, *The City of the Gods* (Macmillan, N.Y. 19650, pp. 217–231, is one such theologian.

12. S. Kierkegaard, *Sickness Unto Death* published with *Fear and Trembling,* tr. Lowrie (Princeton Univ. Press, Princeton, N.J.), p. 146. Hereafter, *SUD.*

13. *SUD,* p. 146.

14. *SUD,* p. 147.

15. *AC,* pp. 69ff.

16. *AC,* p. 69.

17. *AC,* p. 71.

18. *AC,* p. 73.

19. *AC,* pp. xii–xiii. [But cf. ch. 6 ('The Glory Beyond The Grave") in Earle's *Evauscence.*]

20. *AC,* p. 77.

21. *AC,* p. 68.

22. *MR,* pp. 21–22.

23. *MR,* pp. 22–24.

24. *MR,* pp. 26–27.

25. *MR,* p. 27.

26. *MR,* p. 34.

27. *MR,* p. 34.

28. *MR,* p. xi.

29. *MR,* p. 45.

30. *MR,* p. 45.

31. In fact one finds not one but three separate arguments for the existence of God in the third meditation—from degrees of reality, causality and perfection; and the ontological argument is given separately in the fifth meditation.

32. *MR,* pp. 51–52.

33. *MR,* p. 62.

34. I examined this problem at some length in "Parmenides and Mystical Reason: A Metaphysical Dilemma", *The Modern Schoolman* (St. Louis University, St. Louis; Vol. LX, Number 1, Nov. 1982) pp. 30–47.

35. *MR,* pp. 70–71.

36. *MR,* p. 71.

III

Art, Ontology, and Consciousness

Some Reflections on Spinoza's Ethics *as Edifying Ontology*

FORREST WILLIAMS

What each man is to decide is simply what he is to be. . . . If it is a decision that each must make, it cannot be deduced from pure reason, it cannot be generalised from empirical research, and it cannot descend from revelation.

The Autobiographical Consciousness[1]

In our inner professional circles, a more pointed sneer could hardly be found than that a work is edifying.

'Notes on the Death of Culture'[2]

In the many years I have known William Earle, first my teacher at Northwestern University shortly after World War II, then friend and colleague, I have been struck both by the decisive content of his thought and by what I might call his philosophical *voice*. Whether in the classroom, at the podium, or in print, he has always expressed himself, it seems to me, in a style of discourse that is singular and quite unmistakable. He always engages a fundamental issue instantly, and often startlingly—see the opening lines of almost any article, essay, book, or even chapter; moves swiftly toward a sharpening of what is and what is not his theme; insists on the phenomenon, on seeing with one's own eyes what is given "in person," as Husserl would say, disqualifying any deductive, inductive, or causal strategies that lead away from rather than into the original *sense* of the issue; and insists on both the clarity and the limits of clarity offered by the phenomenon. All this in energetic, resilient, witty, often ironic, prose.

95

All who know his work will recognize, I believe, what I am referring to. Like everything concrete and individual, it is hardly definable. That philosophy should exhibit its content in such vivid style, that it should, in consequence, be eminently readable discourse, is far from new, of course. Nevertheless, it is not invariably so in philosophy and perhaps need not always be so. In any event, nowadays, when many of our philosophical publications do make ungrateful reading, and sometimes even appear to have been written in the bland tones of a circumspect committee, I always turn to his writings in secure anticipation of both a singular style and major philosophic contention.

These philosophic virtues were already apparent in the classroom, to the delight of us students, from the day that Bill came to Northwestern University at the invitation of Paul Henle, the new chairman who had himself just left the University of Michigan to accept the assignment of strengthening and expanding the department of philosophy. As a result of this appointment by Paul Henle, Bill was soon to give Continental phenomenology another important base on this side of the Atlantic.

I now realize, however, somewhat to my surprise, that the major thinkers to whom Bill introduced me in my university studies were not figures in modern phenomenology, but earlier philosophers, at that time generally ignored in Anglo-American circles: Hegel, Kierkegaard, Nietzsche, and Spinoza. He did not give a course on Spinoza, but did give a paper about 1948 (as a guest speaker, if I remember correctly, in a seminar conducted by Paul Henle) in which he defended Spinoza's ontological argument. I was a junior, and probably understood little enough at the time (or now?). Nevertheless, it made a strong impression on me, and not least by its incisiveness and vigor. Some 15 years later, remembering the paper, of which I had a reprint, I returned to it, and as a result began studying Spinoza. Some of the following reflections therefore originated, in a sense, in Bill's seminar talk 35 years ago, though they may well not, for all that, represent *his* Spinoza. However, these notes hope at least to reflect the spirit of the passages from the writings quoted above, to which I shall return in the concluding paragraphs.

Despite its title, Spinoza's *Ethics* has been treated by contemporary philosophers largely as metaphysics and epistemology, that is, largely in terms of Books One and Two. Most anthologies used in courses in the history of philosophy choose these themes in Spinoza, and most graduate students similarly limit their study of Spinoza.

There may be some good reasons for this truncated image in the English-speaking world of one of the great works of Western thought. Perhaps it is because Anglo-American philosophy in its approaches to philosophical problems is mainly an extension of the Enlightenment, an outcome of an era of epistemology preoccupied with the rationale of the new natural science. But Spinoza, although commonly associated with such epistemological preoccupations and placed in the company of such thinkers as Descartes, Locke, Hume, and Kant, was not in fact chiefly concerned with founding or justifying the new science, for all his sympathy with its mathematical aspects. To read him as part of this modern sequence leads to a narrowing of his *Ethics* to a modern metaphysical and epistemological project which is then unaccountably followed by a very bulky "hybrid" of "ethics" and "psychology."

The *Ethics* has also to overcome another *parti pris*, a popular conception of moral philosophy which consists almost exclusively of fine-tuning and controversy directed to the rule-moralities of obligation of Kant and the Utilitarians. This characteristically modern approach to moral philosophy is at variance with the tradition of ethical reflection to which Spinoza belongs. Let us make sure, therefore, of what it is that Spinoza was *not* doing in his *Ethics*. For that, we may look briefly at both Kant and the Utilitarians.

These later thinkers, in whom most contemporary moral philosophy is rooted, tried to replace tradition, custom, positive law, and the informally negotiated, usually tacit conventions and manners of everyday intercourse, by universal rules of conduct, or at least, required them to measure up to such philosophically derived rules. Kant, as we know, began with the truism of impartiality, and claimed to deduce from this empty principle of justice, by recourse to reason alone, specific maxims which are obligatory for everyone at all times, for example, the maxim of truth-telling. All differences among persons, circumstances, and social roles, of which "ordinary" pre-philosophical morality takes account, vanish under the white glare of these abstract maxims. A prisoner of war should tell his captors the position of his unit, and diplomats should lay all their cards on the negotiating table. But surely such issues cannot be settled from above by these moralities of universal principles; not, of course, because they are too minute and inconsequential for philosophical genius to bother with, but on the contrary, because they are far too important to human society to be left to philosophical adjudication. Daily questions of obligation and duty would be lifted out of the push and pull of social existence and concrete circumstances; he who disagrees with his fellows should no longer argue, make distinctions, suggest alternative rules, and (if necessary) fight. All such conflicts would instead be determined deductively—not by Immanuel Kant himself, be it noted—but by Reason, *tout court*. And against Reason as such, after all, who could possibly argue? Indeed, would not any rational being, commanding in the name of rationality, and not on behalf of any human desire, be morally entitled to suppress forcibly any and all opposition to such demonstrated moral maxims?

Hence the astuteness of Hegel's observation that the Terror which succeeded the French Revolution was Kant put into practice. The apparent opponents of Kant, the Utilitarians, are quite like him in this respect, as Earle has noted.[3] Their objection is not at all to philosophical demonstration of universal rules of conduct, but to the evident impossibility of moving by reason alone from the vacuity of the principle of impartiality to specific maxims of conduct. A principle only slightly less empty, only slightly less remote from human experience, supplies a trace of content, under the vague names of "pleasure" and "pain." The resulting hedonic maxims, though different from Kant's, are no less obligatory on all of us. As Earle has observed, the "smiling" ethics of "the greatest happiness for the greatest number" resembles the "thin-lipped" ethics of Kant in its issuance of such philosophical rules.[4] Both, of course, fly in the face of "ordinary" moral rules. The one does so in the name of pure reason, the other in the name of a spurious science of utility. Such a priori arguments arriving at universal moral rules of conduct surely end up proving too much. As Hilary Putnam noted recently, "one feels as if one had asked for a subway token and been given a passenger ticket valid for the first interplanetary passenger-carrying space ship instead."[5]

There is of course a thread of moral significance that runs through the Kantian and Utilitarian philosophies of universal rules of conduct, the notion of justice blindfolded, or impartiality. What is sauce for the goose is indeed sauce for the gander. In this negative form, it is a necessity of social existence. In addition, the empty principle of universalization does express, beyond social necessity, a positive moral value: various types of care for other human beings regarded as comparable in value to oneself. Kant, inconsistently with his claim that the emotional fabric of human life cannot occupy a central place in moral theory, focused on this element of morality under the heading of an unique "feeling of respect." Hume, of course, could put a sentiment of human sympathy at the center of his moral philosophy without inconsistency. The pure Utilitarian, which Hume clearly was not, does not even have this much realism about human life, witness the notorious problem as to why any human being, as conceived by Utilitarians, should ever value so many unknown others and act on the principle of utility, unless coerced to do so.

If the impartial treatment according to rules which arises from "the feeling of respect" or "the sentiment of sympathy" for other human beings is indeed of moral as well as social significance, however, this state of affairs may have something to do with what we *are* as human beings, not solely with an emotional side of us, nor solely with a rational side. For we are, after all, both at once. In that case, the issue must have something to do with the entire rational-emotive fabric of human existence, and with the question of the excellence of a human being as a whole being. Impartiality grounded in care for others is certainly a high excellence in certain situations, but surely not the only excellence, nor necessarily an overriding one in every morally significant situation. The fundamental ethical issue, in any case, becomes that of human virtues and vices. The mention of this tradition of philosophy may release us from the dichotomies and sterilities of philosophical theories of universal moral rules, and bring the discussion around to a very different philosophical tradition. Consequently, I should like to look now at Spinoza's *Ethics*, where our ontological status and our actual human composition as modes of a single substance are the grounds of moral life.

It is clear that the term *ethica*, as Spinoza used it, had almost nothing to do with rules of obligation (he does recommend some practical precepts, as we shall see later), and nothing whatsoever to do with the ambition of demonstrating universal maxims.

On the one hand, as we know, the term *ethos* originally meant custom or usage. Customs are indispensable to the moral life, in any society. Spinoza never denied this fact, and never pretended to pre-empt such customs by philosophic argument. His *ethica* obviously reflects, however, the meaning of *ethos* which points to a somewhat different area of decisive concern: the notion of "character" or "disposition." Indeed, there exists an even earlier Indo-European meaning, the root *swedh*, which expresses, I believe, even more accurately the concern of Spinoza's *Ethica*. A compound of the root *dhe*, meaning "place," and the reflexive pronoun *swe*, the Indo-European *swedh* connotes "placing oneself."[6] With the probably allowable assumption that "place" had a figurative meaning, "ethics" on this view would concern the reflexive shaping or locating of one's character or self; or, in Earle's words, it is a matter of "each of us deciding what he is to be." Spinoza's *Ethica*, on this view, is essentially a reflective ontology directed toward the possibilities of human choice. Those possibilities are a function of human existence as *desire*. It belongs, therefore, to a tradition of "treatises on the passions."

Such treatises tend to be discounted by modern philosophers because they seem "merely psychological." At the same time, they tend to be ignored by psychologists today because they are not experimental. At most they merit mention in the psychology textbooks as prescientific gropings. Perhaps it is not entirely out of place, however, to retrieve for the term "psychology" the rich meaning that it still had as recently as a century ago, and still has in some clinical circles. In any event, since I know of no more apt term to designate the bulk of Spinoza's treatise, I shall call "psychological" his study of the emotional life in Books Three, Four, and Five (through Proposition 20). By contrast, I shall call Books One and Two "metaphysical," and the last part of the *Ethics*, Propositions 21 to 42 of Book Five, the "religious" or "yogic" part, in their root sense which connotes "bond" or "union." Considered in their internal connections, these three stages of the *Ethics* seem to me to compose what might be called an "edifying ontology." I would like now to gloss some aspects of these three themes. My remarks, of course, will be extremely selective. I shall not presume to urge Spinoza's ethical views as such. Only the text itself could possibly measure up to that task. But I do want to analyze some of its internal structure, because the *Ethics* is the *sort* of rational discourse on moral issues that usually has no recognized place today, excluded by the aims of experimental psychology, on one side, and by narrowly epistemic philosophies of mind, on the other.

The work rests, as is well known, on two main supports: the so-called "ontological argument" and the threefold distinction between opinion (generalizations from images), rational explanation, and rational intuition. (Book Two, Pr. 40, n.2.)

Regarding the ontological proof of Book One, I take Earle's view to be clearly correct: one cannot plausibly add arguments to Spinoza's thesis without implicitly rejecting its intuitional character.[7] The definitions, axioms, and propositions of Book One can only lay out *ordine geometrico* the conceptual resources within which the intuitional affirmation of the necessity of the existence of substance, or God, can be clearly enacted in an adequate cognition. Consequently, the proof is *in* the adequate idea itself, not in any discursive argument. As Bill notes,

> That [the ontological thesis] is a tautology is true, but whether it is "wretched" or not will depend on what value we wish to place on the analytic clarification of existence.[8]

To assert God's existence, he notes, "is to frame an analytic proposition."[9]

Unfortunately, it is almost impossible today to break the grip of the Kantian vocabulary and the distinctions it imposes. The term "analytic," for example, is almost inevitably associated with Kant's "synthetic," "a priori," and "a posteriori," which he combined and employed to negotiate a particular conception of assertion and truth which was from the start quite foreign to Spinoza's philosophy. The ontological affirmation (that God or substance necessarily exists) is certainly not intended—to employ Kant's philosophical vocabulary— to be the ascription of a predicate to a subject, or a property or attribute to a substance. Hence, it cannot be a synthetic truth. Given the meanings assigned by Kant to the four distinctions, one of the two remaining juxtapositions, "analytic a posteriori," is necessarily nonsensical. Spinoza's thesis, therefore, *must* be classified as "analytic a priori." But analytic a priori assertions are necessarily without any existential import for Kantian epistemology (and *a fortiori* most con- temporary epistemology). Spinoza's most fundamental thesis thus becomes by prior definition a nonthesis.

For Spinoza, of course, the possibility of intellectual intuition, that is, an intuitional idea of the intellect which has existential import, is vital. Kant's notion of "experience," his predicational model of truth and falsehood, and the four features of predicative judgment just alluded to, together serve to deny the possibility of even speaking sensibly of an "intellectual intuition." One can disagree with Kant's philosophy by denying, for example, the possibility of "synthetic a priori" truths, as has been done; one may even go so far as to deny the possibility of distinguishing decisively between "synthetic" and "analytic" truths, as has also been done (though this risks, as in contemporary hermeneutics, an abandonment of founding principles in favor of interpretive practices); but both these disagreements with Kant continue to accept his basic terms. Earle's phrase, "the analytic clarification of existence" seems apposite regarding Spinoza's cos- mology, provided we free "analytic" from the set of interlocking principles which shape its meaning in Kantian and neo-Kantian epistemology, and note the special importance of the term "clarifi- cation." A judgment-model of truth leads to a view of knowledge as an *additive synthesis*, whereas Spinoza's intuitional model leads to a view of knowledge as *a gain in clarity*. The cognitive movement for Spinoza is thus not from judgments to still more judgments, but from relatively confused ideas to clearer ideas.

The point is crucial because it is one with Spinoza's shift from a substance-attribute (or thing-property) metaphysics to a substance- mode metaphysics, which is in turn essential to the subsequent "psychological" discussion. The former metaphysics is Aristotelian and medieval. Kant retained it and reinterpreted it "transcendentally," in his new sense of this term. It is a tradition from which Spinoza, however, had already departed, even though his vocabulary, as compared to Kant's reconstruction of our philosophical language, remained in large part within that venerable tradition. It is an historic instance of a new wine poured into old bottles. Thus, in the *Ethics*, the *fundamental* concern of rational thought is not with beings as qualified by some attribute or property that sets them off generically from other classes of beings ("Potassium is soluble," "Mercury is insoluble," etc.). The fundamental concern is with beings ("modes") which *exist in* another being ("substance"), which does not itself exist in any other being, which is necessarily singular, and which exists necessarily. This state of affairs cannot be formulated according to the traditional subject-predicate conception of truth. It conflicts, accordingly, with any "thing-property" metaphysics or epistemology.

Hence the otherwise puzzling fact that Spinoza's only use for "attribute" is to refer to (the sole) substance itself. The term no longer suggests "predicable property of a substance." Otherwise stated, the grammar of nouns qualified by adjectives, characteristic of the first level of knowledge, or opinion, just is not pertinent at the third level of knowledge in Book One, where it survives only as the way in which one writes. If any familiar grammatical structure is more suitable to Spinoza's ontology—though certainly not within our linguistic practice—it would be the verb-adverb combination. "Substance" is a gerund, referring to something entirely positive and active. "Mode," an adverb in its meaning, cannot be conceived apart from gerundive "substance", and modifies it somewhat as "quickly" modifies, say, "running." Consequently, as an "adverbial expression" of substance, each mode, such as you, I, Mary, Fido, or the apple tree in the yard, is necessarily positive and active to the fullest extent possible. (If the tree falls on me, my quotient of activity as a mode in the universe diminishes due to an external cause: the circulation in the affected part may slow down or stop, my vision may blur, etc.)

From a neo-Kantian perspective, it would be tempting to pursue at this juncture the implications of this substance-mode metaphysics for the natural sciences, as is sometimes done. Certainly, Spinoza seemed to point in the same direction for the progress of natural science as did his seventeenth century contemporaries and their successors in philosophy and science. That is, he saw the first level of language and knowledge, or opinion and generalizations from images, as quite properly the ascription of general properties to classes of things ("Salt is soluble," etc.). The second level would be causal explanation of a transformed, algorithmic sort ("$g = mm_1/d^2$", etc.), just as one finds in modern science. Nevertheless, he did not pursue the subject in the detail of a Kant or his successors. For those who still see the scientific issues as definitive for philosophy, this sketchiness is frustrating. In reading Spinoza, however, we must allow that he was not aiming at a *physica*, and that further inquiry into substance as extension is hardly promising for an *ethica*. Hence he turns, after Book Two, mainly to a discussion of human beings as modes of substance qua thought: as minds.

If I am a mode existing in substance, and if substance is entirely active, then I am not essentially a contemplative thinker, but a striving, a *conatus*, an endeavor, more capable or less capable, according to my finite power, of some degree of thought. I am not a finite mode that exists *and then* strives in certain ways. My very being *is* striving. Any semblance of some negative, non-endeavoring substratum is just my endeavoring self conditioned, limited, thwarted, blocked, or even brought to a near standstill by other finite endeavors in my vicinity. No doubt this is all too familiar a point to the reader; but the important implication, that our peculiarly cognitive abilities are also, first and foremost, expressions of endeavor, is sometimes insufficiently regarded. The result can be a misunderstanding of the nature of Spinoza's "rationalism." The fullest use of intellect is for arriving at truths insofar as these may *benefit* us. What in the sciences may actually benefit us is often not easy to anticipate, of course. Nuclear fission was confidently thought to be safe, clean, and cheap; it turned out to be dangerous, radioactively dirty, and costly. The *fullest* use of reason, however, is to gain such knowledge as may surely provide the greatest possible human satisfaction.

> Thus it is apparent to everyone that I wish to direct all sciences to one end and aim, so that we may attain to the supreme human perfection which we have named; and, therefore, whatsoever in the sciences does not serve to promote our object will have to be rejected as useless.[10]

Hence the shift of Book Three from "cosmology" to "psychology." The aim of such "psychological" knowledge is to *become* more. This is, at the very least, to be less put upon by external causes of our behavior (some, external *simpliciter*; others incorporated or introjected, for example, a disease virus, a hostile *imago*). This aim requires a reflective analysis, in the light of the ontological state of affairs in which we exist, of ourselves as human endeavors. Or, since we are speaking of ourselves as thinking, choosing beings—as minds—the aim is knowledge of ourselves as *desire*.

The "psychological" stage of the *Ethics*, then, is highly tendentious. The supposedly "hyperrationalist" Spinoza does not recommend knowledge for its own sake, but knowledge of a certain sort for the sake of decreased external constraint or increased empowerment, increased freedom. If there were in reality a different path to greater empowerment and freedom than such "psychological self-knowledge"—for example, by great riches, by the multiplication of pleasures, by the subjugation of those around us—then Spinoza would in all consistency have to rewrite his ethical treatise. The bulk of the work, then, consists precisely in the specific case which Spinoza proceeds to make for the path of clarifying self-knowledge, where the self is *essentially* "desire." The *Ethics* thus first comes into its own, it seems to me, *after* the fundamental ontology has been sufficiently but schematically established, with Book Three, "On the Origin and Nature of the Emotions."

Like the natural sciences, the "psychology" must move from the relatively confused, first level of knowledge, or opinion's generalizations from images, to the second level of knowledge, to rational explanations of causes; these are more or less analogous (in the language of ideas) to algorithmic explanations (in the language of extended bodies). I would like to make several points about this complex and lengthy analysis, not to urge its truth here (that each must determine for himself), but to underscore the *sort* of moral philosophy it is, or seems to me to be.

Here, in the realm of the passions, the first level of knowledge does not consist of those ordinary observations and classifications of things in our perceived environment which natural science proceeds to transform into algorithmic explanations. It consists rather of our everyday acquaintance with human endeavor in the form of a multiplicity of familiar emotions, either effects of external causes or active expressions of desire.

Modern psychologists, as we know, far prefer to lead us into laboratories, in order to make their initial observations *ab ovo*, on the assumption that it is not scientifically respectable to begin with any prior acquaintance with one's subject matter. They forget that modern science did not begin with no previous acquaintance with things, but did make a prior conceptual determination of just what information was deemed relevant. The revival of mathematics was the key to physical science, as Spinoza was one of several to propose. In turning from his meta*physica* to his *ethica* proper, however, Spinoza takes as crucially relevant, on the one hand, acquaintance with the spectrum of emotional life that is already available to us by virtue of our living it and talking about it, and on the other hand, the ontological key supplied by Books One and Two. This spectrum of human emotions had already been intelligently studied and inventoried in reflective treatises on the passions from Aristotle to Descartes. Spinoza's philosophical problem is therefore to clarify this rich "psychological" or "psychic" material according to relevant principles, on the basis of the antecedent ontology.

I spoke of the passions scrutinized by Spinoza as a spectrum. Since the list consists of those features of emotional life which matter most in human life, the analogy to the visible spectrum obviously weakens. We may typically find certain colors more or less agreeable (hospital-green is boring, sky-blue pleasing), but they do not express the value of human existence, much less matters for choice. The virtues and vices, by contrast, have to do with our status in being (our *virtus*). It is manifestly impossible to designate such emotional dispositions without at the same time praising or dispraising them. Envy, hatred, courage, cowardice, mirth, hope, dejection, greed, generosity, pity, equanimity, are all dispositions of unparalleled human importance. There is no neutral language in which even to bring them to mind. To characterize envy is to characterize a *vice*, not a virtue; to characterize courage is to characterize a *virtue*, not a vice. And so on.

Spinoza's object, of course, is to move from this first level of knowledge, or opinion, to a second level of knowledge, or rational explanation. Because a human being is an endeavor, such explanation consists of a reflective analysis and clarification of the relationships between emotional dispositions and their accompanying ideas. "Hatred is pain, accompanied by the idea of an external cause." (Book Three, Dfs. of the Emotions, vii.) My idea of the external cause of my hatred may be a mistaken one, of course. For example, the object of my hatred may be someone who only resembles (even, merely seems to me to resemble) someone whom I previously hated. Now, the moral solution for me as an endeavoring mode is not merely to discover the original stimulus of my hatred, just as the psychoanalytic solution to neurosis is not merely to discover that it is really an introjected parent and not the policeman one hates. The real solution is for me to endeavor to transform the disposition itself. Naturally, if I am already brave, merciful, etc., not merely when I am in easy circumstances, but by stable disposition and under stress, I shall not need such transformation. But in fact, as Spinoza notes realistically, without cyncism or rancor, "men are of necessity prone to vengeance more than to mercy."[11] The task of Spinoza's "psychological" analyses, as we know, is to bring those confused ideas which are our vices or weaknesses to sufficient clarity that we may understand our own confusion and loss. We may then discover that courage is indeed empowering, and cowardice, hatred, envy, etc., debilitating. More exactly, in the spirit of the preceding ontology and theory of cognition, the practice of the virtues is shown in these analyses to *be* (not merely to lead in some uncertain future to) an increase of agency, and the practice of a vice to *be* (not merely to result later in) a decrease of agency. For this increased understanding, unlike an increase in my knowledge of planets, genes, or subatomic particles, is at once knowledge of myself as an endeavor and is driven by my need for such knowledge. It affects me as an endeavor.

This affective process presupposes, of course, that my experience has already taught me that I may be missing "some real good." I could certainly read Spinoza's text "between quotation marks," noting its inner logic, and remain quite unaffected by what I had, in a scholarly sense, "learned." But given the identity of rational thought with increase in power, and given the endeavoring nature of the subject matter, an increased understanding of my emotional weaknesses need not be a mere curiosity for me. With respect to the passions, moving from the first level of knowledge to the second is itself a transformation of me as an endeavor, and thus an emotionally significant occurrence. The clarified idea, it must not be forgotten, is not a second idea, but the formerly confused idea itself, now clarified. The emotional energy, if you will, of the confused idea is captured and redirected, available now for different choices and for a different kind of life.

> An emotion . . . becomes more under our control, and the mind is less passive in respect to it [i.e., is less dominated by it as associated with an external cause], in proportion as it is more known to us. (Book Five, Pr. 3, Cor.)

For,

> from the true knowledge of good and evil [viz., of our own disposition] insofar as it [the cognition] is an emotion, necessarily arises desire. (Book Four, Pr. 15, Proof.)

Rationality, therefore, does not displace or even diminish desire, but marshals and redirects desire. The new enthusiasm generated by the increased knowledge, the redirection of ourselves *as desire* through the effective charge on the clearer idea, is what makes the moral difference, according to Spinoza. The process *begins in desire*—"as a sick man struggling with a deadly disease" who is determined to "really get to the root of the matter"[12]—and *eventuates in desire.*

One could not be further from truth for truth's sake (much less, duty for duty's sake), since the highest value of such "psychological" knowledge is not the truth it yields, but the increased satisfaction experienced when one is thereby more self-affirming. From the ontological analysis of Book One to the famous closing line of Book Five, the aim of the philosophy is practical, indeed, the aim is to *edify.* For the text itself can do nothing more—and attempts to do nothing less—than to recommend a specific kind of individual effort on the basis of certain cognitive claims about what we are and about the nature of the universe in which we exist.

In the Proof just referred to, Spinoza recognized realistically that my knowledge of my good and evil dispositions may not be sufficiently empowering to enable me to overcome the force of external causes which repeatedly present themselves (the attraction of ever more possessions, fame, and sensual pleasure). (Book Four, Pr. 15 & Proof.) It is only here, as a pedagogical matter, that something like rules have their inevitable place, according to Spinoza. Lacking perfect knowledge of our emotions, and knowing that we will probably be repeatedly assailed by such temptations, we may choose to "frame a system of right conduct, or practical precepts" and "commit it to memory, to apply forthwith to the particular circumstances which now and again meet us in life." (Book Five, Pr. 10, Note.) These are not universal moral rules in the Kantian or Utilitarian sense, however, but advisable ways of schooling ourselves to certain attitudes by frequent preparatory reflection; for example, by dwelling in advance on responding courageously to possible threats, on responding to hatred with love or highmindedness, and on similar anticipatory devices in the realm of the imagination, where moral weakness and mental confusion may still thrive despite our best efforts.

The last stage of the *Ethics*, concerned with the "intellectual love of God," treats specifically of one's actual identity, insofar as one is an "adequate idea (mind)," with a proper part of God. In Book One, the thesis that every mode exists *in* substance was a formal one, and it has accordingly been much debated as a seemingly abstruse bit of metaphysics. Certainly one may or may not be convinced by this ontological thesis in Book One, and if one is not convinced, one may well read no further. It seems doubtful that Spinoza would even consider it of much importance to be convinced of this ontological claim if one were in fact interested in it only as a bit of metaphysics. For the "psychological" analysis of human existence as desire has to occur before the ontological thesis can not only serve the aim of moral clarification and endeavor, but really matter as a philosophical thesis. Thus, Spinoza opens with an ontology that is edifying because it can lead to clarification of one's emotional life, where the good and evil of human existence originate. Ultimately, if one goes so far, the ontological thesis of Book One also proves to be edifying in a further sense which I have termed "religious" or "yogic." This final stage of edifying knowledge corresponds, if I understand it correctly, to the "mystical reason" of Earle's recent book by that name.[13] Both "religious" and "yogic" are used here in the root sense of "bond," "connection," or "union." The term "yoga" (our word "yoke") means, of course, the conscious realization of one's union with the absolute or whole. In Spinoza's own words, the "chief good" is precisely "knowledge of the union existing between the mind and the whole of nature."[14]

I cited at the outset, and in agreement, a statement from *The Autobiographical Consciousness* which rejects any moral theory that claims to be deduced from pure reason, generalized from empirical research, or descended from revelation. I would like now to note how, it seems to me, the sort of moral discourse represented by Spinoza's *Ethics* passes these three challenges. This can be shown, I believe, quite succinctly, if my previous remarks are correct.

The "psychological" bulk of the work, which is the moral theory proper, does not follow deductively from the metaphysical-epistemological part, though it is certainly governed by Books One and Two. In Book Three Spinoza introduces human beings as conative, just as we find ourselves in everyday life, with our common weaknesses and our much rarer virtues. No one (say, a different intelligent species from another planet) could conceivably arrive by rational deduction or any a priori manner of reasoning at the moral discussion from an understanding of Books One and Two. Human emotions, and desire as "the actual essence of man," provide both the specific discriminations and the very motive power for the inquiry that begins in Book Three.

Spinoza's analyses of the emotional life are not generalizations from scientific research. Science rests, after all, on observation of independently existing things by means of sense perception. The feasibility of Spinoza's *Ethics*, however, rests on the diametrically opposed situation that my emotion and my cognition of it are not independently existing processes, but one and the same reality in different stages of confusion or clarity. Reflective knowledge, the idea of the idea, is not observation of one idea by a different idea, for reflection has no sense with which to observe, and finds nothing observable anyway.[15] It is certainly not kinesthetic perception (of tickles, feels, vague bodily urges, etc.), though psychologists sometimes confound the two under the ambiguous rubric of "introspection" or "inner perception." Reflection is, rather, a *sui generis* cognitive activity which brings a relatively confused mind to clearer awareness.

Third, *amor intellectualis Dei* is no revelation descended from above. It is not rationally disclosed in any creedal text, and is not, strictly speaking, disclosed in any text at all, including the *Ethics*. What Spinoza means by the phrase one could only understand, if one does, through intellectual intuition, at the third level of cognition.

In conclusion, then, what sort of relation to the reader does Spinoza's discourse establish, and how does it differ in this respect from a philosophical theory of moral principles?

Although the moral content is not deducible, the prior metaphysics certainly governs the conception of human existence, the associated conception of emotion, and the particular ranking of the familiar virtues. Human beings are necessarily viewed first and foremost as endeavors in their very being. The life of the intellect is itself an expression of this endeavoring. At a sufficient level of reflexive awareness and knowledge, choice becomes possible. Self-affirmation and related affects (strength of character, courage, and highmindedness) stand in the first rank. Such dispositions as humility and repentance, in marked contrast to the traditional medieval ranking, are downgraded. This reordering of certain human values, no less than the naturalizing of divinity expressed in the recurrent phrase *"Deus sive Natura,"* helped to earn Spinoza his place on the Index as a heretic. Clearly, then, Spinoza's *Ethics* both proposed and reflected a conception of human good that broke in some important ways from the metaphysics, psychology, and ethics of more or less accepted theology and Christian culture. No doubt this ethics was not only an intellectual analysis by Spinoza, but also an expression of Spinoza's individual view of the moral life and an expression of the rare combination of pagan, Jewish, Christian, and Arab culture of his family and forebears.

If the purpose of a rational moral philosophy is to arrive at imperative rules of conduct, then its universal principles must in no way be determined by anyone's individual or cultural experience, and Spinoza's *Ethics* must seem fatally "relativistic." But I believe it was Spinoza's view—and certainly is mine—that commandments are for those in proper authority—rulers, generals, and parents—to issue to subjects, soldiers, and children. Philosophical ethics articulates in terms addressed to intellect a certain understanding of reality, with the goal of thereby clarifying the sphere of human moral concern. Its aim, in that case, cannot be to prove rules that intellect requires us to live by at all times and in all places; nor are there any such rules. Indeed, it cannot *require* anything of us, because the aim is not to order us what to do, but to awaken us to the satisfaction of valuing and strengthing certain emotional dispositions, as well as depreciating and opposing others. The ultimate effect of the discourse, therefore, must be hortatory. It differs from most exhortation ("Hang on!", "Be fair!") in speaking to our capacity for knowledge, rather than directly to our emotions, therefore speaking systematically rather than *ad hoc* or casuistically. This combination of reflective clarification and exhortation in which ontology is brought to bear on our human dispositions is what I should term "philosophical ethics." Such discourse leaves the rules and casuistry of social life where they belong, in the sphere of communal discussion and pressures, which has its own forms of persuasion and debate; where, moreover, a philosophical discourse, as one component of human culture, may at times exert its own significant kind of influence on us.

FORREST WILLIAMS: SOME REFLECTIONS ON SPINOZA'S ETHICS AS EDIFYING ONTOLOGY

Note: All citations of Spinoza are from *The Chief Works of Benedict de Spinoza*, Vols. I & II (New York: Dover, 1951, 1955; R.H.M. Elwes trans.).

1. William Earle, *The Autobiographical Consciousness* (Chicago: Quadrangle, 1972), p. 193.

2. William Earle, 'Notes on the Death of Culture,' in Cecil Hemley (ed.), *Noonday 1* (Chicago: Nooday Press, 1958), p. 7.

3. Cp. *Autobiographical Consciousness*, pp. 187–188.

4. Ibid.

5. Hilary Putnam, 'How Not To Solve Ethical Problems,' (Lindley Lecture, published by University of Kansas, 1983), 3.

6. Cp. C.T. Onions, *The Oxford Dictionary of English Etymology* (Oxford: Oxford University Press, 1969), p. 329.

7. Cp. William Earle, *Mystical Reason* (Chicago: Regnery, 1980), pp. 129–130, 139–140.

8. Ibid., p. 137.

9. Ibid, p. 134.

10. Spinoza, Vol. II, 'On the Improvement of the Understanding,' p. 7.

11. Spinoza, Vol. I, 'A Political Treatise,' p. 289.

12. Spinoza, Vol. II, p. 5.

13. Cp. *Mystical Reason*, p. xi.

14. Spinoza, Vol. II, p. 6.

15. Cp. William Earle, 'Science and Philosophy,' in *Buffalo Studies* (II, July 1966), 62.

Nietzsche as the Last Philosopher of Art

ERICH HELLER

For a philosopher to say 'the good and the beautiful are one' is infamy; if he goes on to add, 'also the true', one ought to thrash him. Truth is ugly.

We possess *art* lest we *perish of the truth.*

This utterance, at once crystalline and tumultuous, brilliant and violent, was written by Nietzsche in 1888, the year preceding his mental collapse. It is contained in one of the posthumous notes that have been collected in *The Will to Power* (MA, XIX, 229 and W, 822)* and has the resonance of last words, words spoken or cried out with that assured despair or hope that allows for no debate; and perhaps it was really meant as Nietzsche's last word concerning a problem of which—à propos his rereading, in the same year, of his youthful *Birth of Tragedy*—he said that it was the earliest which compellingly demanded his serious attention; and even today, he added, this dilemma filled him with "holy terror" (MA, XIV, 326).

---

* In all quotations the translations are my own. As for abbreviations: W, followed by the numeral indicating the numbered section, stands for *The Will to Power*, trans. W. Kaufmann and R. J. Hollingdale (New York, 1967); MA, followed by a Roman numeral indicating the volume and an Arabic numeral the page, stands for the Musarionausgabe of Nietzsche's Work, 23 volumes (Munich, 1920–29). Parts of the present essay were presented at the 1980 meeting of the North American Nietzsche Society in conjunction with the American Philosophical Association, Eastern Division, and subsequently printed in *Nietzsche-Studien* (Berlin and New York, 1983).

The problem, so terrifying to Nietzsche from beginning to end, is the relationship between art and truth. Even in the context of *The Birth of Tragedy* it is exceedingly difficult to grasp. For whatever meaning is given to the word "truth," no common denominator can possibly be found among the endless varieties of "art": a sculpture of ancient Egypt, an archaic Apollo, *Antigone, King Lear*, Michelangelo, Bach, Mozart, Beethoven, Bizet or Offenbach, not to mention a short poem of Goethe's or Mallarmé's. Even if we equate art with ancient tragedy, as *The Birth of Tragedy* might suggest, just as it proclaims tragedy's rebirth in Wagner's music drama, the question is whether the dilemma, whatever its "true" nature, was resolved and the terror diminished by the terrifying "We possess *art* lest we *perish of the truth"*? Has the ugliness of the ugly truth increased so drastically since Plato's time that now anyone associating it with beauty commits a philosophical felony? Has truth become so militantly aggressive that art must serve as a fortification against its invading our lives?

That we should not be able to live with the truth, the whole truth, has surely been said before, and by no one more memorably than by Plato in the cave parable; and it has been repeated again and again, by Lessing, for instance, who, had God given him the choice between the truth and the infinite search for it, would have asked him for the endless striving because the truth, he wrote, was only for God Himself; or by the story of the veiled image of Sais, the mysterious image of "the truth," whose unveiled sight would have been deadly. In all these instances, and many, many more, it is a matter of the whole truth being unattainable or not meant for the treasury of man. But that truth would kill us *because of its devastating ugliness* has never been said—surely not with Nietzsche's aphoristic vehemence. As the "truth" in Nietzsche's saying obviously means the true character of existence, and not merely this or that experience in our individual lives that may shock us to death, what, once more, can "art" mean as its radical contrast and "remedy"? There are many reasons for our reluctance to answer this question.

There is above everything else the indisputable fact that, since the generation of Rilke, George, Mann, the idea of art as the quasi-religious opposite of "life" has run its course. Who among the young can even understand Stefan George's imperial pronouncement that *"kein Ding sei, wo das Wort gebricht"*—there ought to be no thing where language fails in naming it—which in the end meant the same as Karl Kraus' celebrated and notorious declaration that language had to abdicate where the task was to find the right words for the dominion of Hitler: *"Mir fällt zu Hitler nichts ein."* Certainly, there is no artist any more who would look upon his art as an all but ecclesiastical, indeed monastic devotion. "I have many brothers in cassocks," Rilke wrote, and the young Thomas Mann's Tonio Kröger even thought of having to sacrifice "life" in the service to his art: Not one leaf from the laurel tree of art, he said, may be plucked without the artist's paying for it with his life. Meanwhile, art has come to be as "ungodly" as life itself, and the evergreen laurel tree, for Tonio Kröger so dangerously in foliage, has been badly damaged by an autumn in which more has withered than the leaves of trees. "O trees of life, when will your winter come?" Rilke asked at the beginning of the darkest of the *Duino Elegies,* the fourth, written entirely in the deep shadow of the First World War. "Now," is the unison answer of modern literature. It is not for its practitioners to dedicate themselves to literature with that idolatrous religiousness that was Flaubert's, Thomas Mann's, Rilke's, and—amid the endless curses he uttered against the idol—Franz Kafka's. Indeed, art is no longer as *"Heiter,"* as serene, as Schiller believed it should be; yet it has ceased to be as serious as to demand the sacrifice of "life."

Then, there is the unsettling emergence during Nietzsche's lifetime and even before of a species of literature that hardly earned his praise but that, for the sake of his consistency and our intellectual comfort, he ought to have judged even more harshly. Sometimes he did, but only selectively (although when he did so, he discriminated with his unfailing artistic instinct). What I have in mind, is realism and of course naturalism, a term that Nietzsche had to judge utterly inappropriate (W, 864). It is the art—the art? Nietzsche would have asked—of lying as little as possible about the horrors of life. Indeed, "naturalism" prides itself upon forcing the "truth," as these artists saw it, upon the attention of the public. Nietzsche would have approved of our using the word "forcing;" for he once, and more than once, characterized "modern art," above all naturalism, as "the art of tyrannizing." Those "artists," he wrote, were in the habit of employing an "overwhelming mass"—an ugly mass, it is to be presumed—"before which the senses become confused," and "brutality in color, material, desires" (W, 827). One wonders, with regard to both the tyranny and the brutality, what his vocabulary would have been if he had lived to witness the productions of the cinema, a form of presentation that is, quite apart from any content, by its very nature incomparably more "tyrannical" than any art that preceded it: the very darkness in which it is being watched opens the spectators' eyes and minds to the vision of the film's maker with a hypnotic exclusiveness that is unique in the history of the arts; or of Eugene O'Neil or Tennessee Williams or Thomas Bernhard.

Or did he anticipate all this when in 1888 he wrote: "The ugly, that is, the contradiction to art, that which is outside the scope of art, its No; every time decline, impoverishment of life, impotence, disintegration, degeneration are suggested even faintly, the aesthetic man reacts with his No" (W, 809). Or when he said in the same year of the increase in civilization "that it necessarily brings with it an increase in the morbid elements, in the neurotic-psychiatric and criminal" (W, 864) all of which is as "depressing" as it is "the symptom of a depression," and "takes away strength, impoverishes, weighs down . . ." (W, 809). It is exceedingly doubtful whether history is bent upon teaching lessons; but if it does, it proves right the grand gesture with which Nietzsche dismisses the revolutionary claim of "naturalism." A critique of social ills? By no means, a pathological fascination with them and a foreboding of ever more pathology: ". . . the artist, restrained from crime by weakness of will and timidity, and not yet ripe for the *madhouse*" makes himself the bearer of the message "of the Revolution, the establishment of equal rights," and becomes the paragon "of the instincts of decline (of *ressentiment*, discontent, the drive to destroy, anarchism and nihilism), including the slave instincts . . . that have long been kept down" (W, 864).

As examples of the massive tyranny of the arts, Nietzsche quotes the creations of Zola and Wagner. Zola and Wagner may seem a surprising pair of brothers in the art of hypnotic brutality, yet their features do display a family resemblance (of which Thomas Mann, in his most important essay on Wagner [Thomas Mann, *Gesammelte Werke*, Frankfurt 1960, IX,] made a great deal and thus provoked some guardians of the "German genius," intellectual warriors that, under the rule of Hitler, happened to live in 1933 in the "Wagner City" Munich, to that notorious "protest" that certainly helped to keep the author of *Buddenbrooks* outside the frontiers of Germany for the rest of his life).

In the order of aphorisms collected in *The Will to Power* the succinct proclamation of the function of art—to make the unbearable bearable—is preceded by an observation that, of course, denies the possibility of pessimism in art: "There is no such thing as pessimistic art—Art affirms. Job affirms" (W, 821). True, true, although one may not without some scruples accept the abrupt inclusion of the Book of Job in the category of Art. But had we not been prepared for such manoeuvres by Nietzsche's persistently speaking of Art as the power that raises us above the wretchedness of life? It was for this very reason that he denied the very possibility of such a thing as pessimistic art; and there is no mistaking the religious resonance of the voice that pronounces: "What is essential in art remains its being bent upon perfecting existence, its creating perfection and plenitude. Art is essentially *affirmation, blessing, deification* of existence . . . Schopenhauer is *wrong* when he says that certain works of art (what is meant is once more Attic tragedy) serve pessimism." And in case of *The Birth of Tragedy* not yet being understood—as late as 1888— he emphasizes again that tragedy does *not* teach resignation, as Schopenhauer believed. No, for an artist "to represent terrible and questionable things shows in itself his instinct for power and magnificence: he does not fear them" (W, 821), but affirms even evil in its transfiguration through art. He affirms like Job.

To descend from such heights into the lowlands of grammar looks like seeking shelter in banality. Yet is it really banal to enquire whether the verb "affirm," a transitive verb, does not stand in need of an object? My Latin teacher, a kindly Cistercian monk, rigorously insisted on his pupils' asking "whom or what?" to find out whether a verb was transitive. If it responded positively to the question, it was. "Affirm?" he would have said: "whom or what?" and might have failed Rilke on the famous opening line of the Orphic sonnet "Rühmen, das ist's!", "Praising, that's it!" "Whom or what?" he would have asked and waited for a considerably more particular answer than "life as such." "Life is not 'as such'." And indeed, it is only due to Nietzsche and Rilke that the language of poets has become accustomed to the—as it were—intransitive use of such verbs as "affirm" or "praise." This is more than a matter of grammar: grammar, as it often does, mirrors here the grammar of consciousness itself. It is impossible to make articulate sense, and not merely an ecstatic—intoxicated dithyramb, of the praiseworthiness of praise itself, or simply to affirm affirmation. "Ein Gott vermags," "A god may do it," Rilke's third sonnet says; but before Rilke took charge of him, Orpheus was no god. Rilke raised him to the status of a god by merging him with Nietzsche's Dionysus; and he, the god, surely, succeeds where a mere human being is bound to fail: in the lavishing of unconditional yea-saying upon an existence in which the No of disaster, sickness, mass murder, cruelty and senseless death is as inescapable as the Yes of love and happiness. With Job the object is easily supplied—in as un-Nietzschean a manner as can be: Job affirms God. Even so, the story of Job is never easy to take, and had Job received and in the end believed Nietzsche's message of the death of God, it would be a downright unbearable tale.

He who is not inclined to dwell on such questions, may meditate for a while on the song of the Watchman on the Tower in the fifth act of *Faust II*. The first verses of it are one of Goeth's most beautiful lyrical poems, a song of praise intoned by one who is at that moment in the state of pure, will-less contemplation, the ineluctable condition of what Schopenhauer calls aesthetic experience—the experience that is untouched by any self-interest. Lynceus sees, *sees*, and only the happiness of seeing does matter to him. *What* he sees, is almost irrelevant. It is beautiful, because he sees it with eyes that are undistracted by anything that is not pure seeing; nearby the wood and the deer, and high above it the moon and the stars; and beside himself with ecstatic yea-saying, he speaks the words that are always quoted as proof of Goethe's affirmation of life. Yet they lose sight of any definable or even particular grammatical object; for

> Es sei, wie es wolle,
> Es war doch so schön.

(Be it as it may, in the sight of those blissful and blessing eyes— "Ihr glücklichen Augen//was je ihr gesehn . . ."—it has been nothing but beautiful.)

In the whole range of literature, there is no purer lyrical expression of the jubilant yea-saying affirming the world as "aesthetic phenomenon," as young Nietzsche, in *The Birth of Tragedy*, renames what for Schopenhauer was the artist's intuition of the Platonic idea beyond the mere appearance of a thing, an intuitive vision that is undimmed by any self-will. But because Nietzsche, as early as the otherwise faithful Schopenhauerian *Birth of Tragedy*, robs this vision of its transcendental object, the Platonic idea, it is bereft of any object whatever. This is a philosophical act of surgery the consequences of which proved fatal to his philosophy of art.

What in the monologue of the Watchman on the Tower breaks, with catastrophic suddenness, into the celebration of the "ewige Zier" ("kosmos" in Greek), of the "aesthetic phenomenon," is hardly ever quoted. Indeed, it is no longer a song and differs from what precedes it by the changed rhythm: Goethe has separated it from the celebration by the stage instruction "pause". And what a pause is this!

For abruptly the Watchman's aesthetic contemplation finishes when he is reminded of his task as an active human being, placed upon the tower not to celebrate life as an aesthetic phenomenon but to guard Faust's estate against threatening dangers. And what he sees now is the smoke rising from the little house of the dear old couple Philemon and Baucis. It is on fire, as a consequence of Faust's megalomaniac orders to Mephistopheles: to remove the two ancient people from the small holding on Faust's empire; and the fire may spread, destroy not only the two but cause more disasters. Thus the Watchman's glorious yea-saying ends. He now reminds himself of his duty as a Watchman: he was up on his tower not merely in order to delight in the view. "*Nicht allein mich zu ergetzen,//bin ich hier so hochgestellt;*" and is now terrified by the horrible threat from out of the dark world:

Welch ein greuliches Entsetzen
Droht mir aus der finstern Welt.

The indiscriminate object of praise has changed to the accusative of terror. Only a few verse lines before, the Watchman's eyes were happy to see *whatever* it was; but now he deplores that his sight reaches even as far as the burning hut:

Sollt ihr Augen dies erkennen!
Muss ich so weitsichtig sein!

The exact transitiveness of transitive verbs cannot easily be circumvented.

Is this, then, the way in which art affirms even the ugliness of life, "art understood as the potent incentive to living, as the eternal urge to live, to live eternally" (*MA*, XIV, 328)? We only just heard such yea-saying, heard of an art that deifies life and blesses it as Lynceus does before he espies the flames, an art that refutes Schopenhauer's belief that tragedy teaches resignation; and immediately upon the yea-saying Job there follows, with a question mark, Zola, this time not in the company of Wagner but in that of the equally questionable Goncourts. What is wrong with those Frenchmen? "The things they display are ugly: but *that* they display them comes from their pleasure in the ugly." One is tempted to interject: "from the pleasure taken in the truth"? And how does this "pleasure in the ugly" differ from the artist's fearlessness in "representing terrible and questionable things," a courage that shows "his instinct for power and magnificence"? No doubt, this instinct differs from that pleasure. But how? Yet Nietzsche continues: "It's no good! If you think otherwise, you're deceiving yourselves. How liberating is Dostoevsky!" (*W*, 821).

This is a psychological coup and shows Nietzsche's superb literary instinct: praise for Dostoevsky (and Stendhal) despite their practicing "realism" and even "naturalism" in literature. We do not know for certain how much of Dostoevsky Nietzsche had read, but it must have been more than *Notes from Underground* (a book that undoubtedly had prompted him to call himself in the preface to *Dawn*—1881, preface of 1886—an "underground man;" it is likely that he knew *Crime and Punishment*, too. When he chanced upon Dostoevsky late in his life, he said of him not only that finding him was one of the most welcome strokes of good luck in his life (even more so than his "discovery of Stendhal") but also that he was "the only psychologist from whom I had something to learn" (*MA*, XVII, 145). The question "What?" although it lures us into the unknowable, is irresistible. Dostoevsky is "liberating" and different in that from the

Goncourts and Zola, the "naturalists" that took pleasure in showing the ugly, non-artists who did not know that just because the truth of life was its spiritually killing ugliness, we have art, the beautiful illusion, the redeeming untruth, the bewitching lie. Zarathustra himself calls himself a liar insofar as he is an artist. (*MA*, XIII, 166).

The beautiful illusion versus the ugly truth: surely, it cannot be in this aesthetic sense that Dostoevsky could possibly have proved "liberating." His world can be as ugly as any naturalist's, and inelegant is his style. Well then, how is the sentence "We possess *art* lest we *perish of truth*," a dictum that is the extreme formula of the mature Nietzsche's philosophy of art, to be reconciled with his praise of Dostoevsky? The answer is "Not at all." And the same applies to every passage in the *young* Nietzsche's *Birth of Tragedy* that celebrates the Greek redemption of suffering through the "aesthetic phenomenon" of tragedy. What, then, is it that Nietzsche could have learned from Doestoevsky, the *psychologist*, that he might not have learned from, say, Shakespeare, or indeed from himself, incomparable psychologist of crime and criminal that he was, and the tireless, even if sometimes tiresome, explorer of the psychological roots of religion, asceticism and saintliness; the Ivan Karamazov, as he inhabits Dostoevsky's book?

At this point we need only mention the names of Zossima or Alyosha—despite the improbability of Nietzsche's having read *The Brothers Karamazov*—not to feel too insolent in our insolent venture. We venture then, hesitantly, timidly, the answer to our question how the philosopher who called himself "the first psychologist of Europe," had profited from Dostoevsky's "psychological novels" and what, perhaps, might even have "liberated" him. Liberated from what? From the fetters of his own psychology? For reading again and again what Nietzsche, again and again, and in a voice that sounds shriller and shriller as the years go by, says about the origins of "ascetic ideals" and the Christian religion, we sense that this immensely intelligent thinker had sometimes to deafen the still voice which within himself kept insinuating that all was not well with the monotony of his psychologizing. Monotony? True, there are moments when the drumming subsides and the still voice makes itself heard, for instance in *The Genealogy of Morals* when the "torture" of the psychologist's compulsion to guess "the true nature"—and that is, of course, the ugly nature—"of great men" (*MA*, XV, 243) suddenly relents and quite a different tone comes into its own, namely, the psychologist's confession that he, who in his determination to disclose the ugliness beneath the mask of greatness, violates the rule of respect and discretion and, revealing the "truth" about others, only reveals his own character. For greatness and "finer humanity," he says, is also in a man's respect for the mask (*MA*, XV, 246) and in his unwillingness to pursue his psychological curiosity "in the wrong places." It is as if Nietzsche had just read another great psychologist's psychological observation about psychology, the German Romantic Novalis' saying that psychology, or what goes by that name, is one of "the ghosts" "that have usurped the place in the temple where genuine images of the divine ought to be" (Novalis, *Fragmente*, ed. Ernst Kamnitzer, Dresden 1929, 381).

What then, to continue for a little while along the precarious path, could Nietzsche have learned from Dostoevsky? First, that psychology may indeed affect, disastrously or beneficially, a man's pieties but most certainly cannot *establish* the worth or unworth, the beauty or ugliness, the truth or untruth of what has grown from roots sunk deeply into the psyche; as little as botany or soil analysis or meteorology or geology can prove or disprove the justification of the sense of autumnal glory one may have in the sight of that yellowing birchtree before the window or of the play of sunlight on the rugged faces of the mountains that rise beyond it.

That a man may be too weak to endure the tribulations of his existence, its "truth," without faith in God (could Job have endured them?); or that the strongest sensual impulses may have led to Dante's divine love of Beatrice; or that Nietzsche might benefit a little from Freudian persuasiveness even where he is, like Freud, least convincing: in assuming, for instance, that "without a certain overheating of the sexual system a Raphael is unthinkable" or that "making music is another way of making children" (*W*, 800)—all this does not in the slightest touch upon the question of the validity or falseness of the faith; or upon the true nature of Dante's love or the beauty of the poetry celebrating that love; or on Raphael's artistic integrity in painting his chaste madonnas; or on the greatness of Bach's B minor Mass (was he really in need of making music in addition to making twenty children?). If a believer, in the agony of dying, is comforted by the thought of a Beyond, or a pagan hero, deadly wounded, by the promise of national glory, both the believer and the hero may consolingly deceive themselves with illusions. Yet what is certainly *not* proved by the torments that bring forth such consolations, is the absence of a Beyond or the emptiness of posthumous glory.

And Nietzsche's work itself? Would we grasp *anything* of his intellectual passion or of the quality and style of his thought if we merely remembered that he was the son of a mentally endangered Protestant pastor and a mother as ordinary as mothers can be (child of the same parents that a little later produced the notorious, rather than famous, Elisabeth)? Deplorable that it is still necessary to insist upon the obvious: the utter inconclusiveness of all conclusions drawn from origins when we wish to assess the true nature and the moral or aesthetic worth of that which has come from them; particularly when the origins are sought in the physiological, as Nietzsche increasingly did towards the end of his intellectually responsible life. "Countertranscendental reductionism" would be too polite a word for this process. No, this method that defines the value of the pearl by referring to the grain of sand that had pathologically irritated the oyster's mucous membrane does not "reduce" the level of the phenomenon in question; it passes it by, it misses it.

"It is exceptional states that condition the artist—all of them profoundly related to . . . morbid phenomena—so it seems impossible to be an artist and not to be sick," Nietzsche noted in 1888 (W, 811), but at the same time he maintained that "artists if they are worth their salt . . . must be—also physically—of strong disposition, excelling in vigor, powerful animals . . ." (W, 800). This appears to be a tremendous contradiction, yet it is one with which he began to live even two or three years earlier when he knew how to be at his most "healthily" Dionysian. He would at that time ask "in regard to all aesthetic values 'has hunger or superabundance become creative here?' " (W, 846) The question was undoubtedly meant to establish a difference in artistic ranks: Homer, Hafiz, Rubens, Goethe are given as examples of artists who, in the fullness of their cretive powers, "eternalize," "apotheosize" existence while the others, the "hunger artists," are Nietzsche's unloved romantics. Profoundly conscious as he was of the ambiguities that prevail in the relationship between origins and outcomes—unavoidable morbidity and sickness as the source of all art, but then again inexhaustible riches of health and strength—Nietzsche should not have been in need of Dostoevsky's instructions; yet again and again he tempts us to find that he was.

It may have been Dostoevsky, the liberating teacher, whom Nietzsche had in mind, when in the later part of the above note in *The Will to Power* (he almost used it verbatim in the *Joyous Wisdom*, section 370) he acknowledges, as if to make ambiguity still more ambiguous, an art whose abundant sources of energy spring, as it were, from hunger, expressing themselves in "the tyrannic will of one who suffers deeply, who struggles and is tormented" (*MA*, XII, 311). Dostoevsky might indeed have taught him this. But he could have taught him still more, something that audaciously one might call an ontology of human being. It was the psychologist in Nietzsche that was averse to learning it. The lesson is this: it is impossible for the human mind to overcome the compulsion to make fundamental discriminations. No amount of psychology, of "tout comprendre" can possibly lead to "tout pardonner": whatever is felt to be scandalous will keep scandalizing us, whatever the historically changeable occasions of the scandal are; whatever is felt to be outrageous will forever call forth the response of outrage. Surely, the psychological diagnostician Nietzsche, in distinguishing between the soul's plenitude or its starvation as the begetter of different kinds of art, does judge their value. To discriminate in this manner is not simply a bad habit instilled in us by upbringing or language; on the contrary, our discriminating language is merely the expression of an elemental need that will persist as long as the mind is a human mind.

There is no "beyond good and evil" for us. If we miraculously ever reached that terminus, he who deems it desirable that we should would exclaim: "How good it is to have reached the state beyond good and evil!" And what applies to good and evil, does in equal measure apply to the distinction between true and false. *The Twilight of the Idols* (1888), one of the last of the extraordinary books Nietzsche wrote shortly before his mental breakdown, contains an astonishing and astonishingly condensed "narration" entitled "How the 'true world' (once again we have returned to 'truth') finally became a fable" and claims to trace "the history of an error." It ends thus: "We have abolished the true world"—and when he speaks here of the "true world," he means the "world of ideas," the only really real world that ever since Plato has dominated most of our philosophies and religions, the "true world" as distinct from the world of our ordinary experience—well then, this true world "we have abolished: which world is left? Perhaps the apparent one? Certainly not! *Together with the true world we have also abolished the apparent one!*" (MA, XVII, 76). Are we to respond by saying: "How true! The distinction between a true world and an apparent world, and thereby between true and false, is false!"?

Once more, Nietzsche appears to be determined to refute himself and to embrace the very nihilism which he desired to conquer. For if one has even the slightest feeling for the communications of language that, to spite the credulous semioticist, is capable of "meaning" incomparably more than it actually says, then one cannot but doubt that Nietzsche, in his "fable," announced only what is logically self-evident; and the logically self-evident does not need the rhetorical support of the accents of prophecy. As soon as we deny the reality of that ideal world—and Nietzsche is by no means the first to do so—we are clearly left with nothing but the world of our immediate experience, the world that for Plato was merely the world of shadow appearances. If that dualism collapses, there exists only *one* world. Who would doubt that? Every high school boy who has ever heard of the doctrine of positivism, is able to comprehend it. Whereupon

one ought to listen a second time to the conclusion of Nietzsche's
"fable": "We have abolished the true world: which world is left?
Perhaps the apparent one? Certainly not! Together with the *true
world we have also abolished the apparent one!*" What is the appropriate
response to these hammer blows of language? Should we say, "This
is clear enough! What is the agitation about?" No, but rather to
share the deep spiritual apprehension which is conveyed by the voice
that says what the opinion it utters does not say: namely, not merely
that from now onwards we shall have to make ourselves at home
in *one* world, but much more: that now we must be prepared to
exist in *not even one*, at least in no world which allows us truly to
exist. Two or three years before this, Nietzsche drew up a sketch of
a preface—it was replaced by that of 1886—for the new edition of
The Birth of Tragedy. It says: ". . . there is only one world, and this
is false, cruel, contradictory, seductive, without meaning. A world
thus constituted, is the real world" (*W*, 835). And, therefore, one is
lead to ask: a world—false, he calls it—that Nietzsche's *Übermensch*
would experience as beyond good and evil? Not likely, unless he
succeeded in what not even he could succeed in, namely ecstatically
to "transvalue" that world which, in Nietzsche's description, teaches
us that *horror vacui*, the horror of nothingness, of nihilism, that
determines the *style* of the "fable"; and to succeed although he *knows*
that it is in the depth of its nature an evil world?

Can anyone accept such a world which is, decidedly, not a human
world? Even if we achieved the impossible and found the appropriate
language for it, a language that would be able to renounce what
Nietzsche's language cannot do without: namely such words as "true"
or "false," "good" or "evil," would then our inner nature be so
radically changed as to enable us to discard those distinctions?
Perhaps we might; but only if they no longer corresponded to
anything within ourselves. And so we never shall, unless our nature
ceased to be human nature.

Yet if this ever happened, we would no longer know what, for
instance, could possibly be tragic in Sophocles' *Antigone*. It would
seem absolutely senseless to us that a woman should risk her life
by obeying the divinely ordained law which demands the burial of
her slain brother because she deems it superior to the contrary decree
issued by the king. And the tragic metamorphosis that, according to
Nietzsche, is the "true" and "good" effect of tragedy: the transformation of terror into bliss, the ecstatic yea-saying that triumphantly
resists the most forceful temptation to negate, would inevitably be
lost on us. Or we would, reading *King Lear*, no longer perceive any
moral difference between Cordelia and her sisters, or between
Gloucester's sons, and thus judge the whole course of action, the

grand sublimity of the poetry and the ending a tiresome futility; or we would be unable to grasp the extreme brilliance of Nietzsche's paradox: "Truth is the kind of error without which a certain species of life cannot live" (W, 493), or indeed of "We possess *art* lest we *perish of the truth."*

With this we are back at our beginning and forced to ask whether Nietzsche himself, at that time of his life, allows us to make sense of this sentence. Of course, to ask thus goes against the grain. The sentence instantly *shocks* us into understanding it. But do we really? It may appear to us that we know "what he means" and may even marvel at the marvelous power with which "truth" is here endowed: it kills through the force of its ugliness; and by thus cutting short our lives, brings Nietzsche's philosophy of art to its climax. For until Nietzsche arrived on the philosophical scene, it had, at least on that scene, always been regarded as a blessing to live "in the truth." Plato may have looked upon it as a dangerous, even a blinding blessing, but a blessing nonetheless. Has it now transpired that we are so absurdly constituted that one of our deepest, most honorable and most human desires, the desire for truth, would lead to our perdition, if there were no art? But this is an echo from that "once upon a time" which has been mentioned before. Once upon a time, or once in the past, it may have seemed that art could save us from the fatal attacks of truth. In the meantime, it would appear, art has often joined the perpetrators of the ugly, thus becoming the kind of art of which Nietzsche, not even at the time of *The Birth of Tragedy*, could have said that he was "passionately in love" with, seeing art "in everything that is" (MA, II, 68).

Long before Nietzsche wrote that philosophically breath-taking reflection on "how the true world became a fable," this consummation was well-prepared by the very logic of the aesthetics at work in *The Birth of Tragedy*, the book that could not have been written without Schopenhauer, whether it is obedient to him or whether it flagrantly violates his teachings; whether it splendidly supplements it (as, for instance, "rescuing" lyrical poetry for Schopenhauer's code of art by revealing the "objectivity" behind its semblance of "I-saying," its subjectivity: for ". . . we cannot imagine the smallest genuine work of art lacking objectivity and disinterested contemplation," Nietzsche says in the perfect Schopenhauer idiom), or whether he brings about the collapse of Schopenhauer's aesthetics by undermining the foundation on which it rests, namely, the thesis that the work of art is a *revelation of the truth*, truth in the metaphysical sense of Plato's ideas (MA, III, 40f). Without as yet declaring war on Schopenhauer, he quietly topples the "aesthetic phenomenon," the work of art, from its Platonic base, from "truth," letting it bring about *"redemption in illusion."*

The German word is "Schein." It is an uneasy compromise with philosophical respectability: Appearance ("Erscheinung") would be the word that traditionally goes, as its contrast, with the Platonic Reality, the ultimate reality of the Ideas. Or, as Christianity would have it, of that God whose reality is not the reality of "this world." To show the way that leads from Appearance to appearance, "Schein," illusion and finally to that "fable" that "the true world," that ruinous invention of Plato and the Christian religion, was to become, we could quote endlessly from Nietzsche's later writings. We won't. A few passages will have to suffice to make the dramatic point: "Assuming the true world, it could still be a world less valuable for us; precisely the quantum of illusion might be of a higher rank of account of its value for our preservation." And then Nietzsche adds in brackets: "Unless appearance (Schein) were ground for condemnation?" (W, 583 b). Does one dare to counter the question with a question of one's own and ask: who speaks of condemnation? Or, perhaps more damaging: who would be able to believe in the higher rank of the illusion, whatever its quantum, once he *knows* that it is an illusion?

No, this reversal of Platonism will not work. "Assuming," on the contrary, that the empirical world is only apparent, an assemblage of shadows cast by the ideal Truth, who will hinder those who are hungry for initiation into the ultimate knowledge to set out the Platonic quest? They will be unlikely to heed Nietzsche's instructions that the "true" antithesis is "the apparent world and the world invented by a lie," even if "hitherto" this mendaciously invented world has been called the "real world," "truth," "God," all the notions "we have to abolish" (W, 461). Would this not be also the abolition of art? And once we have succeeded in abolishing that world? Then we would have reduced the antithesis of the apparent world and the true world to its "true" meaning, namely "the antithesis 'world' and 'nothing' " (W, 567). This is Nietzsche's most succinct equation between the "true world" of Platonism or Christianity and Nihilism. It is an equation as forceful as that between the *one* world, that "false, cruel, contradictory world," with which we are left after the toppling of Plato's "true world," and the Nihilism of this one world's meaninglessness. Either way leads, it appears, to spiritual Nothingness, at least according to that unpublished preface to the second edition of *The Birth of Tragedy*. Even more than the published one, it would have insisted on the "gloom" and "unpleasantness" of the book's basic conception: the disappearance of the Platonic distinction between a true and an apparent world; and because the *one* that is the "real world" is as it is false, cruel, contradictory, meaningless, *"we have need of lies,* in order to conquer this reality, this 'truth' . . . in order to live." "The terrifying and questionable character of existence" is borne out by this abysmal necessity. But there is worse to come. Remembering that art is an illusion, a lie, and the artist an illusionist, a liar, we shall be struck by the enormity of this sentence: "The will to appearance, to illusion, to deception . . . counts as more profound, primeval, 'metaphysical' than the will to truth, to reality . . ." because "art is worth more than truth" (*W,* 853).

Where the truth is as intolerably ugly as this, a ceaseless offense to the spirit, and the lie as beautiful as the beauty of art (surprising how consistently Nietzsche clings to beauty as the foremost criterion of art); where the "real" is man's worst enemy, and illusion, therefore, becomes the redeeming deceiver, there the human world has been torn asunder. A vast gap has opened, attractiing—irresistibly, it would seem—swarms of demons. Some of them—these need not be failed artists, bad painters—would noisily claim that it is their mission to fuse the severed worlds again by appropriating the real as if it were the raw material for the making of a work of art, a pseudo-aesthetic phenomenon, an unblemished body politic, a perfect society. This is the connection, if any, between the philosopher of art and the devastating usurpers of the human estate. But it is of course only one of modernity's many elements that disastrously connect.

Sartre's Theory of Consciousness and the Zen Doctrine of No Mind[1]

WILLIAM BOSSART

In an essay entitled "Existentialism, Pragmatism and Zen," D.T. Suzuki contrasts the principal features of the Zen experience with those of contemporary existentialism. Zen claims to have developed directly out of Sakyamuni's experience of enlightenment, the core of which is expressed by the doctrine of *sunyata* or emptiness.[2] *Sunyata* is not the result of abstraction or generalization, nor is it a concept or a postulate of some sort. To be experienced, *sunyata* must be grasped as remaining in itself and yet as making itself an object of experience to itself; that is, as dividing itself and yet holding itself together.[3] This experience bears at least a superficial resemblance to Sartre's description of consciousness as a nothingness and as a nihilating activity which is always aware of itself in its activity. Both existentialism and Zen also emphasize the radical freedom of consciousness or mind. Finally, the central experiences of existentialism and Zen are not attained through reason. As Sartre puts it, there is a primacy of being over knowing; what one *is* precedes and grounds what can be known.[4] Similarly Suzuki observes: "Reasoning defeats itself, finds itself altogether futile, in its attempt to reach *sunyata*, because reasoning, instead of trying to see *sunyata* itself in the process of reasoning, strives to reach *sunyata* as the goal of reasoning, that is, when all reasoning comes to an end."[5]

Sartre's view of consciousness, however, remains primarily negative. Consciousness transcends the world and its objects as the negative ground which allows things to appear as something. In itself it is a sheer nihilating freedom which haunts the events of the world without being able to partake of them. In contrast, Zen maintains that when *sunyata* is genuinely awakened to itself, it is experienced positively as *tathata* or suchness, that which makes the existence of anything possible.[5] Whereas *sunyata* denies or rejects everything, *tathata* accepts and upholds everything. They appear to oppose one another from our relativistic point of view. In truth, however, *tathata* is *sunyata* and *sunyata* is *tathata*; things are *tathata* because of their being *sunyata*.[7] Hence despite their similarities, Zen and existentialism also diverge from one another.

> Zen does not find anything frightening in infinite possibilities, unlimited freedom, neverending responsibilities. Zen moves along with infinite possibilities; Zen enjoys unlimited freedom because Zen is freedom itself; however unending and unbearable responsibility may be, Zen bears it as if not bearing it at all. . . . The existentialist generally interprets freedom on the plane of relativity where there is no freedom in its higher sense. Freedom can be predicated only of *tathata* and its experience. The existentialist looks into the abyss of *tathata* and trembles. . . . Zen would tell him: Why not plunge right into the abyss and see what is there? The idea of individualism fatally holds him back from throwing himself into the devil's maw.[8]

In what follows I shall examine Sartre's theory of consciousness as it is formulated in *The Transcendence of the Ego* and developed in *Being and Nothingness*. I shall then examine the Zen experience as it is presented by Hui-neng in his doctrine of unconsciousness or no-mind. Finally, I shall argue that although Sartre's initial description of consciousness confirms Hui-neng's understanding of the Zen experience, Sartre closes himself off from that experience, for he is blinded by his pursuit of an authentic selfhood which is forbidden by his theory.

I

Sartre's theory of consciousness originates as a critique of certain doctrines which compromise Husserl's insights into the nature of consciousness. The primary motivation of Husserl's thought is epistemological—he seeks to found knowledge upon a starting point which is absolutely given and indubitable. Husserl holds that such givenness is attainable only within the sphere of the *cogito*.[9] Unlike Descartes, however, he does not seek to employ the *cogito* as the ground of our knowledge of an independently existing world. On the contrary, Husserl sees our belief in the independent existence of objects which wholly transcend consciousness as the principal barrier to apodictic knowledge; for we can never check the immediate data of consciousness against these things as they are in themselves. Thus to obtain apodictic knowledge we must exercise the phenomenological reduction or *epoché* by suspending our natural belief in the independent existence of objects and focus our attention on the data of consciousness as they are immediately given to us.

The *epoché*, however, has no effect upon the *content* of experience because consciousness is fundamentally intentional; that is, it is always consciousness of a datum or 'object' from which, except in the case of self-consciousness, it must also be distinguished. Thus the task of phenomenology becomes the clarification of every aspect of the phenomenal field through an intuitive grasp of the structures which give it meaning. According to Husserl, however, this intuitive apprehension of essences is not merely a passive inspection of what is given to consciousness. It is an act of the transcendental subject which constitutes the essential structures in question. Constitution, Husserl tells us, is not arbitrary but takes place in accordance with the basic laws of reason.[10] Husserl never discusses these laws in any detail but he seems to hold that the fundamental law of reason is the principle of identity. Only the self-identical can be an object of apodictic knowledge. Furthermore since an object is always more than what is actually given to consciousness at any given moment, its constitution must take place successively in time. Therefore rational consciousness, which effects the synthesis of identity, must also conform to the fundamental form of all synthesis, the inner consciousness of time.[11] To recognize the role played by time in the constitution of objectivity is to acknowledge that knowledge is a growth, that not every cognition is possible to every subject at every time. Hence Husserl concludes that the transcendental ego is inescapably personal. It is a concrete subject whose 'world' reflects the personal character which makes it unique.[12]

Sartre maintains that the doctrine of a personal transcendental consciousness is neither necessary to nor compatible with the description of consciousness given by Husserl. The existence of a transcendental subject is allegedly justified by the need to account for the unity of experience and the individuality of consciousness.[13] Sartre points out, however, that phenomenology has no need to appeal to a transcendental ego to account for either. In regard to what might be called the objective unity of experience, the unity of my diverse consciousnesses of "2 plus 2 equals 4" or of my perceptual awareness of my desk, no ego is needed; for it is in the object, which transcends each momentary consciousness intending it, that the unity of these various consciousnesses is to be found. It might be objected that a subjective unity of experience is nevertheless required to ensure that these moments of consciousness will all be states of one and the same consciousness. Consciousness must be a continual synthesis of past, present and future moments or, to put it in Kantian terms, all experiences must be part of one and the same experience. Sartre agrees, but he points out that in his study of the subjective unity of consciousness Husserl never had recourse to the synthetic power of an ego. On the contrary: "It is consciousness which unifies itself, concretely, by a play of 'transversal' intentionalities which are concrete and real retentions of past consciousnesses. Thus consciousness refers perceptually to itself. Whoever says 'a consciousness' says 'the whole of consciousness,' and this singular property belongs to consciousness itself, aside from whatever relations it may have to the I."[14] Finally, if consciousness accounts for the subjective synthesis of its states, it also accounts for its individuality. It is individual in the sense that it can be limited only by itself. Its individuality is its self-containment. Hence the I is not a condition of individuality but merely its expression and the transcendental ego has no *raison d'être*.

But the transcendental ego is not merely superfluous. "If it existed it would tear consciousness from itself; it would divide consciousness; it would slide into consciousness like an opaque blade. The transcendental *I* is the death of consciousness. Indeed, the existence of consciousness is an absolute because consciousness is consciousness of itself. This is to say that the type of existence of consciousness is to be consciousness of itself. And consciousness is aware of itself *in so far as it is consciousness of a transcendent object*. All is therefore clear and lucid in consciousness: the object with its characteristic opacity is before consciousness, but consciousness is purely and simply consciousness of being consciousness of that object. This is the law of its existence."[15] Consciousness, then, is a spontaneous and lucid awareness of its object. To add to this consciousness a personal ego, weighted down with the structures and laws of its personality, would be to compromise the lucidity and spontaneity of consciousness which make phenomenological description of the structures of experience possible. And yet the illusion of a personal consciousness persists.

The *cogito* is undeniably personal. It would appear, therefore, that there is no act of consciousness which is not accompanied by an I. But the *cogito* is a reflective operation. It is performed by a consciousness which is directed toward a consciousness, one which takes consciousness as its object. The reflecting consciousness, however, does not take itself as its object; the ego whose presence it affirms concerns only the reflected consciousness. Hence we must ask whether the I also accompanies consciousness on the pre-reflective level or whether it is reflection which gives birth to the I. At first glance this question seems impossible to answer, for every examination of consciousness appears to take place in reflection. Yet since every unreflected consciousness of an object is also a non-positional self-consciousness, it must leave a non-positional memory which one can consult. I must not posit that consciousness as an object of reflection. Rather I must direct my attention to the revived objects, but *"without losing sight of the unreflected consciousness."*[16] If, for example, I direct my attention to a non-reflective memory of reading a novel, I must attend primarily to the characters and events which are related in the story. The result, Sartre maintains, is clear: there is no place for an ego in the unreflected consciousness; there is simply a consciousness of the characters and events in question. The I never appears except on the occasion of a reflective act. It is a transcendent existent which appears to an intuition of a special kind which apprehends it, always inadequately, behind the reflected consciousness. As transcendent the ego must fall before the phenomenological reduction— the *cogito* affirms too much.[17]

How, then, is the ego constituted in conscious life and why do we treat it as an inhabitant of consciousness rather than one of its objects? The ego appears only to reflection; therefore it is only on the reflective level that the ego life has its place. Sartre's thesis is that the ego, of which the I and the me are but two aspects, is the ideal and indirect objective unity of the infinite series of our reflected consciousness. The I is the unity of actions and the me is the unity of states and qualities.[18] There are, for example, the different consciousnesses of disgust, repugnance and dislike for Peter which are unified by the state which is my hatred of Peter. My hatred in turn may be seen as the actualization of a certain quality of my psyche, *my* spiteful disposition. Finally, the ego is the unity of my various states and qualities. These unities are, however, always transcendent. Just as my hatred transcends my immediate dislike of Peter, the ego is the transcendent unity of my states and qualities. The ego, Sartre tells us, is related to psychical objects as the world is to things.[19] As transcendent these unities are also questionable. Do I really hate Peter or am I merely irritated by him at this moment? Indeed the ego itself is always capable of being contradicted by subsequent intuitions. This is why I may deceive myself in thinking that I have such a me.

Each new state is given to consciousness as fastened directly (or indirectly by a quality) to the ego as its origin. Yet we do not apprehend the ego as a pure creative source beside its states nor as a skeletal pole apart from its qualities. Rather the ego appears to create its states and to sustain its qualities by a sort of spontaneity. "But this spontaneity must not be confused with the spontaneity of consciousness. Indeed, the ego, being an object, is *passive*. It is a question, therefore, of a pseudo-spontaneity which is suitably symbolized by the spurting of a spring, a geyser, etc. . . . Genuine spontaneity must be perfectly clear: it *is* what it produces and can be nothing else."[20] Hence the relation of the ego to its states and qualities remains, unintelligible, for the ego is an irrational synthesis of passivity and spontaneity.

Sartre now explains how the ego, which is a transcendent object for the reflecting consciousness, comes to be taken as an inhabitant of that consciousness. "The ego is an object apprehended, but also an object *constituted*, by reflective consciousness. The ego is a virtual locus of unity, and consciousness constitutes it in *a direction contrary* to that actually taken by the production: *really*, consciousnesses are first, through these are constituted states; and then, through the latter, the ego is constituted. But, as the order is reversed by a consciousness which imprisons itself in the world in order to flee from itself, consciousness is given as emanating from states, and states as produced by the ego. It follows that consciousness projects its spontaneity into the ego-object in order to confer on the go the creative power which is absolutely necessary to it. But this spontaneity, *represented* and *hypostatized* in an object, becomes a degraded and bastard spontaneity, which magically preserves its creative power even while becoming passive. Whence the profound irrationality of the notion of an ego."[21]

As a transcendent object, therefore, the ego must submit to the phenomenological reduction, thus effecting the complete liberation of transcendental consciousness. In a sense this consciousness is *nothing* since all truths, objects and values lie outside it. But this nothing is also *all* since it is consciousness of these various structures. Transcendental consciousness is an impersonal spontaneity which determines its own existence without being able to conceive of anything which precedes it. It follows that there is no longer an inner life, and all doubts, remorse and deliberations are nothing more than sheer performance. At this level, however, each of us has the impression of ceaselessly escaping from himself. Consciousness, Sartre tells us, is frightened by its own spontaneity, for it senses this spontaneity as beyond freedom. Hence he suggests that the essential role of the ego may be to mask this spontaneity from consciousness.[22] This suggestion becomes, of course, the central theme of *Being and Nothingness*.

Sartre begins his discussion of consciousness in *Being and Nothingness* by reaffirming both the intentionality of consciousness and the thesis that all non-reflective consciousness is non-positional self-consciousness, "for if my consciousness were not consciousness of being consciousness of the table, it would then be consciousness of the table without consciousness of being so. In other words, it would be a consciousness ignorant of itself, an unconscious—which is absurd."[23] Hence cognitive or positional consciousness is grounded in a non-positional self-consciousness which I *am* but which is not an object of knowledge. Consequently Sartre argues against the primacy of knowledge. To defend the view that "to know is to know that one knows" is to introduce into consciousness the subject-object relation which characterizes knowledge. This, in turn, leads to an infinite regress of consciousness in which one is the knower and the other the known. To avoid such a regress we must acknowledge that consciousness of self is not dual—that there is an immediate, noncognitive relation of consciousness to itself.[24] Hence Sartre names consciousness *pour-soi* or the for-itself to underline its fundamental character of self-awareness and to distinguish consciousness from its object or that which is wholly *en-soi* or in-itself.

In contrast to the reflecting consciousness which posits the reflected consciousness as its object, the immediate consciousness of perceiving does not *know* its perception, for it does not posit it. The entire intention of this immediate consciousness is directed toward the outside, toward the world. But this spontaneous consciousness of my perceiving consciousness is constitutive of that perceiving consciousness. "In other words, every positional consciousness of an object is at the same time a non-positional consciousness of itself. If I count the cigarettes which are in that case, I have the impression of disclosing an objective property of this collection of cigarettes: they are a dozen. This property appears to my consciousness as a property existing in the world. It is very possible that I have no positional consciousness of counting them. Then I do not know myself as counting. . . . Yet at the moment when these cigarettes are revealed to me as a dozen, I have a non-thetic consciousness of my adding activity. If anyone questioned me, indeed, if anyone should ask, 'What are you doing there?' I should reply at once, 'I am counting.' Thus in order to count, it is necessary to be conscious of counting."[25]

Reflective consciousness, therefore, has its ground in the pre-reflective consciousness of self, or, as Sartre now chooses to put it, there is a pre-reflective *cogito* which is the condition of the Cartesian *cogito*. Consciousness, therefore, appears as its own source, and that, we have seen is the mean of its spontaneity. Thus, Sartre concludes, once again taking up a theme from the *Transcendence of the Ego*, "by abandoning the primacy of knowledge, we have discovered the being of the knower and encountered the absolute, that same absolute which the rationalists of the seventeenth century had defined and logically constituted as an object of knowledge. But precisely because the question concerns an absolute of existence and not of knowledge, it is not subject to that famous objection according to which a known absolute is no longer an absolute because it is relative to the knowledge one has of it."[25]

What must the relation of intentionality be for consciousness to be aware of an object? Our question itself provides the clue to its answer. The attitude of questioning presupposes that I stand in ignorance; it entails as well the possibility of a negative response; and a positive response will exclude other possible answers. To question presupposes each of these different modalities of negation. It is only because consciousness transcends the world and its objects in the sense of not being an object that it can intend and interrogate them. Consciousness is an original disengagement, a nihilating withdrawal in relation to the in-itself.[27] Hence it is not subject to the causal order which governs the objective world, and this testifies once more to its basic spontaneity, to the fact that there can be no preceding state of affairs which is its cause.

As a fundamental nihilation of its object, consciousness must also continually separate itself from its past and its future. It is its past and its future only in the mode of not being them. To recognize this is to realize that my past provides no determining structure on which I can rely, and that my future is merely possible, for I am not now the self that I will be. This recognition, according to Sartre, takes place in anguish. Anguish is the mode of being in which consciousness experiences its radical spontaneity, that is to say, its freedom. Freedom, manifesting itself through anguish, engenders a recognition of the radical transcendence of consciousness which is characterized by a constantly renewed obligation to re-invent the self which I am only in the mode of not being it.[28]

Since freedom is the very being of consciousness, Sartre must explain why anguish is such a rare occurrence. To experience my freedom I must experience the fact that I transcend my situation in the world, my past and my future. This occurs in reflection, when I see that situation and the structures which compose it as so many possibilities. Reflection opens up a gap between them and me. I transcend them as *my* possibilities and they can be actualized only by a free commitment on my part. On the pre-reflective level, however, I am already in a situation and there are only actions to be undertaken—my awareness, for example, is of the alarm which has me up at its summons. Only when an undertaking is interrupted or held at a distance do I realize that it is I who give meaning to the alarm clock by allowing it to make me rise or who, by acknowledging a sign, forbids himself to pick the flowers in the park.

Anguish, however, can be avoided even on the level of reflection in particular modes of flight. Anguish is the recognition of all possibilities as *my* possibilities; that is to say, the recognition that nothing in its past or its future can determine consciousness to act except consciousness itself. Flight before the future attempts to disarm the threat of this freedom which erupts at the very core of what I take myself to be. Flight recognizes possibilities but not as *mine;* for example, I shall keep the appointment I have made but *one* might also not keep it. Or I shall meet my obligations as a professor of philosophy but *one* might also refuse to meet those obligations. Similarly flight before the past seeks to veil the fact that the past can affect me only insofar as I choose to reaffirm it as my own. Instead I assert that I am my past and that an act is truly free when it coincides with or reflects my essential nature. This, Sartre observes, is a matter of apprehending my freedom as if it were the freedom of another.[29] Yet we cannot overcome anguish, for we are anguish. Fleeing anguish presupposes experiencing it; hence flight is an act of self-negation. This observation announces the central theme of *Being and Nothingness,* the attitude of bad faith.

Consciousness is a lucid spontaneous awareness of an object but it is also not its object. It transcends all objective structures including the self as the nihilating spontaneity which is their awareness and nothing more. But this spontaneity is compromised by its own activity, for it must have something to negate. Thus the being of consciousness is ontologically tied to something which it is not and of which it is not the ground. In *Being and Nothingness* the ego serves as a kind of mediator between consciousness and the world. As in the earlier essay, the ego or self is not in consciousness yet it is not merely one objective structure among others, for it provides to consciousness its mode of access to the world.[30] The world is always seen from a certain point of view. No perceptual object can ever be exhausted by the varying perspectives I may have on it. This Sartre calls the object's transphenomenality. Thus each consciousness is a particular point of view on the world—it apprehends the world through a particular situation which constitutes its facticity. It is through my situation in the world that I give meaning to the world. It is the practical and conceptual frameworks within which my activities take place which determine what things and events will be meaningful to me. Facticity is the counterphenomenon to transcendence, for although consciousness transcends the world and its situation in it, its transcendence is also a transcendence toward its possibilities which are constituted by its situation. Consciousness, then, is both a self-originating spontaneity and a lack. Sartre expresses this dual aspect by describing the *pour-soi* as being what it is not (facticity) and as not being what it is (transcendence).[31]

Bad faith is a fundamental mode of consciousness which plays on the duality of facticity and transcendence. These two aspects ought to be capable of coordination but bad faith neither wants to coordinate them nor surmount them in a synthesis. Rather it seeks to affirm their identity while preserving their difference. It affirms facticity as *being* transcended and transcendence as *being* facticity, so that when a person apprehends one, he can find himself abruptly faced with the other.[32] Thus the ambiguity essential to bad faith comes from the affirmation that I am transcendence in the mode of being a thing. In this way I can escape all reproaches. I identify myself with my role as a university professor. My obligations to my students and my colleagues and my involvement with my scholarly research all conspire to aid me in my flight from the spontaneity of my freedom. I have a job to do and I must get on with it. But this identification is never complete, for I am also none of these things, or rather I am but in the mode of not being them, and I am able to make use of this fact whenever things turn out badly. A paper is rejected for publication, a course is unpopular or a promotion is not forthcoming. What of it? It's too bad but of course my being a university professor is a role which I play and nothing more. It is certainly not my life. I am separated from being a professor as consciousness is from its object, by nothing. And yet I *am* a professor since being a professor is an essential part of my situation in the world. Otherwise I could call myself something else. Bad faith, then, is the acceptance of not believing what one believes. Hence bad faith is itself in bad faith.[33]

Bad faith is basically inauthentic. In it I recognize two aspects of my being, my facticity and transcendence, only by fleeing each in making use of the other. What, then, of authenticity? Is there a mode of being in which I can genuinely recognize and be what I am, or am I, as a being which is what he is not and is not what he is, doomed to inauthenticity? Unfortunately Sartre says very little about authentic existence and most of what he says in *Being and Nothingness* is said *en passant*, a series of undeveloped suggestions and *aperçus*. Thus in a note to his discussion of bad faith he observes: "If it is indifferent whether one is in good or in bad faith, because bad faith reapprehends good faith and slides to the very origin of the project of good faith, that does not mean that we cannot radically escape bad faith. But this supposes a self-recovery of being which was corrupted by itself. This recovery we shall call authenticity, the description of which has no place here."[34] Farther on, in his discussion of relations with others, he suggests that there are two authentic attitudes: "that by which I recognize the Other as the subject through whom I get my object-ness—this is shame; and that by which I apprehend myself as the free object by which the Other gets his being-other—this is arrogance or the affirmation of my freedom confronting the Other-as-object."[35] Finally, there is an interesting passage in his discussion of play. The act of play, Sartre tells us, "is not its own goal for itself; neither does its explicit end represent its goal and its profound meaning; but the function of the act is to make manifest and to present to *itself* the absolute freedom which is the very being of the person."[36] Here we seem to have at least a clue to the recovery spoken of above. Yet once again Sartre declines to develop this suggestion. He acknowledges that the project of play is radically different from all other projects in that it aims at a radically different type of being but declines to investigate it here. "It belongs rather to an *Ethics* and it supposes that there has been a preliminary definition of nature and the role of a purifying reflection."[37]

Despite Sartre's reluctance to develop these suggestions, we can, I think, glean some idea of what Sartrean authenticity might be like, given his theory of consciousness and certain passages in the closing sections of *Being and Nothingness*. On the one hand consciousness is nothing more than the radical spontaneity which is its freedom. As such, however, it is literally nothing at all. Furthermore, its spontaneity is basically intentional; it can express this nothingness only by negating its objects as not itself. Hence consciousness is also its situation in the world. Being in a situation defines its presence to the world. And this situation is the organized totality of my facticity interpreted and lived toward the end and the values with which I endow it.

"It is this steep and dusty road, this burning thirst which I have, the refusal of these people to give me anything to drink because I have no money or am not of their country or of their race; it is my abandonment in the midst of these hostile populations along with this fatigue which will perhaps prevent me from reaching the goal which I had fixed for myself. But it is also precisely this goal, not insofar as I formulate it clearly and explicitly, but insofar as it is there, everywhere around me, as that which unifies and explains all these facts, that which organizes them in a totality capable of description instead of making of them a disordered nightmare."[38]

The end which illuminates the details of my situation is, however, chosen and not merely given, for nothing whatever can determine consciousness. Thus insofar as it is present to the world consciousness finds itself given over to a situation not of its own making yet the meaning of which it freely determines by the choices which it makes and the goals which it sets for itself. These choices, which are wholly undetermined yet unavoidable, make me inescapably responsible for my situation.

"Thus, totally free, indistinguishable from the period of which I have chosen to be the meaning, as profoundly responsible for the war, as if I myself had declared it, unable to live anything without integrating it into *my* situation, engaging myself wholly in it and marking it with my seal, I must be without remorse or regrets as I am without excuse, for, from the instant of my emergence into being, I carry the weight of the world on myself entirely alone, without anything or anybody being able to lighten the burden."[39]

And Sartre concludes: "It is precisely for this reason that the *pour-soi* apprehends itself in anguish, that is to say, as a being who is not the foundation of its own being, nor of the being of the other, nor of the *en-soi* which from the world, but who is constrained to decide on the meaning of being, in himself and everywhere outside himself. The one who realizes in anguish his condition of *being* thrown into a responsibility which goes back to his very abandonment has no longer remorse nor regret, nor excuse; he is no more than a freedom which reveals itself perfectly and whose being resides in this very revelation. But, as was pointed out at the beginning of this work, most of the time we free anguish in bad faith."[40]

II

Hui-neng was the sixth patriarch of Chinese Buddhism and is generally regarded as the Chinese founder of Zen. His principal pronouncement, "from the first not a thing is," is directed against the view which understands mind as originally pure and undefiled. In this view the task of the yogin is to clarify this original Buddha-nature by brushing the dust, which results from the confusion enveloping individual mind, from the mirror of this original and undefiled consciousness.[40] Hui-neng sees this serene contemplation of the purity of original mind as a denial of life, and it is against this denial that he launches his attack. "When you sit quietly with an emptied mind, this is falling into a blank emptiness." "There are some people with the confused notion that the greatest achievement is to sit quietly with an emptied mind, where not a thought is to be conceived." In opposition to this kind of quietistic meditation Hui-neng advises "neither to cling to the notion of a mind, nor to cling to the notion of purity, nor to cherish the thought of immovability; for these are not our meditation." "When you cherish the notion of purity and cling to it, you turn purity into falsehood. . . . Purity has neither form nor shape, and when you claim an achievement by establishing a form to be known as purity, you obstruct your own self-nature, you are purity-bound."[41] Thus Hui-neng's utterance, "from the first not a thing is," affirms the fundamental nothingness *(sunyata)* of consciousness, sweeping away at a stroke all logical and psychological supports and leaving one with nowhere to stand.

According to Hui-neng there is no pure seeing into original mind, for original mind cannot be experienced apart from the activities of individual mind. Hui-neng agrees with Sartre that these activities are fundamentally intentional, that individual consciousness is always a consciousness of objects, and that objects are objects only for such a consciousness. Original mind, on the other hand, is *sunyata* or nothingness; hence it cannot become the object of a specific act of consciousness. Rather it is in being aware of its objects that consciousness also becomes conscious of itself in its activity. Therefore seeing into one's self-nature or *dhyana* cannot be understood apart from the illumination of the world of multiplicity by the light of *prajna*. *Prajna* is one of the three traditional subjects of Buddhism: morality *(sila)*, meditation *(dhyana)* and wisdom *(prajna)*. Suzuki explains that this triple discipline gradually became split into three separate areas of study and practice. The separation of *dhyana* and *prajna* was particularly unfortunate. "Dhyana became the exercise of killing life, of keeping the mind in a state of torpor and making the Yogins socially useless; while Prajna, left to itself, lost its profundity, for it was identified with intellectual subtleties which dealt in concepts and their analyses."[42] According to Hui-neng's opponents, *dhyana*, understood as dust-wiping, is first and *prajna* follows. For Hui-neng, however, *dhyana* without *prajna* leads to a grave error but when *prajna* is genuine, *dhyana* comes along with it. Hence *dhyana* is *prajna* and *prajna* is *dhyana*, and unless this relation of identity is grasped there will be no emancipation.[43]

Hui-neng defines *dhyana* as follows: "Dhyana is not to get attached to the mind, is not to get attached to purity, nor is it to concern itself with immovability. . . . When, outwardly, a man is attached to form, his inner mind is disturbed. But when outwardly he is not attached to form, his mind is not disturbed. His original nature is pure and quiet as it is in itself; *only when it recognizes an objective world and thinks of it as something, is it disturbed. Those who recognize an objective world, and yet find their mind undisturbed, are in true Dhyana. . . ."[44] Seeing into self-nature does not take place independently of a consciousness of the world, but since self-nature is *sunyata* or nothingness, this seeing can have no specific reference to a particular state of consciousness. It is non-reflective, therefore non-positional, with regard to consciousness, and this is why it is designated negatively as no-thought or no-mind. Hence Hui-neng's understanding of *dhyana* embraces the fundamental nothingness of consciousness, its intentional relation to its objects, and its non-reflective awareness of itself in its consciousness of its objects.

Suzuki points out that the relation between *prajna* and *dhyana* can be better understood by invoking the concepts which Mahayana Buddhism employs to explain the relation between substance and its function: body, form, and use. "Body corresponds to substance, Form to appearance, and Use to function. The apple is a reddish, round-shaped object: this is its Form, in which it appears to our senses. Form belongs to the world of senses, i.e., appearance. Its Use includes all that it does and stands for, its value, its utility, its function, and so on. The body of the apple is what constitutes its appleship, without which it loses its being, and no apple, even with all the appearances and functions ascribed to it, is an apple without it. To be a real object these three concepts, Body, Form and Use, must be accounted for."[45]

In the case of consciousness or subjectivity, self-nature is the Body and *prajna* is its Use but there is nothing which corresponds to Form since the subject transcends the world of form. The object of Zen is to realize the Buddha-nature which is present in all things. This is possible because self-nature is self-knowledge; all consciousness is consciousness of self. This "self-nature finds its own being when it sees itself, and this seeing takes place by Prajna. But as Prajna is another name given to self-nature when the latter sees itself, there is no Prajna outside self-nature."[46] This seeing, however, is also an experiencing, an enlightenment, and this is *dhyana*. *Dhyana* is the body of *prajna* and *prajna* is the Use of *dhyana*. When *prajna* is taken up, *dhyana* is in *prajna* and when *dhyana* is taken up, *prajna* is in it. "It is," Hui-neng tells us, "like the lamp and its light. As there is a lamp, there is light; if no lamp, no light. The lamp is the Body of the light, and the light is the Use of the lamp. They are differently designated, but in substance they are one. The relation between Dhyana and Prajna is to be understood in like manner."[47]

An understanding of the relation between *dhyana* and *prajna* also enables us to bring together *sunyata* and *tathata*. *Sunyata* expresses the nothingness of consciousness while *tathata* is the positive aspect of self-nature or consciousness—its suchness. "Suchness is the Body of Consciousness, and Consciousness is the use of Suchness. It is the self-nature of Suchness to become conscious of itself."[48] Suchness is the absolute, something which is not subject to the laws of relativity and which cannot be grasped by means of form. Hence *tathata* express the unity, self-identity and transcendence of consciousness. But insofar as its transcends the realm of forms or things, *tathata* is also the undeterminable, the formless or *sunyata*. Furthermore, the consciousness of self referred to above does not have a circumscribed consciousness as its object—it is not reflective or positional self-consciousness. Consciousness, however, is non-reflectively self-conscious only insofar as it is directly consciousness of something; that is, insofar as it recognizes a world of objects but is undisturbed by that world. This in turn reveals the positive aspect of *sunyata*, for things are illuminated by consciousness only insofar as they are determined or discriminated, and discrimination is a function of what Sartre calls nihilation. In this sense, *sunyata* is also *tathata,* for *tathata* is that which makes the existence of anything possible.

For both Hui-neng and Sartre consciousness is devoid of any structure which would compromise its spontaneity and lucidity. Both agree that consciousness cannot really be affected in anyway. For both, consciousness is aware of an objective world which must be distinguished from consciousness and of which consciousness is not a part. Contrasted with "the ten thousand things" consciousness is nothing and it is in this nothingness, this transcendence, that its freedom consists. Furthermore, no matter what objects it intends, consciousness always *is* also a non-positional awareness of itself. To be consciousness is to be consciousness of being consciousness. Hence both Sartre and Hui-neng attack the primacy of reflection whether it is the Cartesian *cogito* which seeks to found being in knowing, or static meditation which passively polishes the mirror of consciousness. For both, consciousness is also the source of the meaning of things. Its negativity allows things to stand out as something. Hence they agree with Hegel and Spinoza that all determination is negation. Finally, Hui-neng and Sartre maintain that in becoming aware of the true nature of consciousness we encounter an absolute. It is, however, on the nature of this absolute that Zen and Sartrean existentialism part company.[49]

Sartre's early description of consciousness as a lucid and impersonal spontaneity corresponds with the core of the Zen experience. But Sartre turns away from that experience to pursue a unity of consciousness and self which his description forbids. This turn in Sartre's thought is signaled most obviously by his use of the first person singular in referring to consciousness in his later work. Furthermore, where The *Transcendence of the Ego* merely suggests that the function of the ego may be to mask the spontaneity of consciousness from itself, *Being and Nothingness* makes this function its central theme. Sartre's description of consciousness as an absolute which is compromised by contingency announces the direction which his thought ultimately takes. In itself consciousness is an absolute spontaneity which is its own source. Yet as an intentionality which negates its object as not-itself, consciousness must depend on its objects if it is to function at all. Hence to stabilize its being, to render itself truly absolute, consciousness seeks to rejoin the self-structure of the ego, to become *pour-soi-en-soi*. Consequently each of us attempts to identify with his situation in the world through which we endow the world with meaning. In doing so we undertake a fundamental project, a certain style of life, through which our experience of the world is inevitably filtered. Thus the transcendence of consciousness is not merely a transcendence of the world and its objects but at the same time a transcendence toward a not yet actualized self, an absence which haunts the present and which we call 'value.' "The self," Sartre writes, "is individual; it is the individual completion of the self which haunts the for itself."[50] Consciousness is haunted by a self which it can never become. Its attempt to rejoin the self is the attempt to purge consciousness of all contingency and thus become truly absolute. Sartre identifies this project as the desire to be God— the fundamental project of being human. But as a synthesis of two mutually exclusive types of being, the concept of God is fundamentally contradictory. Hence man acts in vain. The themes of anguish, bad faith and the absurdity of being responsible for a world of which I am not the maker and which I am forbidden to join, express the futility of this project.

In contrast to Sartre, the attitude of Zen is positive—it claims to emerge from "the abyss of *tathata*" beyond anguish and futility and to bear responsibility as if not bearing it at all. Yet Zen also recognizes the dangers of the abyss. "Hui-neng's concept of nothingness may push one down in to a bottomless abyss, which will no doubt create a feeling of utter forlornness. The philosophy of Prajnaparamita which is also that of Hui-neng, generally has this effect."[51] Zen aims at nothing less than the conversion of this negative encounter with *sunyata* into a positive one which sets us free from all forms of bondage. This conversion is not to be sought in the world, in the teachings of a master, a text, or in a series of practices but in ourselves; for if each of us is the problem—the existential encounter with anguish and bad faith—then each of us is equally the solution to that problem. The goal of Zen is "to waken the mind while abiding nowhere."[52] But this is not a turning away from the world. Hui-neng's teaching rejects all forms of quietistic retreat into the self. It is rather to see *nirvana* or emancipation in the midst of *samsara*, the worldly cycle of birth and death.[53] How, then, is this possible if we take Sartre's description of consciousness as our model?

A moment ago I was perceiving the pad of paper on which I am writing, as well as the movements of the pen traced by the ink along the surface of the paper. I was not reflecting; there was no I present in my experience. My consciousness was nothing but consciousness of the pad, the writing, and the ideas I was trying to formulate. According to Sartre, however, such a consciousness is also a consciousness of being consciousness of the pad, the pen, the flow of ink and those ideas. It is non-positional consciousness of itself. But what is the intentional object of such an awareness? Not the pad and the writing, nor the ideas, for they are the objects of the prereflective consciousness which posits them. Nor can the object of this self-consciousness be consciousness, for then it would be a reflective consciousness which posits a consciousness as its object. Hence this non-positional self-consciousness, which accompanies all positional consciousness, seems to have no intentional object at all. In ascribing intentionality to every mode of consciousness, Sartre has exceeded the limits of his own analysis and obscured the very thing he is seeking—consciousness understood as an unconditioned absolute.

The *prajna* of Hui-neng describes this non-positional self-consciousness as follows: "To perceive the mind unmoved, and yet to raise no thoughts as to its immovability; to perceive the mind pure and undefiled, and yet to raise no thoughts as to its purity; to discriminate what is bad from what is good, and yet to feel no defilement by them, and to be absolute master of itself: This is known as Prajna."[54] *Prajna*, then, is awakening the mind to this nonreflective awareness of itself. Although it accompanies an intentionally directed consciousness of an object, *prajna* consciousness is entirely nonpositional. That is why it goes untouched by the objects of the discriminating consciousness, why it abides nowhere and why it is absolute.

Sartre not only insists that each and every act of consciousness must be intentional, he also draws some unwarranted conclusions about intentionality itself. For Sartre consciousness is intentional in a double sense. There is first of all the fact that consciousness is consciousness *of* something. Hence perceptual consciousness requires a perceptual object, conceptual consciousness an intellectual object and so on, if these various modes of consciousness are to function at all. "Intend," however, may be understood either personally or impersonally. The impersonal rendering would, of course, be consistent with Sartre's critique of Husserl in the *Transcendence of the Ego*. But an intentional act can also be understood as one purposely performed by a particular subject with a certain end or project in view; for example, I may intend to finish my supper early so that I can go to a movie tonight, or to inspect the tree to see why it is losing its leaves. This second sense of intend appears to be inescapably personal. But the first sense of intend, clearly does not entail the second. For the Sartre of *Being and Nothingness*, however, a purely impersonal intending is impossible; for although it transcends the world, consciousness intends its objects only through that situation which constitutes its presence to the world. Thus despite his remarks about the impersonality of consciousness, Sartre's position is really not very different from Husserl's, for intending, understood as giving meaning to the world, is always *my* intention, the projection of my meanings and my values, the shaping of the world in the image of my individual self.

For Hui-neng and his followers the recognition that consciousness is the condition under which things appear to us as something does not necessarily lead to the conclusion that all intentions are personal. For although consciousness endows the world with meaning through the mediation of its situation, it need not strive to identify itself with that situation. "When a mind, thoroughly understanding the emptiness of all things, faces forms, it at once realizes their emptiness. With it emptiness is there all the time, whether it faces forms or not, whether it discriminates or not. . . . Why is it so? Because all things in their self-nature are empty; and wherever we go we find this emptiness. As all is empty, no attachment takes place; and on account of this non-attachment there is a simultaneous Use (of Dhyana and Prajna). The Bodhisattva always knows how to make Use of emptiness and thereby he attains the Ultimate. Therefore it is said that by the oneness of Dhyana and Prajna is meant Emancipation."[55] Thus seeing into emptiness or nothingness, which is the ground of all distinction, may have an effect quite the opposite of that which Sartre describes. To see into emptiness is to realize that the events of the world do not touch that aspect of consciousness which accompanies intentional consciousness. The world and its objects are essential only to positional consciousness which is directly aware of them. To realize, however, that these objects appear to consciousness only on the ground of negation, is to recognize that ultimately—on the level of non-positional self-consciousness—there is no dependence or attachment whatsoever.

This state of consciousness is also called *unconsciousness* by Hui-neng, to indicate its non-intentional character. His definition of unconsciousness is: ". . . not to have the Mind tainted while in contact with the conditions of life—this is to be Unconscious. It is to be always detached from objective conditions in one's own consciousness, not to let one's mind be roused by coming in contact with objective conditions."[56] Hui-neng maintains that this state of consciousness is fundamentally non-attainable. It is non-attainable since in self-nature there is from the first not a thing which is attainable. "This self-nature in terms of the *Prajnaparamita* is Suchness (*tathata*), and Emptiness (*sunyata*). Suchness means the Absolute, something which is not subject to the laws of relativity, and therefore which cannot be grasped by means of form. Suchness is thus formlessness. In Buddhism, form *(rupa)* stands against formlessness *(arupa)*, which is the unconditioned. This unconditioned is not a negative idea, nor does it mean privation, but as it is not in the realm of names and forms it is called emptiness, or nothingness, or the Void."[57] This consciousness is without form since it is not a circumscribed mode of consciousness (for example, a perceiving, a conceiving, an imagining) which could become the object of a reflective inquiry. It is experienced only as non-positional consciousness of itself. Emptiness or formlessness is also unattainable in the sense that it cannot be sought as something to be acquired or achieved. To seek to acquire or achieve something presupposes a goal of the action and a lack on the part of the agent. It is, therefore, a mode of intentional consciousness. But these conditions are altogether absent in the experience in question. Emptiness, then, is unattainable because it is beyond perception, conception, or any other kind of grasping whatsoever. It is beyond the duality of being and non-being, of objects, and our conscious intending of them. It is unattainable since the brightness of non-positional self-consciousness is present all along.

Thus "Prajna, which is the awakening of consciousness in the Unconscious, functions in a twofold direction. The one is towards the Unconscious and the other towards the conscious. The Prajna which is oriented to the Unconscious is *Prajna* properly so-called, while the Prajana of consciousness is now called mind with the small initial letter. From this mind a dualistic world takes its rise: subject and object, the inner self and the external world, and so on. In the Mind, therefore, two aspects are also distinguishable: Prajna-mind of non-discrimination and dualistic mind. The mind of the first aspect belongs to this world, but so long as it is linked with Prajna it is in direct communication with the Unconscious, it is the Mind; whereas the mind of the second aspect is wholly of this world and delighted with it, and mixes itself with all its multiplicities."[58] Discriminating mind is intentional consciousness which is dependent upon its objects. Non-discriminating mind or unconsciousness is non-positional self-consciousness which accompanies all positional or discriminating consciousness. In itself non-discriminating consciousness is entirely formless, sheer nothingness or *sunyata;* for since it is without objects, it is not a determinate mode of consciousness. But all discriminating consciousness is accompanied by and grounded in non-discriminating consciousness, since discrimination is nihilation—the Use of nothingness to allow something to stand out as something. Understood in this way, non-discriminating consciousness is suchness or *tathata,* that which makes the existence of anything possible.

From the standpoint of Zen, Sartre has failed to distinguish two different aspects of the spontaneity of consciousness. Borrowing a phrase from Kant, we might call the first freedom in the negative sense. It stems from the fact that consciousness is not a thing and transcends, therefore, the network of causal interactions which characterizes things. But, as Suzuki has pointed out, this aspect of freedom is always relative because discriminating consciousness is always related to that which it discriminates and from which it distinguishes itself. The second aspect of spontaneity is emancipation or freedom in its positive sense. It does not cancel out the relative freedom of discriminating consciousness but accompanies it as the non-positional self-consciousness which is its ground. This aspect of spontaneity is called non-discriminating mind by the Zen masters because it is free from all affections. Being unaffected its freedom is absolute. Not being consciousness of this or that object as seen through this or that situation in the world, non-discriminating mind is the pure lucidity presupposed in all discrimination. "Thus, 'non-discriminating Prajna', 'to be free from affections', 'from the first not a thing is'— all these expressions point to the same source which is the fountainhead of Zen experience."[59]

The contrast between discriminating consciousness and non-discriminating absolute consciousness is also brought out in Hui-neng's understanding of the doctrine of *karma*. The doctrine of *karma* holds that one's state in this life is a result of both physical and mental actions in past incarnations, and that actions in this life can determine one's destiny in future incarnations. *Karma* is a natural, impersonal, moral law of cause and effect which is held to be universally applicable, and only those who have attained emancipation can transcend it. According to Hui-neng, however, since non-discriminating consciousness is wholly free from affection, the law of *karma* is effective only on the level of discriminating consciousness, and only when there is no recognition that discrimination has its ground in non-discriminating consciousness which always accompanies it. So long as one refers to working out one's *karma*, *karma* is already there.[60] *Karma*, then, is a result of the attempt to complete the self, to take it as real. As long as I fail to recognize that consciousness is fundamentally impersonal, I am delivered over to the karmic determinations of my situation in the world. But these determinations are ultimately illusory, for they can never affect the source of all discriminating consciousness which is *sunyata* or nothingness. They affect me only as long as the continual presence of non-discriminating consciousness is veiled. But since non-discriminating consciousness always accompanies discriminating consciousness, it is never entirely concealed. The laws of *karma* bind me, therefore, only so long as I am in bad faith.

For Sartre the only alternative to bad faith seems to be an anguished responsibility for a world which I never made and can never really inhabit. Elsewhere he hints at an authenticity which requires a "self-recovery," and in his discussion of play he speaks of "a purifying reflection" which would allow us to understand play as a presentation to itself of the absolute freedom which constitutes the very being of the person. His few remaining remarks suggest, however, that play must ultimately be analyzed as a mode of intentional consciousness which seeks to appropriate its objects. He tells us that play involves a certain degree of appropriation; that sport, like art, transforms the environment into a supporting element of its action.[61] Skiing, for example, is an instrumental appropriation of the snowfield. "It is *my* field of snow; I have traversed it a hundred times, a hundred times I have through my speed produced in it this force of condensation and support; it is *mine*."[62] Thus play must be analyzed on the model of the fundamental project which is man, the desire to be God. "Art, science, play are activities of appropriation, either wholly or in part, and what they want to appropriate beyond the concrete object of their quest is being itself, the absolute being of the in-itself."[63]

In making play one more form of appropriation, Sartre denies the very phenomenon he set out to describe. Play cannot be understood as an attempt to appropriate the absolute being of the *en-soi*, for appropriation is an expression of contingency and dependence. It takes place on the level of discriminating consciousness which enjoys only relative freedom. As the presentation of absolute freedom to itself, play must be an expression of non-positional self-consciousness which is absolutely free, since it is completely unaffected by the objects of positional consciousness. But this aspect of consciousness is not isolated from positional consciousness and its objects. Rather non-discriminating consciousness always accompanies discriminating consciousness. Hence we should expect to find its freedom manifested in the activities of daily life. Zen does just this. It performs such activities as painting, gardening, and drinking tea as activities without purpose, thus transforming them into so many expressions of play.

The Zen understanding of play is brought out clearly in the work of the Sumiye painter. He uses the frailest of materials—ink made of glue and soot, highly absorbent paper and a brush of sheep or badger hair which soaks up a great deal of fluid. The nature of his materials dictate that the artist must work as quickly and economically as possible. Only the essentials are permitted and they must be executed without deliberation, erasure, repetition or retouching. Once executed, the brush strokes are irrevocable. As Suzuki describes it:

"The artist must follow his inspiration as spontaneously and absolutely and instantly as it moves; he just lets his arm, his fingers, his brush be guided by it as if they were all mere instruments, together with his whole being, in the hands of somebody else who has temporarily taken possession of him. Or we may say that the brush by itself executes the work quite outside the artist, who just lets it move on without his conscious efforts. If any logic or reflection comes between brush and paper, the whole effort is spoiled."[64]

The Sumiye painter does not seek to represent an objective reality in his art. And though there may be some relation between his marks and objective nature, this is not an essential element of his work. Rather the painting has its own merit beyond any resemblance it may have to the forms of nature. Its birds or leaves come into being simultaneously with the work and exist only within it. The line of the painter is as final and as inevitable as a flash of lightning; the artist himself cannot undo it; from this issues the beauty of the line. "Things are beautiful where they are inevitable, that is, when they are free exhibitions of a spirit."[65] The Sumiye artist works so that no explicit purpose is discernible in his work. As an instantaneous record of an act which is both impersonal and without purpose, Sumiye painting expresses the absolute freedom of play which is the Zen attitude toward life.

The art of Zen and its attitude toward life are essentially egoless. The doctrine of no mind or non-ego is also the doctrine of the unconscious. "The Unconscious evolves silently through our empirical individual consciousnesses, and as it thus works the latter takes it for an ego-soul, free, unconditioned, and permanent. But when this concept takes hold of our consciousness, the really free actions of the Unconscious meet obstructions on all sides. Emotionally, this is the source of torments, and life becomes impossible. To restore peace in the most practical manner, Buddhism now teaches us to abandon the thought of an ego-soul, to be free from this clinging, to dry up this main spring of constant annoyance; for it is thus that the Unconscious regains its original creativity."[66] In his conception of consciousness as a lucid, impersonal spontaneity which is always non-positionally aware of itself, Sartre has touched the center of the Zen experience. But he turns away from his original insight which purifies consciousness of the self. In contrast to Zen art, Sartre's stories, plays and novels are always personal. They are so many descriptions of a freedom which seeks to ground itself by completing itself in something other; of an impersonal spontaneity seeking to render itself personal. Whereas Sartre discovers dependence at the heart of freedom thus rendering man a useless passion, Zen discovers freedom in the midst of dependence, discrimination and multiplicity.

It releases consciousness from its fascination with the self, thus allowing impersonal consciousness to act without goal, without care, and without anguish.

WILLIAM BOSSART: SARTRE'S THEORY OF CONSCIOUSNESS AND THE ZEN DOCTRINE OF NO MIND

1. This paper originated in an impromptu discussion of the problem of authenticity in Sartre. I subsequently reread a good deal of literature on Buddhism drawn particularly from the work of D.T. Suzuki. All references to Zen Buddhism are from the edition of his selected writings: *Zen Buddhism*, ed. William Barrett (Garden City, N.Y.: Doubleday Anchor Books, 1956).

2. Suzuki, Chapter 9.

3. Suzuki, p. 262.

4. *L'être et le néant* (Paris, 1943), pp. 18–23; English translation *Being and Nothingness* by Hazel Barnes (N.Y., 1956), pp. l–lvi. Hereafter abbreviated *EN*. Page references to the French edition followed by the English edition in parentheses.

5. Suzuki, p. 263.

6. Suzuki, p. 261.

7. Suzuki, p. 264.

8. Suzuki, pp. 264–65.

9. The *cogito* is certainly not the only way into Husserl's phenomenology but it is the entrée appropriate to Sartre's interpretation of Husserl. For a discussion of other starting points see Iso Kern, *Husserl und Kant* (The Hague, 1964); also "The Three Ways to the Transcendental Phenomenological Reduction in the Philosophy of Edmund Husserl" in F. Elliston & P. McCormick eds., *Husserl: Explanation and Appraisals* (South Bend, 1976), pp. 126–149. See also Husserl, *Die Krisis der Europäischenwissenschaften* (The Hague, 1962), part III.

10. E.g., *Cartesianische Meditationen* (The Hague, 1950), *Meditation III*.

11. *Cartesianische Meditationen*, #18, 37; also *Ideen I* (The Hague, 1950), #81.

12. E.g., *Cartesianische Meditationen*, #30–33; also *Krisis*, #28–55.

13. Sartre, *The Transcendence of the Ego*, trans. F. Williams and R. Kirkpatrick (New York, 1957), pp. 37–38. Hereafter abbreviated as *TE*.

14. *TE*, p. 39. See also *Cartesianische Meditationen*, #18, #37.

15. *TE*, p. 40.

16. *TE*, p. 46.

17. *TE*, p. 53.

18. *TE*, pp. 60–61.

19. *TE*, p. 75.

20. *TE*, p. 79.

21. *TE*, p. 81.

22. *TE*, p. 100.

23. *EN*, p. 18 (ii).

24. *EN*, p. 19 (ii–liii).

25. *EN*, pp. 19–20 (liii).

26. *EN*, p. 23 (lvi).

27. *EN*, pp. 37–40 (3–6).

28. *EN*, pp. 40–47 (9–12).

29. *EN*, p. 80 (42).

30. E.g., *EN*, pp. 121–127, 561–638 (79–84), (481–556).

31. *EN*, pp. 94–108 (55–67).

32. *EN*, pp. 95 (46).

33. *EN*, pp. 108–111 (67–70).

34. *EN*, p. 111 (70).

35. *EN*, p. 351 (290).

36. *EN*, p. 670 (581).

37. *EN*, p. 670 (581).

38. *EN*, p. 634 (549), my translation.

39. *EN*, p. 641 (555), my translation.

40. *EN*, p. 642 (556), my translation.

41. Suzuki, p. 161.

42. Suzuki, p. 166.

43. Suzuki, p. 167.

44. Suzuki, p. 167. My emphasis.

45. Suzuki, p. 174.

46. Suzuki, p. 178.

47. Suzuki, p. 179.

48. Suzuki, p. 190.

49. There are, of course, other parallels between the thought of Sartre and of Hui-neng, particularly the interrelation of theory and praxis, but we cannot go into them here.

50. *EN*, p. 134–135 (91).

51. Suzuki, p. 159.

52. Suzuki, pp. 264–65.

53. Suzuki, p. 15.

54. Suzuki, p. 196.

55. Suzuki, p. 181.

56. Suzuki, p. 189.

57. Suzuki, p. 190.

58. Suzuki, p. 211.

59. Suzuki, p. 183.

60. Suzuki, p. 203.

61. *EN*, p. 670 (581).

62. *EN*, p. 674 (585) my translation.

63. *EN*, p. 675 (585).

64. Suzuki, pp. 279–80. The same can be said, of course, of certain works of western art—the *croquis* of Marquet, certain drawings of Matisse and some abstract expressionist paintings come immediately to mind. For an extended discussion of the role of play in culture see J. Huizinga, *Homo Ludens* (Boston: Beacon Press, 1960). For a discussion of play and art see William Bossart,

"Form and meaning in the Visual Arts," *The British Journal of Aesthetics*, VI, 3 (July 1966), 259–71.
   65. Suzuki, p. 281.
   66. Suzuki, pp. 289–90.

IV

Morality and War, Surrealism and Memory

Earle's "Rejection" of Morality

HUGH MERCER CURTLER

"Good Lord," they'll scream at you, "you can't possibly deny that: twice two IS four! Never does nature ask you for your opinion; she does not care a damn for your wishes or whether you like her or not. . . . A stone wall, that is, is a stone wall. . . . But, goodness gracious me, what do I care for the laws of nature and arithmetic if for some reason I don't like those laws of twice-two? No doubt I shall never be able to break through such a strone wall with my forehead, if I do not possess the strength to do it, but I shall not reconcile myself to it just because I have to deal with the stone wall and haven't the strength to break it down.—Dostoevsky: Notes from the Underground

William Earle insists that philosophy somewhere took a wrong turn. It began with "high hopes and brave promises" and has run aground on a "depressing mess of common sense" and "banality." The problem, apparently, is the spirit of abstraction, the desire for "essence, concept and definition."[1] Thus, Earle's philosophy stands as a protest against this spirit, an expression of his outrage against the pristine, clinical abstractions of the neo-positivists and linguists who dominate Anglo-American philosophy in our century. In its place Earle prefers "the articulation in thought of one man's deepest concerns."[2] He seeks to restore the sublime and the mysterious to a discipline that has become cold and lifeless. Following Hegel, he would replace "the coldly progressing necessity of the subject matter" with "fermenting enthusiasm," and, like Hegel, he would hope that

> The Spirit is turning away from the husks and, confessing that it is in trouble and cursing, it now demands from philosophy not so much self-knowledge as that philosophy should help the Spirit to establish . . . substantiality and the solidity of

153

being. Philosophy is asked to answer this need by supressing the discriminating concept, and by establishing the feeling of things, granting not so much insight as edification.[3]

In a spirit that is, to be sure, wholistic, Earle rejects the current reduction of "experience" to "sense experience"; "reason" to "logic"; "reality" to what can be found in graduated cylinders, microscopes and beakers. As it happens, however, his rejections are so vehement that he often finds himself looking out from under the burden of an extreme position that, though opposite from the position he attacks, is nonetheless extreme for all that. This, I think, is a great part of the charm and appeal of Earle's thinking. But it is also problematic from another point of view.

In this essay I shall examine, sympathetically but nevertheless critically, one sample of the tendency I find in Earle's thought that leads him from an acute sense of the flaws and dangers of one point of view to its opposite, with little concern for the middle ground. I shall be most concerned to examine his rejection of traditional moral philosophy in what is possibly his best book to date, *The Autobiographical Consciousness*. To prepare the way I shall say a few words about his general tendency toward exclusivity which I have alluded to above.

I

Earle's rejection of much of contemporary philosophizing comes from within the tradition of German idealism, and ultimately stems from Descartes. It is fascinating to watch him wrestle the two bears of Idealism in its Hegelian mode and the strong existential tendencies that abhor such systematic straightjackets. Any success he might enjoy in this struggle, I suspect, results from his adaptation of the Kierkagaardian notion of "subjective truth." In this view truth is not "correspondence"; it is not "coherence"; rather, it is "troth," or loyalty to human experience as it is lived.[4] Earle does not, however, insist that truth is relative or *merely* personal in the sense that it is so for me but not for you. Truth is, rather, "disclosure," or strict adherence to experience as it reveals itself to human consciousness—whether it be yours or mind. Thus, Earle espouses subjectiv*ity* rather than subjectiv*ism*, which is to say, he would direct attention to subjective consciousness as the proper seat of inquiry without reducing all we find there to mere opinion. He seeks the "unique, singular, unrepeatable, the historical and autobiographical;" but his autobiography is ontological, concerned with an object that has pertinence for all other subjects. It is Earle's ties with Husserl that make the ramifications of his subjective truth clear. As Earle says

Intentional or dialectical analysis, then, is not in the least tracing my own meanings and intentions as they wander here and there, but tracing those intentions only insofar as they are in strict correlation with the objective significations of the given object. Otherwise I have not analyzed the object but only myself. . . .[5]

Earle's reluctance to identify his position in any simple way with Husserl results more from a difference of stress or concern than it does from ideological differences. Husserl was not interested in what lies outside the limits of shared human experience; Earle regards the "accidental as essential."[6] He pushes Husserl's method to its limits— and beyond. His own searches have led him to the very boundaries of philosophy where it blends into poetry and these searches have resulted in a series of captivating studies of surrealism, mysticism, and much of the territory that separates philosophy and poetry.

In his explorations Earle has discovered signs of a decaying culture that renders much of what passes for truth and wisdom irrelevant to contemporary human existence. Earle struggles against the wave of self-indulgent youth worshippers that reek of the stench of a diseased culture, while at the same time he senses genuine hope in the casting off of the dead husks of a forgotten past. One senses in Earle's "public sorrow" a strong current of conservatism that strains against his sympathies with those who propose radically new ways of thinking and feeling.

If we survive, we are told by presumed experts that we are coming to a totally new consciousness, higher levels of intuition, development of the right hemisphere of the human brain, greater tolerance for "esoteric" ways of knowing.[7] One can infer that the new consciousness will be less philosophical and more poetic, less discursive and remote and closer to life as it is lived. Like a handful of others who are sensitive to the prophesies of poets and artists who have seen these changes coming for nearly a century, Earle finds in the signs of the new consciousness the seeds of both hope and despair. Despite his sorrow over the "radical madness" that attacks the carcass of our decaying civilization, he hopes for a "private recuperation of the spirit altogether beyond civilization."[8]

One is not surprised, then, to find Earle the philosopher arguing for the supremacy of poetry as a vehicle of truth on the grounds that

the singular unrepeatable aspects of singular lives are what the arts are admirably equipped to show; what might be called the "existential"; the conceptualization of the existential is but a questionable flight from it, one which can moreover only be proven correct or incorrect by a return precisely to that intuition from which it took its flight.[9]

The central idea here, and one which is vital to Earle's position, is that any attempt to talk *about* experience involves conceptualization and since concepts are static they necessarily distort the dynamic human experience that is forced through them. As Earle puts it, "philosophy is inherently *disruptive* of whatever unity or coherence truth might have."[10] Direct awareness of human experience as it is lived is more nearly poetic than philosophical, imagination is more vital than understanding. Poets do not argue; they show! ". . . the need for proof must be considered an inherent fault, the consequence philosophy reaps for having abandoned reality in the first place via the concept."[11]

The poet takes us beyond the realm of what we usually refer to as "reality" to the realm of the surreal. It is, for Earle, a realm of "private pleasures" that involve those aspects of human experience that most interest him and that have given rise to some of his most fscinating discoveries over the years. It is a realm *beyond* civilization in the dialectical progression of the human spirit from nature, through culture, to civilization, where "everything is discontinuous, dislocated, disoriented, nonadditive, and not a world at all."[12] It is not a journey for the timid or the faint at heart. But, one asks almost involuntarily, assuming one can find his way to this place, how is it possible to get one's bearings?

How are we to know that the radicals, for instance, are not the prophets of the surreal, "beyond civilization, an effort at an absolute recuperation of the spirit, but not on the plane of reason, reflection or civilization. . . ."[13] How does this realm differ from the utopia of the mad radicals who also attack discursive reason and traditional ways of knowing? The ideas of "freedom, poetry, and mad love" have, after all, been extolled before—although in an entirely different context from the one in which Earle would place them. It is also difficult to distinguish the realm of the surreal, which lies "beyond" civilization, from the primitive culture which preceded civilization. How do we distinguish the true prophets (Earle, or perhaps, André Breton) from the frauds? We must, surely. Earle himself would lead the way. But his path is *his own* and we look to him for guidance in vain. Which way to go? Whom do we follow? How are we to distinguish a concern for "consciousness of the transitory life of the transcendental ego" from a preoccupation with self that characterizes the mad radicals and the youth worshippers?

Whatever the answers to these questions might be—and I am left with them after first raising them in print in 1976—Earle leaves us with some fascinating puzzles and profound difficulties alongside the startling revelations and vivid descriptions of such phenomena as time, memory, and horror. Doubtless this is a consequence of the forbidding nature of the territory he has chosen to explore, coupled with the enthusiasm and energy with which he has undertaken that journey.

Earle the philosopher yearns for poetic vision and rejects the cardboard abstractions of philosophers past and present who force human experience through the static categories of human understanding until it loses what is essential. He should welcome the signs that suggest that our civilization is in its death throes and that whatever replaces it will be more sympathetic to the revelations of the "higher intuition" than is our neo-positivistic age. But he does not. He senses that the new self-consciousness might be no more than self-indulgence, genuine intuitions might be difficult to make out and impossible to distinguish from pseudo-intuitions. Above all, the rejection of old ways of thinking may, in the end, extract too great a price, since consciousness is above all else *human* and it requires conceptualization in addition to imagination and heightened intuitive power if it is to understand and control the world and not merely experience it.

Earle knows all this, though at times he tends to forget in his efforts to reject the "degenerative tendency" of philosophy that leads it to "ape the mathematical and natural sciences."[15] It is necessary, however, to listen to the still, small voice of reason that seeks to strike a balance. It is this voice that we can hear when we turn to Earle's rejection of traditional morality, which he calls the "immorality of morality," and it is this discussion we shall now consider as a case in point, an example of some of the general tendencies noted above.

II

In the ninth chapter of *The Autobiographical Consciousness*, Earle lists several propositions that form the rejection of moral principles:

(1) that every morality, whether religiously expressed as commandments of God or philosophically expressed as reason applied to the conduct of life, depends upon principle;

(2) that, in the question to which all moralities address themselves, no exceptions can be admitted;

(3) that no universal principle offered by any morality can have any bearing at all on life;

(4) that all moralities turn themselves immediately into their opposite, the immoral . . .; and

(5) that, if the whole religious and philosophical theory of moral principle is disastrous, we must find another way of illuminating this most decisive area of our concerns, a way that we may hope will not simply introduce one more principle.[16]

Of major concern, here as elsewhere, is the spontaneity of human experience that can only be diminished, if not altogether relinquished, by the espousal of universal directives and proscriptions. Earle suspects any moral theory, or indeed, "any supposed descent from ontology or any general theory of value into the existent human scene."[17] But he goes further. He argues "no universal principle offered by any morality can have any bearing at all on life."[18]

It is clear that Earle, with his concern for the "accident as essential," must be unfriendly toward moral absolutism and the tendencies of moralists to command and condemn. It is what is unique about a person's life that is of chief interest to Earle and the moralist's instincts drive him in another direction entirely. At the same time, one must question Earle's logic in the above argument, since there is certainly something wrong between steps #2 and #3 in the above list which are, I take it, steps deducible from one another in Earle's view. From the claim that principles must not allow of exceptions he argues that such principles cannot have any place in human experience where the exception is the rule. That is to say, he argues that since principles do not (cannot?) *always* apply to human experience, they therefore *never* apply. But this does not follow, since the denial of a universal proposition does not imply the truth of its contrary. It is possible that principles do not always apply to human experience, but they may nevertheless apply *some* of the time. Let us take a concrete example.

Imagine the case of Emanuelle, a thoroughgoing Kantian who always seeks to do the right thing but who finds herself confronted by a dilemma in which she is forced to lie or betray a friend. She is asked where her friend is and despite her knowledge of her friend's whereabouts she says she does *not* know because she has good reason to believe that her friend will be harmed if she tells the truth.

Now, like the rest of us no doubt, Earle would certainly approve of Emanuelle's action in this case. I suspect that Kant would also, but that is another story for another time. The question is whether Emanuelle's decision can be said to be based on a moral principle.

As a Kantian, Emanuelle knows it is wrong to lie. That is a general principle and as such allows of no exceptions. It arises from an application of the Categorical Imperative that would make lying "self-defeating." In the face of Emanuelle's dilemma, however, it would *also* be wrong to tell the truth in this case since that would bring harm to her friend, and that, too, would be "self-defeating." Indeed, it would be worse to tell the truth than it would be to lie, since the categorical imperative rests systemically on the grounds of the inviolability of persons. Telling a lie in this case would be, as we say, the "lesser of two evils." What this means is that it is always wrong to lie, but in this case it would be worse to tell the truth. Emanuelle did a wrong thing, her action lacked moral worth in Kant's view, but it was the only thing she could do—morally speaking—under the circumstances.

Now, as we are all aware, Kant seldom if ever dealt with conflicts between duties, since he was enamored of the simpler case of conflicts between desires and duties. Thus we cannot say for certain that this is what he would have Emanuelle do in this case. But it matters not. What is important is that Emanuelle has remained true to her principles, she has retained her integrity, while at the same time exercizing her free choice to elect one principle over another.

Despite the fact that principles do not entail actions in a logical way, they do not lose their universality. It is always wrong to lie, under any circumstances even if in a particular case one must lie to avoid a greater wrong. But even if this were not the case, it is not clear that because moral principles allow of exceptions and, (say,) are not, strictly, universal they therefore do not have *any* application whatever. From the fact that a principle is not universal it does not follow that "it has no bearing at all on life."

As if we weren't confused enough about this issue, Earle takes the position one step further. He reasons that the idea of morality is "ludicrous," since one cannot "dream here and now what everyone *must* do, of establishing standards for all men, past present, and future."[19] But moral principles do not establish what all men "must" do; they establish (if they establish anything) what all men *ought* to do. And this is quite different. The same problem surfaces in Earle's final claim in chapter nine that ideals "predetermine" human conduct and therefore destroy its spontaneity. Ideals do not predetermine conduct; they *direct* it and (as we have seen) not faultlessly by any means. Human life remains the same confusing, buzzing, confounding mess it always was with or without the guidance of principles—as long as we realize that principles only guide actions, they do not determine them, and as long as human beings remain free *not* to obey principles. "Ought" implies "can," as Kant knew. It does not imply necessity any more than Earle's position implies necessity. We can be moral or not: it is a matter of choice.

What is clearly of interest to William Earle throughout this discussion is the maintenance of genuine options in our moral life. But his image of the Melanesian mask in the Museum of Paris with its chalklike pallor, its sunken cheeks and its terrified eyes, with which he begins his discussion is a parody of morality at its dogmatic worst and not a fair characterization of all moral systems.[20] To espouse moral principles is to limit action somewhat. That much is clear. But it does not entail a loss of freedom, since one must still choose among principles once he has decided to act morally—which also remains an option. Unlike the laws of Newton, the universality of moral principles does not entail inviolability on the level of human action: principles must simply be acknowledged to be binding *prima facie*. All persons ought to try to be honest, fair, judicious, good humored, kind, and generous. But they cannot always be so. This does not mean that universal principles allow of exceptions (which would be a contradiction, as Earle insists), but that they do not always apply because they conflict with other principles in a specific case and must give way before their greater force.

It is curious that Earle did not spot the analogy between moral principles and values, which he regards as relative in respect to human actions but, in another respect, "as absolutes, borne of things in their relations to other existents that need them. An experienced value is the experience of a mode or moment of complete or absolute being."[21] While this admission does not allow for deductions from values to specific courses of action, as Earle insists, it does not necessarily force us to conclude, as Earle goes on to do, that they do not allow us to "reach any conclusions whatever about human experience."[22] Once again, Earle seems to have overstated his case, since (as we have seen in the case of moral principles) values can have considerable practical use in the guidance of human actions, though as such they are not binding on all people at all times and in all places. Values, as Earle allows, are both transcendent and immanent ". . . in both places, and not forever an abstract 'ought.' "[23]

In any event, there seem to be two major difficulties with Earle's rejection of morality in *The Autobiographical Consciousness*. (1) Even if we insist that principles cannot allow of exceptions, it does not follow that they have no bearing whatever on human actions. (2) Since principles are not laws they are not binding except as directives to human actions. Thus while they cannot allow of exceptions (for example, it is *always* wrong to lie), they may conflict with other principles at times and we are then forced to choose among them. This does not deprive us of our freedom, it presupposes our freedom to choose among principles or to ignore them altogether.

One misses a great deal in his writings if he ignores Earle's sense of the ironic. This, coupled with his tendency toward overstatement in the face of what he considers an immoral morality, makes one wonder just where Earle does, in fact, sit on the issue of morality (to take only the case in point). In his final chapter in *Mystical Reason*, for example, Earle has a lengthy discussion of "the Ethical" that has strong Kantian overtones—to the extent that he is led to insist that "the answer" to "the problem of morality . . . places the sacredness or dignity of the person as both the origin and end of morality."[24] Now while this conviction does not bind Earle to any sort of moral absolutism it is a far cry from the notion that all moralities are immoral.

It is clear that Earle shrinks at the thought of the Melanesian mask and all forms of intolerance and proselytising that often accompany moral absolutism. The sanctity of the person and the value of love that form a part of the warp and woof of Earle's ethical position allow him the flexibility he demands in order to give full rein to human choice and allow for the luxury of human error. But one can reject the "nay-sayers" of proscriptive moral systems without rejecting morality as such. Indeed, this is, I think, where Earle ends up. His insistence on the sanctity of the person, coupled with his concern for "transcendental love," and "the mystical source of excellence" which is God, suggest that his rejection of morality is less radical than it might appear at first blush.

III

Earle always startles and provokes. He is never dull, and we can only regret that there aren't more around like him. Whether or not one agrees with him, one cannot ignore his arguments. Many of the difficulties that one encounters when reading his writings are obviously a result of his attempts to say the unsayable, to report his findings in areas most philosophers have been too timid to explore because of the rough terrain and the lack of map and compass. In the end, though, one finds throughout his writings pairs of dichotomies: intuition, not argument; subject, not object; concrete, not abstract; immanent, not transcendent; imagination, not conceptualization; immorality, not morality. To follow Earle is, at some point, to make some very basic choices. In the end, however, I find myself unable to make those choices because I cannot agree that they are necessary. Perhaps I lack Earle's courage: I sometimes think this is the case. I want to have it both ways. I, too, want to reject the nay-sayers of absolutistic morality who see in the Melanesian mask an ideal of human nature. But a rejection of the mask does not involve a rejection of all moral systems *per se,* or all attempts to deal systematically with our moral life. I want to insist that both intuition and argument, imagination and conceptualization, the concrete and the abstract, can find their place at the philosopher's table.

It is possible that Earle is not only more courageous than I, but also more honest, and that one cannot have it both ways. If I reach that conclusion in the end it will be because he has persuaded me that such a point of view is the only one a philosopher can take. In the meantime I reserve final judgment and await further arguments with some anxiety, but also with a decided sense of excitement.

HUGH MERCER CURTLER: EARLE'S "REJECTION" OF MORALITY

1. *Public Sorrows and Private Pleasures* (Bloomington: Indiana University Press, 1976), p. 141.

2. Ibid., p. 173.

3. Hegel, Preface to *The Phenomenology of Mind*, I.3.

4. *Mystical Reason* (Chicago: Regnery, 1981), p. 106.

5. Ibid., p. 12.

6. *Public Sorrows and Private Pleasures*, p. 152.

7. See, for example, Jantsch and Waddington, eds. *Evolution and Consciousness: Human Systems in Transition* (Reading, Mass.: Addison Wesley, 1976).

8. *Public Sorrows and Private Pleasures*, p. xii.

9. Ibid., p. 129.

10. Ibid., p. 134.

11. Ibid., p. 135.

12. Ibid., p. 145.

13. Ibid., p. 119.

14. See Hugh M. Curtler, "A Refuge from Rebellion," *Modern Age* (Fall, 1976). This was a review of *Public Sorrows and Private Pleasures.*

15. *Public Sorrows and Private Pleasures*, pp. 125 ff.

16. On these five points, see *The Autobiographical Consciousness* (Chicago: Quadrangle Press, 1972), pp. 185–86.

17. *Autobiographical Consciousness*, p. 178.

18. Ibid., p. 185.

19. Ibid., p. 195.

20. Cf. ibid., p. 184.

21. Ibid., p. 178.

22. Ibid.

23. Ibid., p. 183.

24. *Mystical Reason*, p. 90.

On the Indefensibility of War

ERROL E. HARRIS

Praise and sympathetic exposition of philosophies with which one agree are not without value, but critical disagreement is usually more interesting and often more fruitful. Those who did not know it before have learnt from Kant that all genuine philosophy is criticism; though it does not, of course, follow that all criticism is negative, and we should also have learnt from Hegel that negative criticism always has a positive result.

In honoring my friend and colleague, William Earle, I have not chosen, therefore, to write about that wide area of philosophical conviction in which we are agreed, or to comment on those of his writings that I most admire, but I have chosen one of the few topics (if not perhaps the only one) on which our expressed opinions diverge. Yet, even here, the disagreement may be only in the visible expressions of our views, for I more than suspect that the underlying principles on which they both rest are more at one than our published opinions may suggest.

In his book, *Public Sorrows and Private Pleasures*,[1] Earle has written 'A Defense of War'. He does concede that war is a public sorrow, but he is nevertheless prepared to defend it in principle. As is always the case with his writing, the essay is a scintillating model of English style; but philosophically it leaves something to be desired and seems to mark the one occasion on which Earle has allowed his emotional aversion to sentimental pacifism to get the better of his intellectual judgment. For the essay does not really offer a reasoned philosophical defense of war, so much as rhetorical and sarcastic polemic against bad arguments for peace, which the author himself, for the most

---

[1] Indiana University Press, 1976.

part, admits to be irrelevant. The cause of peace cannot be harmed by the refutation of bad arguments in its defense; but neither is the cause of war thereby advanced. In effect, the only clear argument Earle offers in favor of war is that it requires courage—which nobody should deny—but, as it equally requires courage, often much more and of a more resolute nature, to face the threat of violence without physical resistance, this argument is two-edged and fails of its objective.

It will be apparent from what follows that I am no pacifist, and I do not advocate non-violence in principle, least of all for the sort of 'reasons' castigated by my colleague, so my own withers are unwrung by his polemic.

"The justification of war is existence," writes Earle; "to will to exist is to affirm war as its means and condition." This he expands to include individuation: the existent 'I', with its 'mine', also identifying with others as 'we' with 'ours', as against 'you' with 'yours'. This, he says, is "the ineluctable ground of war." (*Public Sorrows,* 59f.) Indeed, the ineluctable ground it well may be, but what is an ineluctable ground is not automatically justification.

We come nearer the mark when it is admitted that mere existence, or bare life, is not enough to justify: "men have always thought it justifiable to fight not merely to preserve their physical being, but also for those additional things that make that life worth living: fertile lands, access to the sea, minerals, a government of their choice, laws and customs, religion and finally peace itself." (*Public Sorrows,* p. 60.)

With all this one can hardly disagree, but we should be wary lest "what men have always thought" should prove, in certain circumstances and under unprecedented conditions, to be false. For this argument also might turn against itself should the weapons of war and the inescapable effects of their use be such as to destroy not only the physical being of the combatants but, at the same time, those very things which make life worth living, the entire community and its government, its heritage, its fertile lands, in short (to quote Earle further), "all those concrete values which illuminate and glorify existence"—everything worth fighting for. Existence then, so far from justifying war, might well imperatively demand its prohibition.

Self-preservation and individuation certainly involve the move from 'I' to 'we'. No human individual can survive or develop a personality of his own in isolation from other fellow human beings. Society is as essential to genuine human existence and to human satisfaction as is food or water. It is so, moreover, not simply as an expression of gregarious instinct, but as the locus of intelligent cooperation efficiently to obtain and to preserve the requirements of physical existence and whatever else is desirable to make it worth preserving. "The state," Aristotle told us, "comes into existence for the sake of the bare needs of life, and continues in existence for the sake of the good life." And it is between states that war is waged, also, when the occasion demands, for the sake (as Earle concurs) of the good life. That aim, and that alone, can justify war.

The state is a system of organized social activity which can persist only if ordered and regulated by law; and just because men are not perfectly rational, because they are corruptible, envious, rapacious, covetous and, in fact, susceptible to every sort of vice, laws must be enforced, to maintain, so far as possible, order and concord— what, in medieval times was called "the King's peace." The result is a more or less civilized community, for the protection of which from outside aggression its members may be, and throughout the ages have been, called upon to fight. But the fundamental purpose, even in this case, be it noted, is the peace of the realm. Moreover, for the maintenance of peace and order within its borders, the citizens of the state must be compelled to obey its laws. Though fear of penalties is never the only motive for compliance, it is, in a society of fallible humans, an indispensable condition of the preservation of law and order. But force may not rightly be exercised arbitrarily, nor by unauthorized agencies, and power must be vested in a recognized authority such as no individual citizen can legitimately or successfully defy. This is the sovereign authority of the state, empowered to make, administer, and enforce its laws within its own borders, and to defend its territory against invasion from without. As such it is supreme and is subject to no superior law and to no superior terrestrial power. Its function is to govern in the common interest of its subjects and to defend them against attack.

We must notice, however, that there is another feature of sovereignty besides its supreme power, a feature which grounds both power and supremacy. That is authority. The state is authorized by the consent of the governed, either tacit or declared, and by that alone. Only from the loyalty and collaboration of its citizens is its power derived, in default of which that power withers away. "*Le plus fort*," wrote Rousseau, "*n'est jamais assez fort pour être toujours le maître, s'il ne transforme sa force en droit et l'obeissance en devoir.*"

With this condition, sovereigns are legally subject to no constraint and are said to be independent. Other sovereigns can coerce them only by the threat of superior force, to defy which they have only their own strength on which to rely. Thus every sovereign state exerts itself to the utmost to ensure its own safety and to provide to the best of its ability its own defense. In so doing, as Earle very rightly maintains, it cannot rely on treaties, for there is no superior power to secure their observance. As sovereigns are not subject to any higher law, the national interest is ultimately the only determinant of their action. They cannot therefore be trusted or expected to fulfil treaty 'obligations' unless it will serve that interest to do so. Their future policies can never be reliably predicted, for they may change them at will. Their alliances, when made, are never stable, and may be wrecked at any time by a mere change of government. So every state can but regard every other as a potential enemy (except where national interests temporarily coincide), and must needs seek to maintain its defensive power sufficiently to repel any anticipated attack.

The natural consequence is that all international relations are determined by power considerations, all international politics are power politics, and all international action is a manoeuvering to maintain a power balance. An arms race is the inevitable result with its attendant ever-increasing tensions and 'cold war'. International 'incidents' result and recur, international crises are intermittent, and war breaks out as soon as the balance of power, which is always unstable, breaks down. *This* is "the ineluctable ground" of war— rooted in existence, no doubt, but in the existence, in external relations, of sovereign states.

The cause of war is not instinctive pugnacity, or even human irrationality (again Earle is right). On the contrary, it derives from the rational tendencies of human beings to cooperate for their mutual good and so to found sovereign communities. War is a social institution, arising inevitably from the competitive relations between sovereign independent powers. What alone can 'justify' war is the interest of their citizens in what they take to be 'the good life'.

Thus far, I have little doubt, Bill Earle would raise no demur. And, until the middle of the twentieth century, one could perhaps, like him, have acclaimed war as the ultimate test of courage and nobility (as did Hitler and his Nazis). But since the invention and prodigious multiplication of nuclear weapons, while the conditions outlined above still persist, our value judgments must drastically be changed. The ever-present threat of war has now become the risk of ultimate annihilation. To embark upon war today is to invite total destruction, not only of human life but also of the very means of sustaining it. The vast indiscriminate destructive power of nuclear weapons threatens not just the decimation of populations but the total dissolution of organized life. It threatens besides the poisoning of the earth and its waters with radioactive dust and the disruption and pollution of the life-giving and protective envelope of the atmosphere. This destruction would not be limited to a restricted area, to which, after the holocaust, aid might be brought from others left unscathed. It would almost inevitably be world-wide. Survivors, such as may be, would be exposed for long periods to debilitating radioactive fall-out, which, if not immediately fatal, would impregnate them with inherent defects condemning their progeny to congenital disabilities for the foreseeable future. No possible conception of a good life could survive, much less be defended by, nuclear war.

This failure of justification, moreover, today infects all warfare of whatever kind, because the development of modern technocracy is such that the nations and the regions of the earth are all interdependent and the vital interests of the major powers embrace conditions and resources the world over. Conflicts arising anywhere and for any reason are therefore liable to involve everybody, and any threat to any nation may become a threat to all. War today cannot be restricted to any so-called 'theater'. Its method of conduct cannot be prescribed. If by the use of 'conventional' weapons combatants cannot succeed, they will resort to nuclear weapons to escape defeat. This the United States is already pledged to do in defense of Western Europe. No enemy can ever be relied on to respect any desired limitation in the use of 'tactical' weapons of any kind. The fear that nuclear weapons may be used against any party must prompt its resort to a preemptive first strike. Fear of a preemptive first strike gives pretext for the preparation of an automatic launch, on warning, of a second strike in retaliation. Such preparation is currently known as 'deterrence'.

But deterrence cannot deter. Not only because delusory wishful thinking seeks to persuade us and our leaders that nuclear war is controllable, is limitable and may be survived (perhaps even won); and such delusions could tempt some ebulient politician to take unwarrantable risks. But more essentially the policy of so-called deterrence is founded upon nothing other than the age-old doctrine of the balance of power, a balance which is inherently unstable, if only because, with the inevitable obsolescence of weaponry and with every advance in destructive techniques, one side or the other must gain some advantage. Thus is the arms race built into the policy of deterrence, resulting, as has been said, in inevitable tensions, persistent threats, recurrent crises and all the other destabilizing consequences of power politics. So the threat of war continually mounts and the growing menace of nuclear annihilation.

The balance of power has never prevented war in the past and at best has only postponed major world conflicts; nor, for the reasons given, can it ever be more salutary. Likewise deterrence cannot indefinitely deter nuclear war, still less can it limit prospective belligerents to the use of conventional weapons. And, as nuclear war would be destructive of any semblance of the good life, there is no longer any conceivable justification for war.

This conclusion, I am convinced, is incontrovertible; and clearly it is now imperative that nuclear war must be prevented at all costs. Yet so long as international relations continue to be power politics it will not and cannot be prevented in the long run. What then is the remedy? Obviously the only feasible remedy is to remove the root source of power politics, namely, national sovereignty. The United Nations, as at present constituted, is of no avail, for it upholds sovereign independence for its members. International law can provide no mitigation, for sovereigns are not and cannot be compelled to obey it. Disarmament agreements cannot palliate the situation, because they are but treaties, the observance of which can be insured, if at all, only by the use of the very armaments the treaty seeks to limit. There is but one practicable course: the submission of all nations to a single world authority invested with real power to enforce a genuine world law. Nationality must henceforth refer, not to the sovereign independent state, but to the cultural heritage of a community. In this new sense an international authority is required, which will absorb the several sovereignties of separate nations and exercise the power to maintain the security of all, to enforce the observance of international undertakings and to ensure the pacific settlement of disputes. This means, of course, the establishment of some form (no doubt very complex) of world federation, achieved either by reconstructing the United Nations (more appropriately to its name), or by a deliberately convened constitutional conference.

The proposal will undoubtedly be ridiculed as utopian, though I cannot see it as less realistic than the illusory expectation of victory in nuclear war. It is deprecated by Earle as "a totalitarian monstrosity," but I do not see why. The United States of America is a federation of former (if only briefly) sovereign states. Is it a totalitarian monstrosity? There is not the least necessity that a 'world state' should be a dictatorship; in fact, the contrary is far more compelling. World government could not be totalitarian, because if it were it could not command the consent of the governed, and so could not maintain its authority or its power. It could come into existence only if the nations agreed that it should not be totalitarian and wrote into its constitution and its law provisions guaranteeing freedom and security to its members.

Earle maintains that such a world authority, even if feasible, would make no essential difference. It would simply convert interstate war into civil war or insurrection. Possibly, but if the control of nuclear power were concentrated in the hands of the international authority, resistance to its power could not be by means of nuclear weapons, so that internal warfare, should it ever occur, would still leave hope of survival and continued civilized life. But the likelihood of such internal conflicts must be substantially reduced when the decisions of the courts can be enforced and the disputes between members legally adjudicated. Enforcement, moreover, would not be against sovereign states, but upon legal persons, and it would be by legal penalty and not by war.

Yet, it may be asked, would not the monopoly of power, especially of nuclear power, by a world authority lead inevitably to totalitarianism? For who then could resist its tyranny? The question is based upon a spurious presupposition that a world authority must be some abstract, unrepresentative agency remote from the peoples who constitute it. Can we, as individuals, resist the power of our present governments? Is their power not immeasurably superior to our personal physical strength? How then do we prevent them from tyrannizing us? Only by constitutional means—and such means would be equally available in a world federation. Political power is never merely physical force. No government of any sort can exert force which is not provided by its own subjects. All political power is the fruit of social organization, and that is why every nation gets the government it deserves. The control of power, nuclear or other, must be placed in the hands of the peoples' representatives, to be exercized in their common interest.

It is, of course, always possible that power may get into the wrong hands. But that is a possibility present in every society. It is an ever present risk—one that we constantly face even in national sovereign states. Many may think it too great a risk for a nation to forfeit its national soveeignty; yet no risk can be as great as that of nuclear extinction, which we now run with constantly increasing peril. It is the risk of final destruction to everything that we prize—a risk inherent in, and ineradicable from, the prevailing character of interstate politics, which can be eliminated only by converting the separate sovereignties into a genuine community of nations.

The establishment of a world political community is so far from being utopian that it is the only practical course genuinely open to mankind. Today we are plagued by world problems quite independent of the threat of nuclear war, none of which can be solved within the limits of jurisdiction of national sovereign states, and all of which demand international action, joint and concerted, regulated and controlled by an international authority. Without such action, the destruction of the environment, already well advanced, will continue unabated. Life can exist on earth only because the earth is a rare planet harboring conditions favorable and conducive to life; but those conditions are being steadily eroded by industrial pollution of air and water, the destruction of rain forests and the exhaustion of energy supplies. These and kindred evils can be counteracted only by concerted international planning and the strict and effective control of the conduct of peoples in every part of the world. Only an international authority would be competent to do what is needed.

It would, indeed, be rash to suggest that the establishment of such an authority would be easy, or to imagine that the attempt would not be hedged around with pitfalls, and that it involves no risks. But that should not deter us, least of all William Earle, who commends courage in the maintenance of existence and the pursuit of the good life. Plato defined courage as the right opinion about what ought to be feared. Never were men and women more in need of this virtue, nor can there be any doubt at this time about what ought more to be feared, nuclear annihilation or the relinquishment of national sovereignty. The latter would offer at least some chance of the good life for future generations, the former none whatsoever.

In the above argument I have not made any demand for 'equality', or even for 'justice'; I have made no appeal to a feckless 'idealism' or to mawkish sentimentalism, all of which are anathema to my friend Bill Earle. I have not sought to enlist sympathy for the miseries of serving soldiers, or for the sufferings of the innocent victims of hostilities. I have made no reference to 'pity choked by custom of fell deeds'. I have not psychoanalysed political leaders, or castigated warmongers as 'materialists', nor have I sanctified the peacemakers as the heralds of the millenium. I have not canvassed the opinions of G.I.s or consulted the feelings of the masses; nor have I consulted the 'media' or the findings of the pollsters. I have not even condemned the use of force—how otherwise could law and order be maintained? Such shenanigans, perhaps understandably, have moved Earle to indignation and contemptuous scorn. Rather my appeal has been to practical good sense, to the lessons of history (which, admittedly, few ever learn), and to the implications of existing facts, on an issue which is essentially one of practical politics.

Human reason and the exercise of intelligence is what makes social order and political organization possible, the issue of which is the sovereign state. In the present age, reason and intelligence, proceeding along the same line of logical implication should lead sovereign states to combine under a central authority, just as, in the past, individuals, families and village communities have done. All political structure is in general character federal, and the process of federation does not inexorably stop with the national sovereign. As the natural relationship between sovereign nations is, in the words of Thomas Hobbes, "a posture of war," and as in our day war with nuclear weapons spells extermination, sound reason which has led us so far should take us one step further to an universal 'city of mankind'.

Reason, I must concede, has not always been highly rated by William Earle. And there are more kinds of rationalism than one, not all of them commendable. Since he has written *Mystical Reason*, however, he seems to have softened towards at least one form of rationalism. His insight there into its absolute validity and its ineradicable ingredience in every form of excellence, may now just possibly make him more receptive to the suggestion that what must eventually prove destructive of the very bases of civilized life and of every medium of human excellence, namely, modern warfare, can on no pretext and in no imaginable circumstances any longer be justifiably defended.

Surrealism and the Movies: From A to Miss Zed

WILLIAM FOWKES

For more than a decade William Earle tried to publish a book of his entitled *A Surrealism of the Movies*.[1] During those years a number of his other works appeared, including *Public Sorrows and Private Pleasures*[2] and *Mystical Reason*,[3] yet his book on film continued to make the rounds of publishing houses with no luck.

This book has happily found a publisher at last; however, I think I know why this particular work met with such resistance: the book is a celebration in honor of a guest who refuses to show up. Earle has made all the preparations and delivered characteristically eloquent toasts, but is finally forced to admit to all assembled that they must content themselves with distant memories of the honored guest or perhaps with a distant cousin or two. The truly surrealist movie does not exist and perhaps never did.

"Are there any such movies?" he asks halfway through the book (p. 72). In the Introduction, he confesses, "Alas, there have been so few excellent examples of surrealist film . . . that I have had to content myself with some few old chestnuts" (p. 8).

However, rather than jump to the conclusion that Earle has simply concocted some odd species with very few specimens, we must understand that the surrealist movie that Earle seeks is an ideal. It is something not easy to come by, because "it is certainly difficult to sustain the intensity of poetry required for any great length, which says something I hope against length and not against surrealism" (p. 127).

Successful surrealist films, then, are few and far between, but that should not prevent us from following Earle as he leads us to the spirit underlying these films. However, before discussing that spirit and Earle's journey there—and as a roundabout introduction to that discussion—I would like to reflect upon the fact that realism is so pervasive in film.

As Earle notes, movies took two directions right at the start, as exemplified by the work of the Lumière brothers on the one hand and Georges Méliès on the other, and both kinds of movie shows captivated their audience. In the end, which kind one prefers is a matter of sensibility and Earle does not wish to denigrate realism. Nevertheless, if one followed and agreed with the "argument" of the book, one would never look upon realism and surrealism as equally valuable options. Clearly, if forced to choose between the two, Earle would opt enthusiastically for the latter—which is fine.

But why then is he in such a minority? Putting aside the vast audiences of Hollywood "blockbusters" and limiting ourselves to the more-or-less serious viewers of film and the relatively few "good" films available to them, we must still acknowledge that realism predominates. What draws these people to such films? For Earle, the realist sensibility is one which is most comfortable among things that are familiar, recognizable, and comprehensible (p. 46). And indeed he goes on to show that these are essential features of perceived reality. He also grants that the pleasures of such a sensibility are "genuine." Nevertheless, the competing sensibility finds such a reality "the very home of the boring and a serious invitation to spiritual death" (p. 46).

It's all right, then, to admit a preference for realist films, but you open yourself to the charge of being boring—a charge which always has the last word, because there's no other notion which must be summoned up to support it. But worse than this, Earle implies that the spectator of realist films is fooling himself if he thinks that the real world—or the real world as reflected in the film—has anything new to show him. That is because a realist film is constrained to showing a world of *real* possibilities, and real possibilities are already implied by the situation before the spectator. Such a film, then, merely shows "specifications of the real possibilities in what he is looking at. And yet he must already *know* those" (p. 64). In short, "the realist film can disclose nothing but what is already prefigured in the initial data of the film" (p. 64).

Is the spectator of realist films fairly characterized as someone who seeks the comfort of a familiar and therefore boring world and whose chief delight is seeing what number comes up on the die of plot resolutions, even though he already knows what's on every side of the die? Surely there are viewers like this. But perhaps realism will get more of its due if we consider theorists like Siegfried Kracauer and André Bazin.

The main delight of film, as described by these theorists, is its ability to bring us face to face with the physical and social world in a way that no other art ever could. The "redemption of physical reality," to use Kracauer's phrase, is made possible through the decreased amount of human intervention required in this medium. That is to say, a relatively automatic recording of the world is possible. Whatever the desirability of following such a practice, the fact is that a film-maker can capture a vast array of phenomena beyond his control or explicit choice. I can, if I wish, start the camera rolling and film *something* with a minimum of selectivity.

Earle, on the other hand, is correct to point out that there is no guarantee that the product of such a practice will be interesting (he speculates that even Andy Warhol has probably never endured his own eight hour filming of the Empire State Building [p. 122]) and that, furthermore, the "reality" of what is shot is spurious. We learn nothing about a person or object by merely "shooting" it. The subjectivity of a film-maker is required to make sense of—or give meaning to—the world to be filmed.

Is there some more exalted explanation for our fascination with realist films than the need for comfort and predictability, on the one hand, and a "blind" staring at physical phenomena, on the other? I leave aside all the various arguments which amount to using films for comparison with the world beyond the screen (that is, film as instruction about the world, film as political statement, etc.). Earle easily disposes of such arguments, all of which have a point, but none of which get to the heart of what is so compelling about film.

I see two possibilities. One is that Earle is right, that what we cherish in realist films are certain fleeting moments or scenes which are best understood as actually "surrealist." The other is that the Kracauer-Bazin school of theory is on the right track, provided we do not interpret it as shallowly as I have done above.

In the end, I believe both possibilities will lead us to the same place, but to show how this is possible I must now take us, finally, to Earle's notion of surrealism. Earle is careful to differentiate surrealism from "sensory art," meaning by the latter works which try to offer us sensation rather than perception, works aiming at a "systematic defeat of every built-in expectation of perception" (p. 54). The abstractly visual is not Earle's idea of what is surrealist, because such abstractions (for example, colors in themselves) are virtually meaningless and surrealism is far from meaningless.

On the other hand, if what surrealism starts with are meaningful objects (or objects composable into meaningful compositions), these objects nevertheless do not have the meaning of "essences," "types," or "concepts." An eyeball (such as the one used in the jarring image of "Le Chien Andalou") is not the display of an ideal type or an indication of the essence "eyeballness."

Surrealism, as Earle conceives of it, occupies a space somewhere between these two poles. It begins with meaningful objects (that is, "It at minimum demands that we see something "[p. 3]), but it uses these as a point of departure, inviting us to see with the imagination. It is this link to the imagination which is the key to Earle's notion of surrealism. The film itself, he says, "is nothing but an occasion for partially controlled dreams" (p. 69). This suggests that much of what makes a surrealist film "work" is the "work" that we, the viewers, undertake. (This also perhaps explains why surrealist films do *not* "work" for many people. It also explains, for Earle, why a film-maker who has no guarantee that the combination of images which has a magical, evocative power for him will also have the same power for others is quick to take flight from surrealism back to realism.) (Cf. p. 68.)

The imagination, taking what is offered on screen, must synthesize what is given into a different kind of world, perhaps one "structured by magical correspondences" (p. 71). Without such a synthesis, what is shown is indeed a puzzling and ultimately boring series of images. Ultimately, then, a surrealist film does make sense, though it may be the sense of dreams. One of the reasons such a sense is possible is that the film is, after all, the creation of another person. It is here that surrealism parts company with dadaism. Though dadaist methods may have been tried by surrealists along the way, it was merely as one attempt among others to produce evocative images and not as an ultimate giving-in to automatism or chance.

A surrealist film is the expression of a spirit. Here Earle is Hegelian in his insistence that the so-called intentional fallacy is hardly a fallacy because the film itself implies a maker and motivates an interest in its maker. This spirit can never exhaust itself in a single work just as the viewer's imagination is not exhausted by a single work. The film becomes something like a point of intersection or convergence of two spirits. The experience of the two spirits is not the same, just as the experience of any two viewers cannot be the same, but the film implies something shared. This sharing is possible because of the not-fully-synthesized nature of the work.

The nature of the presentation thus is an important point of difference between realism and surrealism for Earle. The attempt to reduce an audience to a state of utter passivity in the presence of an overwhelming visual assault is the ultimate act of effrontery committed by the realist. I assume the same charge would apply to those who succeed at carefully and unambiguously manipulating an audience's emotional response.

By contrast to this "nazism of the spirit" what the surrealist attempts is nothing more or less than a free offering to free persons. (p. 90) For such an offering to spark imaginative poetry or communion, clearly the external circumstances play an important role. The circumstances surrounding the production, distribution, and exhibition of most films make it unlikely that they could be offered or experienced in this way.

It is here that we hit upon the core of Earle's conception of surrealist film and come to understand his own special relation to the world of film:

> Should we not inaugurate an era of private films, made for one, a few, shown under private circumstances at home, at a time when one *wishes* to see the film, in short an aristocratic privacy and intimacy of experience rather than the hopelessly mediocre *populist* ideal of vast audiences throughout the world, all laughing and crying at the same cues? (pp. 68–69)

If such an era has yet to be inaugurated, William Earle nevertheless has emulated this ideal in his own setting, for he has made several surrealist movies over the years and for the most part has chosen this format for exhibiting and sharing them. To be in a group invited to a showing of "The Memories of Miss Zed" (his most familiar work) in his living room—a room filled with enough evocative objects to constitute a surrealist work in its own right—is like being admitted into an exclusive club of the spirit. (Indeed it has been almost a rite of passage for many of his graduate students.) The generosity of spirit required for the surrealist film to "work" is reflected in the invitation to share such special screenings.

The notions of imagination, privacy, and shared offering, then, are at the center of Earle's notion of surrealism. The "epicenter" of all this, however, is the transcendental ego (which, of course, is the focus of much of his work). It is ultimately the transcendental ego which offers and receives the surrealist presentation. It is the transcendental ego which "dreams." All of this requires giving the transcendental ego a larger role to play than that found in Husserl's work. (See pp. 116–117.)

The transcendental ego is understood as ultimately free (it is the focus of imagination and creativity) and as constitutive of meaning in the world. In a sense, what it sees in a work of art is its own constitutive power at work or a possibility of meaningfulness. Put differently, a work of art offers a variation on the real world or invites participation in the creation of one or more variations and thereby offers confirmation of the transcendental ego's meaning-conferring activity. In Earle's terms, "surrealism offers a unique opportunity for the mind to experience its own transcendental freedom" (p. 119). It is in this context that we can understand his claim that "the ultimate accomplishment of the surrealist experience is to see the most banal as the most extraordinary" (p. 119).

Having said all this, I must now return to the observation that the vast majority of films watched even by "serious" viewers are realist and that Earle himself has been known to watch and enjoy a realist movie or two. Why is this so, if the surrealist film holds out the possibility of the incomparable delights discussed above?

One possibility is that we go to the movies (or watch movies on cable or on our VCR) for more mundane reasons—to be mildly entertained, to be somewhat passive, to relax, to see people and situations somewhat like ourselves and our own and be comforted, and so on. This, I think, is the case and accounts for the major portion of our interest in this activity.

However, the remaining portion, I would suggest, is based on something akin to Kracauer's "redemption of physical reality." There can be no denying that the material nature of a movie's presentation (whether a large, luminous projection in a dark theater or a much smaller and more mysterious reception that can be summoned up at home by pushing a button) is conducive to a certain amount of aesthetic distance toward the world shown. And there can be no denying that sometimes a movie can seem to be (and almost in fact be) an automatic recording of the world and for part of the time, at least, not imply (phenomenologically) the existence of a film-maker.

Given these two descriptive facts, I am led to conclude that at certain special moments what we are attuned to is a bit of reality revealing itself to us without explicit interference or interpretation on our part. Such an experience is perhaps another instance of seeing the most banal as the most extraordinary.

Here, I think, we have reached a point of contact between realism and surrealism. In neither case are we talking about the "abstractly visual" because both present us with a meaningful world. Where there is meaning, there must also be the transcendental ego, and thus both cases amount to a kind of transcendental self-enjoyment. What differentiates the two is the way in which this is achieved— in the one case by offering a composition of carefully chosen images and objects for the purpose of an imaginative synthesis or reconstruction; in the other case by letting a well-placed camera roll on a bit and give us a unique, self-disclosing glimpse of the world. In one case the transcendental ego dreams; in the other it observes. In both cases it "makes sense" or confers meaning on what might, with less effort, be merely boring.

Returning to William Earle and his difficulties in publishing his book—his celebrated guest has still not shown up. In the closing paragraph, he apologizes again for the scarcity of references to specific films in the book (I've made only two references here myself) and confesses disappointment at the scarcity of surrealist films in actuality, yet holds out hope for escape from boredom by pointing to "those films not yet made. . . ."

But perhaps escape is closer at hand . . . in private screening rooms like Earle's and . . . if he'll allow . . . in a realist film or two.

WILLIAM FOWKES: SURREALISM AND THE MOVIES

1. All page references are to the unpublished manuscript as it existed in August 1983. It is to appear in print in 1986 (Precedent Press, Chicago).

2. *Public Sorrow and Private Pleasures* (Bloomington: Indiana University Press, 1976).

3. *Mystical Reason* (Chicago: Regnery Gateway, Inc., 1980).

Earle on Memory and the Past

EDWARD S. CASEY

Memory, therefore, is our immediate awareness of past experience. *(The Autobiographical Consciousness)*

It is perhaps doubly appropriate to honor William Earle by discussing the subject of memory. Not only has he written engagingly on the topic of memory itself—as we shall witness at some length below—but he is the source of many important memories for the contributors to this volume. When such memorability as a person combines with a concerted memory-mindedness as a writer, it is tempting indeed to enter into matters of memory. To do so is to commemorate Earle the man and Earle the philosopher, re-membering his work in one's own.

I

Let us take as a starting-point Aristotle's conception of memory. This conception is the very archetype of the views which Earle is seeking to oppose in his own considerations. It is unequivocal in its assumption that memory *(mnēmoneuein)* is "of the past."[1] But it is equally unequivocal in holding that memory is not of the past in any direct way. As a state *(hexis)* or affection *(pathos)* belonging to "the primary perceptive part" of the soul, memory deals with objects for which "time has elapsed" *(DM,* 449 b 25–26). This means that the objects or events we remember have been subject to change since we first experienced them and that any *present* access to them in their pristine state must be indirect—where the premise is that direct access to anything we experience in the present is paradigmatically realized in perception.[2] Put another way: past objects presently remembered must be given to us in a mediated relation.

179

Such a relation is provided precisely by images *(phantasmata)* of the past. In and for the soul, images alone bridge the gap between present and past, providing that continuity (that is, magnitude-*cum*-change)[3] which remembering requires. Thus, if "all memory involves time" (449 b 28), all memory involves images as well. It is time's toll that calls for the image. Therefore, "memory, even the memory of objects of thought, is not without an image."[4] But by what property does an image lead us back to the past? Taken in isolation, an image is a sheer phantasmal presentation; it is the very emblem of self-containment. As William James remarks, "a farther condition is required before the present image can be held to stand for a past original."[5] It might be tempting to claim that this condition is supplied by causality. But if a causal connection between a present image and its past original is a necessary condition for the way this image can stand for that original, it is still not a *sufficient* condition: many things besides memory-images have causal connections to the past without standing for them in a relation of remembrance—without being "reminders" (as Aristotle sometimes terms such images).[6]

What then *is* the sufficient condition? According to Aristotle, what makes an image into a genuine reminder of the past is the fact (if it is a fact) that it *copies* that past. More exactly, it is the likeness that such copying provides which represents the critical "farther condition" in question. The memory-image, in short, operates "like a sort of picture" (450 a 29); it is "like an imprint or drawing in us" (450 b 16). How can this be? How can something as purely present as an image be *of* the past? Only by being *like* it: by being its likeness. The memory-image, the image qua reminder, is at one and the same time a "figure" *(zōon)* and a "copy" *(eikōn):*

> . . . one can contemplate it both as a figure and as a copy.
> . . . In so far, then, as [the memory-image] is something in its own right, it is an object of contemplation or an image. But in so far as it is of another thing, it is a sort of copy and a reminder . . . the one image occurs simply as a thought, the other, because it is a copy . . . is a reminder. (450 b 23–451 a 1)

Notice especially the last claim here: *because the image acts as a copy of a past original*, it can serve as a reminder of it. The picturing bears the brunt of the relation to the past, which is therefore conveyed into the present of remembering by pictographic means. An image has memorial status and powers insofar as it depicts a past by copying it. And precisely as a copy, the memory-image preserves the same proportions, the same shape as the original: such had been the basis for Plato's distinction between *eikastikē* and *phantastikē*.[7]

Admittedly, the resemblance need not be exact; but some significant degree of isomorphism must nonetheless be present for remembering to occur.

II

Following Aristotle, the copy theory of memory had a very considerable history—which it cannot be our present purpose to discern.[8] Suffice it to say that from Hobbes and Hume to Russell and Price there has been a continual recrudescence of the view that the past can be retrieved in memory only through images that bear a quasi-pictorial likeness to it, whether these images be called "decaying sense" or "ideas," "representations" or simply "memory-images." So tenacious is this tradition of thought that even philosophers like Bergson and James, otherwise such trenchant critics of the associationism with which the copy theory is so characteristically affiliated, still adhere to the ideas that memory is essentially mediated by images. Thus Bergson, while recognizing the importance of "habit memory" (which is strictly non-representational) nevertheless considers "memory par excellence"[9] to be that which "records, in the form of memory-images, all the events of our daily life as they occur in time."[10] And James considers an indispensable part of "secondary memory" (that is, recollection) to be "the revival in the mind of an image or copy of the original event."[11] Such memory, unlike the "primary memory" of retentional fringes around the present, is in fact "a very complex representation, that of the fact to be recalled *plus* its associates, the whole forming one 'object'."[12] Here James moves beyond the view that the recollected past is contained in an image or copy as a "simple shape, as a separate 'idea'."[13] Such factors as name, date, and place; "a general feeling of the past direction in time"; a certain "warmth and intimacy" that allow me to appropriate a past experience as my own—all these are also required in any full analysis of memory.[14] Nonetheless, even such a complex representation as this *remains a representation;* it is an ideational complex,[15] and as such it is no less a copy of the past than Aristotle's *phantasma.*

III

It is precisely James' view that Earle takes as emblematic of the copy theory:

> In principle, the theory is remarkably simple. Memory is the
> feeling or belief that a certain complex image, formed in my

imagination, resembles the past. The complex image in which
I believe has three factors: the *event imaged*, its *reference to the
past*, and its reference *to my past*. . . . Such, I believe, are the
basic elements of any copy theory.[16]

Earle's insightful critique of the copy theory follows forthwith, attacking in turn each of the three elements just distinguished:

(1) the *event [as] imaged:* here Earle finds a twofold problem. On
the one hand, the image is simply a superfluous term; when I
remember something, there is "no sense in which I can be said to
form an image, copy, or representation of anything" (*AC,* 147). On
the other hand, the positing of such entities gives rise to insoluble
logical dilemmas. Either I already know (and thus remember) the
past of which I have a copy in mind—how else am I to declare the
copy to be a copy in the first place?—or else the past with which
I compare my memory-image is itself a copy. In other words, either
I have independent and direct access to the past to start with,
rendering any copy of it useless; or, if I do have recourse to image-
copies, I am involved in an infinite regress. In Earle's words, "if the
image is to appear in any form whatsoever as a representation of
anything, both it and what it copies must appear; but that implies
that eventually the past itself, and not just an image of it, must
appear to the remembering mind."[17]

(2) *reference to the past:* precisely because the very notion of a
memory-image separates it from its own past original, we are left
with the problem of how the thus cast-off image refers back to the
original. We have seen that two traditional answers have been "causality" and "similarity"—each of which has its problems.[18] Earle does
not take these particular problems up, concentrating instead on the
difficulties inherent in *any* kind of backward reference. Once more,
these are two in nature. First, how will we distinguish memory-
images (which presumably do refer to the past) from purely imaginary
images (which make no such reference)—except by some internal
mark carried on their phenomenal surface? "Vivacity," the traditional
such mark, is notoriously unreliable and brings with it the questionable premise that imagination and memory differ in degree only.[19]
Without any satisfactory criterion by which to differentiate the images
of imagination from those of memory, any retro-reference becomes
baseless or gratuitous. Second, we soon find ourselves impaled on
the horns of yet another dilemma: "either memory is identical with
the act of 'referring', in which case we have explained nothing, or
the two [the image and the original] are distinct, in which case the
act of referring becomes arbitrary" (*AC,* 151).

(3) *reference to my past:* building on James' statement that a memory-image "must be dated in *my* past,"[20] Earle disputes the criterion of "warmth and intimacy" by which James attempts to establish the sense of *Jemeinigkeit*.[21] More basic than intimacy itself—indeed, required if intimacy with one's own experience is to become possible—is a *recognition* of one's past as one's own: "it is quite insufficient to assimilate our recognition of our past with a present feeling of intimacy" (*AC,* 152). It is revealing that in Earle's tripartite critique of the copy theory of memory he is briefest and least convincing on this last count—a point to which I shall return. For now, let us hear Earle's own superb summary of this critique:

> In short, the copy theory must find the remembering mind enclosed within a gallery of present images, embarrassed by its task of choosing which are to be regarded as memories and frustrated by the very *significance* of regarding them as memories. To make the rickety theory work, we must be both within and without our minds at the same time, we must both credit and discredit our only access to the past, and we must be endowed with faculties for measuring quantities of strength, vivacity, warmth, and intimacy, which have, as we have seen, no particular signifiance anyway. (*AC,* 152–53; his italics)

IV

Memory, said Aristotle, is "of the past." On this point, Aristotle, his disciples, and his critics (including William Earle) are in happy accord. The divergences begin to arise when we ask whether memory is of the past *directly* or not. For Aristotle, as for James and many others, we cannot know the past directly, head-on, when we remember it; rather, we know it *through* images which recaptitulate the past in quasi-pictorial format. Against this mediationist view, Earle (joining forces with Reid and Alexander)[22] proclaims forthrightly that memory is "a direct vision of the genuine past" (*AC,* 154) and is "our immediate awareness of past existence" (*AC,* 142–43). What are we to make of this positive position, which supervenes on Earle's incisive critique of the copy theory?

The position derives from three "phenomenological observations" of memory's eidetic structure. Each is essential to Earle's direct realism of the past; and each has special difficulties.

(1) *reflexivity of memorial consciousness.* Instead of image-copies mediating between my present awareness and the past, a close look at remembering reveals that my contemporary awareness connects

directly with the past experience I am recalling: where "past experience" includes both the original *act* of consciousness and its *object*. The fact that we tend to thematize the object alone ("the building burning yesterday") leads us to overlook the act-dimension ("myself looking at [the burning building]"). But we retain an at least implicit awareness of the act—such that we can formulate the entire situation as "I now remember (myself looking at) a burning building" (*AC*, 155). Here nothing copies anything; only two consciousnesses connect. So far so good. But there are two unanswered questions here. First, is implicit awareness really a requirement? Isn't the role of past awareness a logically, not a psychologically, necessary one? There needs to have been such an original act of mind, but need it be revived (however dimly) now in remembrance? I doubt it.[23] Second, how do the two consciousnesses, past and present, connect? Just *where* do they connect—at their outer fringes? How can we avoid the question of point-of-contact, and yet how can we say in principle precisely where they will interact without unduly spatializing the two consciousnesses? Nor will it help to say that "memory is a reflexive act of awareness wherein a present act of awareness has as its direct and unmediated *object* a past awareness of some object" (*AC*, 156; my italics). Then there would be *two* (intentional) objects in remembering: the past act as such *and* its own object. Surely this would disrupt the very continuity which the notion of self-reflexivity of consciousness is designed to establish.

(2) *pastness of memorial content.* That which we remember (that is, the thematized object of the past act) does not bear pastness on its shoulder like an epaulette. But what then does account for our abiding conviction as to the pastness of what we remember? Earle's answer is disarmingly straightforward: "descriptively, what more can be said but that I now am simply aware that I was aware of something before?" (*AC*, 157) The awareness of pastness, in other words, is at once intuitive (unmediated by any mark or sign) and "lateral or implicit" (ibid.). Does this mean that we now have two implicit awarenesses, one attaching to the past act of consciousness (not aware of itself as past) and one to its inherent pastness? The matter only becomes more complicated when it is added that "the conjunction of past and present occurs within reflexive mind, and is a genuine conjunction of the actual past of consciousness with the actual present of consciousness" (ibid.). Once more: just how is the conjunction effected? The connection between the past and the present of consciousness is surely just as mysterious as the connection made between any two acts of consciousness themselves—in whatever temporal dimension. And if we have to do with one consciousness only (as the just-cited passage suggests), how will we distinguish

between the "actual past" and the "actual present" except by the very "internal properties" (*AC*, 156) which Earle considers to be nonexistent?

(3) *the source of mineness.* A putative answer to these last questions is furnished by the third phenomenological feature of memory, which is deemed the "most important" (*AC*, 158). If there are at least two acts of consciousness involved in remembering, they belong nonetheless to *one* self. It is just here that Earle expands upon his abbreviated third objection to the copy theory by furnishing his own most audacious hypothesis: the eternity of the self. The argument is as follows. If we agree with James that what we recall "must be dated in *my* past," we will go on to ask the question, "what does it mean for me now to recognize some past experience as mine?" (*AC*, 158). It means, according to Earle, that there must be (a) a strict identity between remembering and remembering selves ("I am numerically identical now and then . . . there is only one I that once had some experiences I now recall as mine" [*AC*, 158]); and (b) an atemporality or eternity of such an 'I': "if the I is identical now and then, it is, of course, atemporal" (ibid.). By this bold move both of the potentially divisive dichotomies specified above (that is, remembering vs. remembered consciousness; actual past vs. actual present of consciousness) are unified at a single stroke:

> . . . there is an intrinsic binding together of past and present
> in the identity of the self that both experienced the past event
> and now recollects it . . . the presence to me now of what is
> no more is rendered possible by the self that was identically
> present at both times. There is a genuine gap between the
> past and the present acts; but to say this is not to say the last
> word. . . . The gap must be bridged by the self that presided
> over both occasions, the same and identical self. (*AC*, 160)

In saying this, Earle has not moved as far from James as he would like to think he has. Speaking precisely of the cleavage between past and present experiences of one and the same person, James writes:

> . . . consciousness remains sensibly continuous and one. What
> now is the common whole? The natural name for it is *myself*,
> *I*, or *me* . . . whatever past feelings appear with those
> qualities [of warmth and intimacy] must be admitted to receive
> the greeting of the present mental state, to be owned by it,
> and accepted as belonging together with it in a common self.
> This community of self is what the time-gap cannot break in
> twain.[24]

I juxtapose James and Earle not so much to vindicate James from Earle's rather abrupt dismissal as to indicate that the phenomenon of memory can very well drive one to posit the "same and identical self" (Earle) or "a common self" (James) *without* having to press further toward the much stronger thesis of "the eternal being of consciousness" (*AC*, 172). It is striking that James, surveying the same "time-gap" as does Earle, prefers to speak of the "community of self" rather than the "identity of the self." Whereas community implies a shared temporality, identity naturally suggests atemporality. And atemporality in turn intimates eternity. The logic is inexorable: "the eternal dimension of consciousness, which is identical now and then, and which is consciously so identical, we have called the eternal ego or self" (*AC*, 172).

But the inexorability depends on a tenet which James would question: the strict distinguishability between the self and its acts. For Earle, the former exists independently of time altogether, while the latter is strictly time-bound: "The self in its core is therefore atemporal, while its various acts take place in time. Time differentiates only the acts, not the self that does the acting" (*AC*, 159). But wait! If the self were rigorously atemporal, how could it relate to its *own* temporalized acts, including the act of being conscious of its own identity amidst change? Earle admits at one crucial point that "the I is of course related to passing events, or time itself would be an illusion" (*AC*, 158). How is it so related? Presumably "by its acts of consciousness, which are temporal acts, unrepeatable and separated in time" (*AC*, 158–59). Yet if these acts are acts of *my* own consciousness, they must link up with my superintending self in a manner that cannot itself be timeless; and if such is required, this same self must be, if not rankly temporal, at least predisposed to temporality, able to "receive the greeting" (in James' phrase) of its own thoroughly temporal acts. Otherwise, the self, myself, would be irretrievably alien from its own acts and would lose the very self-identity that is essential to its conscious continuity as selfsame over (if not through) time. Moreover, need it be deeply corrupting to such a self that it be at least pre-temporal by carrying the seeds—if not the full fruit—of time within it? Could it not play the same bridging or unifying role on which Earle insists (cf. *AC*, 160) without having to be atemporal, much less eternal? Indeed, could it not (as James hints) play it all the more effectively if it could realize a meaningful sense of "community" as belonging to the same "stream of thought, of consciousness, of subjective life"[25] as its own acts? What is to be lost—other than the eternal?

V

Earle will have none of this. To lose the "eternal dimension" of the self is to lose the self itself: the self in the only sense that matters in memory, as in transcendental life generally. Nevertheless, he might be willing to accept a compromise along the following lines. Let an atemporal or even eternal self be posited as a *formal* feature of the continuity between past and present consciousness as these connect in memory. *Something* after all must remain unchanging and selfsame if two or more acts of mind are to achieve more than more contiguity in time—if what James terms a "common whole" is to be realized (as it manifestly *is* realized in each and every veridical experience of remembering). This "something" is not, however, a substantial, much less a material, self: for the only such self which is genuinely eternal is that belonging to God.[26] It is ineluctably a formal self, or a formal dimension of the self or layer of self, that remains "same and identical" (*AC*, 160) in remembering and remembered acts of mind. That this is indeed the case is suggested in Earle's admissions that "the 'mine' therefore indicates the *relation* that unites past with present" (*AC*, 158; my italics) and that the eternal ego is "the third *aspect* of the total phenomenon [of remembering]" (*AC*, 160; my italics). What else are relations and aspects but formal factors?

If this formal status of the atemporal self is allowed, it becomes less vexing to imagine how temporality enters the scene. The particular acts of such a self encroach upon its formality by giving to its *material* dimension an irrevocably temporal complexion. Rather than being divisively alienated from the timeless self, they are its own other side, its materialization in time—which is less an alien than a complementary modality of its total being. Thus the crucial sentence cited above could be rewritten: "the self in its [formal] core is therefore atemporal, while its [own material] acts take place in time" (*AC*, 159).

Putting it this way has the additional advantage of not committing us to any claim as to the *consciousness* of the self's own eternity. Indeed, we would not even have to claim that the "awareness of our own eternity" is "lateral" (*AC*, 159), much less present in our consciousness of our own selfsame identity over time (cf. *AC*, 172). As a purely formal dimension of our being, such eternity need not be a mode of awareness or consciousness to begin with; it can remain just that: a form, even an essential form, of our being. This would allow *all* acts of awareness and consciousness to be temporal, however diversely or paradoxically they may be so. Then we would connect with our own past in and through, and not only over, the very acts by which we retrieve this past for ourselves, reappropriating it and *making it our own:* which is also part of recognizing it *as* our own. An active memory—the counterpart of Nietzsche's "active forget-fulness"—requires time for its realization. It is in no way incompatible with the existence of an eternal-formal self.

VI

Here we must ask: *do* we in fact have direct access to the past? The bulk of the evidence speaks against this possibility. Most of the avenues which we take into the past come heavily freighted with mediating factors: for example, monuments and other memorials, ritualistic bodily actions (such as commemorative rituals), habitual bodily behavior, texts of many kinds, and inhabited places. Quite apart from images as mediations, such factors as those just mentioned act to convey the past to us in non-recollective modes. Indeed, whenever we venture beyond the paradigm of recollection or sec-ondary memory, we find the past being borne down upon us by precisely such non-imagistic go-betweens. I would claim that precisely this concrete intermediation between past and present is in fact the rule: against which any form of direct access must appear as an exception. Thus the "hypermnesic" states with which Freud was so fascinated—when the past returns in "ultra-clear," quasi-hallucinatory intensity—are confined, by Freud's own admission, to dreaming and to the regressive revival of traumatic experiences. Therefore, if the past does "rise before us" *in propria persona* and without any material or psychical bearers, it is a rare event indeed. Even Freud fell back on memory traces as indispensable bearers of the past.[27]

So we come to ask: does any one really believe in an absolutely pure re-presentation of the past, *sans* mediation of any sort? I doubt it. Earle himself can be seen to bring in mediation by the back door, especially if we focus on that aspect of his position which could be designated as *act-immanentism.* As we have seen, he argues em-phatically for the genuine immanence of past acts of mind in present acts of mind. Setting aside the questions raised above, let us grant him this much: one's past experience qua act of cognition can very well ingress in a present act of cognition (for example, remembering itself). But the *object* of the past act—that which we characteristically thematize in recollection—is not available to us *except through this past act itself.* If we are in immediate contact with the act, then we cannot be in any comparably immediate contact with its object. One cannot have it both ways: such is the lesson, indeed the fate, of the intentional analysis to which Earle is committed as a practicing phenomenologist. The intentional objects of past experiences are mediated by the very acts to which we have such strikingly direct access in remembering.[28] Act-immanentism of the past is one thing; direct realism of the past—qua act *and* object—is something else again. In other words, even if the remembered past does not come mediated by images, it does come mediated by acts of mind.

VII

But can we continue to assume, despite Earle's own convincing critique, that the image plays no role at all in remembering the past? His critique concerns images only insofar as they are *eikons* or strict likenesses, whether these likenesses be straightforward copies (as in Aristotle) or "very complex representations" (as for James). This is to construe the term "image" in a very narrow way. Or, more exactly, it is to magnify likeness, an indispensable property of most—perhaps even all—images, into a dominant trait. What if likeness is only a minimal condition of being an image, or just one trait among others? At the very least, we might then not be forced into the rigid option of either defending it as the sole basis of remembering (Aristotle)[29] or attacking it as the primary villain (Earle). This option is, I believe, a forced and most unfortunate one. There *is* a place for imaging in remembering, but this is precisely *not* in its copying capacity.

Hans Jonas has argued persuasively in "Image-making and the Freedom of Man" that 'image' should not be confused with 'imitation'—indeed, that imaging may even lose what is distinctive of it if it is too readily assimilated to imitating. On this view, an image properly understood captures, in its sheer appearing, the *eidos* of what it represents. Merely to repeat this *eidos* or aspect is to become an *eidolon* or replica only; and it is to court the danger of confusing the image with its own original:

> The likeness [of an image to its original] is not complete. A duplication of all the properties of the original would result in the duplication of the object itself—in another instance of the same kind of object, not in the image. . . . The incompleteness of the likeness must be perceptible . . . else the beholder would suppose himself to be in the presence of the object and not of its image only.[30]

In fact, we can even go so far as to say that many degrees of likeness are allowable in images—up to, and including, a pronounced *un*-likeness. More than "incompleteness" we can speak of "positive difference" between image and original: of active *dis*similarity by means of selection and omission, displacement or schematization.[31] A simple caricature, for example, can convey the *eidos* of its subject by a few deft strokes, none of which is isomorphically exact.

At the limit, rather than having to take recourse to the non-imagistic, physicalistic bearers mentioned above (body, text, place, ritual, etc.), memory might subsist perfectly well on a non-physicalistic, purely formal likeness that is unreducible to a copy-relation. In other words, likeness itself (in whatever degree and however diversely realized) may become the bearer of memory, its essential mediation.[32] With this claim, Earle's position is contested twice over: not only is our access to the past mediated but it is mediated precisely by likeness. But where likeness is at once material and highlighted as such in the copy-relation that is the specific target of the Earlian critique, likeness is now being construed as formal (*eidetic* in the root sense of 'seen aspect') and as subordinated.

Subordinated to what? To a general power of representation which knows many modes and, as such, is an essential expression of human freedom: such is Jonas' larger thesis. For present purposes, we need only notice the effect on our conception of memory. It is *animal*, not human, memory that is bound to images in their *eikonic* or *eidolic* avatars: to exact representations of objects of desire or aversion. Here, paradoxically, the past *is* brought back in person—as that very object or its indistinguishable replica (for example, the decoy, the scarecrow).[33]

In human remembering, in contrast, the image, not being bound to replicating the past, can actively discriminate it: indeed, can *imagine* it more fully and richly than its strict re-presentation can achieve. Neither voluntary nor involuntary, such memory proceeds by the employment of "the truly reproductive faculty of imagination"[34] no longer constrained by the requirements of iconicity or even by the laws of association (as is still the case in Kantian reproductive imagination). Imagination becomes an ingredient in memory itself—as Aristotle had proleptically, albeit reductively, claimed: "it is the objects of imagination that are remembered in their own right" (*DM* 450 a 24–5). These objects are precisely *images*, not iconic but free images. Their very freedom—freedom from mandates of association or duplication—is what allows them to convey the past more adequately than would be the case if memory were confined to repeating it without nuance or variation.

A final paradox is that such images, in placing us farther from the past *per se* by being creatively translucent and not merely transparent conveyers of it, end by giving us a deeper, if not a more direct, access to it:

> Imagination separates the remembered *eidos* from the
> occurrence of the individual encounter with it, freeing its
> possession from the accidents of space and time. The freedom

so gained—to ponder things in imagination—is one of distance and control at once.[35]

Instead of act-immanentism, with its *sub rosa* mediation of the past in memory, I would advocate an image-activism in which the *eidos* of the past comes to full expression in memory-images that no longer copy but transfigure. Such a view is not only compatible with the life of the transcendental ego but may be said to constitute the very basis for its ontological autobiography.

EDWARD S. CASEY: EARLE ON MEMORY AND THE PAST

1. Aristotle, *De Memoria et Reminiscentia* 449 a 15. I am employing the excellent translation of Richard Sorabji, included in his *Aristotle on Memory* (London: 1972, Duckworth). Further references to Aristotle's text will be to *DM*.

2. "Perception is of the present" (*DM*, 449 b 27).

3. "It is not possible to think of anything without continuity . . . it is necessary that magnitude and change should be known by the same means [i.e., the image] as time. And an image is an affection belonging to the common sense" (*DM*, 450 a 6–10).

4. *DM*, 450 a 11–12. "Even the memory of objects of thought" is mediated by images partly because of the nature of passive intellect (which requires a sensuous medium) and partly because of the fact that the *past cognition* of objects of thought is subject to time's decay. (On this last point, see Sorabji, op. cit., pp. 13–14).

5. *The Principles of Psychology* (New York: Dover, 1950), I, 650. James italicizes the last two words.

6. See *DM* 450 b 28; 451 a 1; 451 a 12. The term for "reminder" is *mnēmoneuma*.

7. See *Sophist* 235 d–236 c.

8. A brief sketch is offered in Norman Malcolm, *Memory and Mind* (Ithaca: Cornell University Press, 1979), pp. 30–37.

9. Henri Bergson, *Matter and Memory*, trans. N.M. Paul and W.S. Palmer (New York: Anchor, 1959), p. 72.

10. Ibid., p. 69.

11. William James, *The Principles of Psychology*, I, 649.

12. Ibid., p. 651.

13. Ibid., p. 650.

14. The foregoing factors are discussed in ibid., p. 650.

15. This term is suggested by James' revealing diagram in ibid., p. 655.

16. William Earle, *The Autobiographical Consciousness* (Chicago: Quadrangle, 1972), p. 147; his italics. (Hereafter referred to as *AC*.)

17. *AC*, 149. Another way to put this is to say that there is "a very confused alternation of standpoints" (*AC*, 148) as we consider first the image and then its original—the latter requiring us to step "outside the mind altogether" (ibid.).

18. Causality, as we saw, is not sufficiently specific. As for similarity: how will we determine in advance just how much similarity is required for meaningful retro-reference?

19. See *AC*, 150–51. Nor will "date" do. Although James and Bergson both make much of this (cf. *Matter and Memory*, p. 69; *Principles of Psychology*, I, 650), Earle does not consider it, perhaps because it is clearly not an *internal* mark of memories.

20. *The Principles of Psychology*, I, p. 650. James' italics.

21. See ibid., p. 650 and pp. 238–39.

22. See Thomas Reid, *Essays on the Intellectual Powers of Man*, ed. Woozley (London: Dent, 1941), Essay III; Samuel Alexander, *Space, Time, and Deity* (London: Macmillan, 1920), I, 113–17. Malcolm discusses both positions, along with Earle's, in *Memory and Mind*, pp. 30–34.

23. For a different expression of much the same concern, see Malcolm, *Memory and Mind*, pp. 24–26, where Earle (among others) is taken to task on this point.

24. *The Principles of Psychology*, I, 238–9. His italics.

25. *The Principles of Psychology*, I, 239, in italics in the text.

26. I leave aside here Earle's later contention (in *Mystical Reason*) that the transcendental ego and God are indeed difficult to distinguish.

27. See letter 52 to Fliess in *The Standard Edition of the Complete Psychological Works of Sigmund Freud* (London: Hogarth, 1966), I, 233–35; and ibid., V, 538–9, 540n., 565, 578. On hypermnesic states, see ibid., IV, 11–17, 57, 64.

28. The degree of awareness of the past act is not decisive here. Earle himself grants that this awareness can be quite "implicit" or "lateral." My point is that even if we have *no* consciousness of the past act, it is still required as mediation.

29. Recall Aristotle's dictum: Memory is "not without an image" (*DM* 450 a 12). So too James, who, however, considers "an image or copy of the original event" the "first element" among others in an adequate account of memory (*The Principles of Psychology*, I, 649).

30. Hans Jonas, "Image-making and the Freedom of Man" in *The Phenomenon of Life* (Chicago: University of Chicago Press, 1982), pp. 159–60.

31. For Jonas' discussion of this point, see ibid., pp. 161–62. On the notion of "degrees of likeness" cf. ibid., p. 166.

32. Although he is not speaking of memory at the time, Jonas suggests the same idea: "through likeness as the intermediary the directly perceived object is apprehended not as itself but as standing for another object" (ibid., p. 167).

33. "For the animal mere similitude does not exist" (Jonas, op. cit., p. 166). Only the thing itself or its precise replica bears the past for the animal, whose memory is thus bound to "actual sensation" and not to images proper (cf. p. 170).

34. Ibid., p. 171.

35. Ibid.

Afterword

WILLIAM EARLE

The very first and last thing I would like to express to the contributors to this volume is my deepest gratitude. It can not be often that a writer has such distinguished friends willing to take the time from their own work to reexamine his. My own thanks, I thought, could best be expressed not by detailed, refutative argument, but in a more general response. The truth is I rarely have any defensive refutations at all and hate that mode of discourse, but was delighted by these essays. They invited me to reacquaint myself with what I have thought and written over some thirty years; I did, sometimes with embarrassment, sometimes with something like reaffirmation, but usually learning something new. And very special thanks to Donald Morano and Edward Casey for originating the project, and for the endless trouble of seeing it through to publication; also, needless to say, for their own contributions to this volume.

I. IN GENERAL

Unquestionably, Asher Moore's essay occupies the center of this group of essays. He understands me and my work best; and while we hardly agree on every point, and I must add I don't always agree with myself, nevertheless this comes closest to what both of us have been talking over for many, many years. I do not refer to his concocted dialogue with me on the ontological argument; at least, my version is available in *Mystical Reason*. But the tone of the whole is absolutely and subtly right. What he has modestly omitted is his own contribution to my thought. I have never known a more honest or clearer head than that of Asher Moore. But perhaps that is of more interest to ourselves than to the outside reader.

193

Moore is absolutely right in thinking that the ontological argument is a central pivot of my general argument; the other, of course, is the transcendentality of the self or ego. In *Mystical Reason* and beforehand, that Ego and the Absolute God of the philosophers are argued to have a point of *identity*. One passion behind that insistence is to save the intuition of reason from being a phantastical hypothesis in which both reason and all its works float in some domain more or less verbal, hypothetical, or imaginary. The ontological argument anchors the ultimate intuition of the transcendental ego in a reality which is both its and absolute. Moore here is, at least for me, completely right. And yet, the whole of our thought hardly consists in repeating an old argument which, in fact, is not an argument at all, but a simple, clear intuition, arguable only negatively: any denial is absurd, or worse, *blinding* both rationally and spiritually. When the philosopher's God passes into the meaningless, has not the very center of sense, passion, and truth vanished? Surely the matter is not of passing interest, nor either of monomaniacal self-absorption.

The "personal" to which Asher Moore repeatedly refers is, of course, our very own existences as experienced first-personally—the "autobiographical." And if the ontological "argument" turns the mind to what is absolutely eternal and transcendental, the "existential" aspect of our total life turns it toward the unrepeatable, transient and singular. I myself have always had an inextinguishable fascination with both sides, the eternal, best explored by a rational phenomenology, and existential thought, that which is engaged in and equally fascinated by the singular and accidental, in short, the life in life. Love, hate, indifference, action, inaction, in other words, *where we find ourselves*, the world in which we are born, are now living, and out of which we die—well, anyone who thinks all this of no consequence, or of philosophical value only as illustrations of theories, such a person, if one could be found, would be profoundly unsympathetic with my own concerns as well as his own. Can one not think of both? And are they indeed such hostile facets of the human totality that they raise insuperable problems for the mind?

I myself, as Asher Moore emphasizes, am equally obsessed with these apparently opposite and irreconcilable aspects, seemingly so irreconcilable that there can be no thought of the one which does not exclude the other. And yet, I am very far from being sure. The issue, as I have posed it, is too crude to be subject to fruitful discussion. But then I have read enough Hegel to have an enormous intellectual sympathy with that final synthesis which does *not* see these as ultimate contrasts but, while *remaining* contrasted, also join in a sacred and intelligible synthesis; is not that synthesis the only thing which *is* intelligible or final? That our existences are the playing out *seriatum* of what can also and most profoundly be taken eternally, *totum simul*—both give whatever significance might obtain for our lives, and save the eternal from being a dead abstraction. Perhaps I have said a bit more about this in an essay in *Evanescence* called "The Glory Beyond the Grave." This polarity in my thought irritates a number of my critics; and yet I stand with it. Otherwise I can see nothing but a sterile eternity and a meaningless existence, neither of which is rationally conceivable nor true. That it is not true would require a dialectical discussion wholly out of place in a discussion of this sort.

James Edie addresses himself to one of the same problems: am I a "phenomenologist" or an "existentialist"? And he repeats a warning of Herbert Spiegelberg, not to "sell out" to a "mess of existential pottage." Well! I must, of course, thank both gentlemen for their merciful concern to save me from myself, but nevertheless decline their own singular paths of salvation. "Fidelity to Edmund Husserl" admirable as it might be, is hardly applicable to me since I have never taken any oath in his support; moreover he has done well enough by himself.

The philosophical issue, if there is any, locates itself in the question whether a strict eidetic phenomenology urged by Edie is indeed an appropriate approach to certain issues, the chief of which is *life itself.* But life, as Kierkegaard said, is not a problem to be solved but something to be lived. When strict phenomenology turns its attention to life, in order to extract certain "structures" it may indeed do so; anything whatsoever can offer up something like its structure. And yet there remains an unbridgeable chasm between the structure or sense of anything and that thing itself in its living freedom and presence. Edie quotes extensively, and well if I may say so, from my essay on love. The chief point of that "extraordinarily romantic" essay was not to characterize universally *all* love, nor to ring changes on the word, "love," but to show that at least in *some* cases the whole thing might very well be that lived synthesis of the temporal and eternal, existing eternity, found unintelligible by "school logic". In no sense was it intended to evaporate love into a structure, or to imagine that the *value* of love was to be found in whatever structure it might exhibit.

Thought and language can be directed to anything whatsoever; they can comment on the passing scene and, more importantly, both are acts within existence, "performative" as J. L. Austin and his followers have emphasized perhaps too much. In all of this, life or human existence is one thing, a transcendental explication of it another, and my chief emphasis is that while remaining related yet ultimately they are abysmally different. Now does this constitute a "love-hate" affair between phenomenology and existential thought? Or some dilemma in which I must be impaled on one horn or the other? I fail to see it. The truth is that thought and existence itself both use whatever approach is appropriate to the given problem, or they miss their target.

I hope this does not seem like some eclecticism. But it is indeed an openness to a variety of methods, whatever in fact is appropriate to its subject matter. In my own case, I would detest phenomenology if it ever lost sight of what it methodically "brackets," to wit, the *existence* of anything, the chance, the accidental, in short, the life in life, in order to concentrate itself on essential meanings. I would equally shun existential thinkers who thought that life offered up nothing whatsoever intelligible. But then why detest anything useful? The spirit has many standpoints, and many occupations. Is there anything to be gained but impoverishment by some misguided "fidelity to Husserl?" Is Husserl faithful to himself? I hope not.

II. TRANSCENDENTALISM AND AUTOBIOGRAPHY

Professor Mohanty does not focus his attention on my own thought, but at the same time he touches on themes dear to my heart.

Without intervening in the dispute between Mohanty and Davidson, I must say Mohanty makes a very strong case for a transcendental philosophy. In fact, it is unintelligible to me how anyone can deny the transcendental point of view. To deny it is to affirm it, and the resulting whirl of self-contradictions only takes us back into the ancient refutations of an absolute relativism or absolute skepticism. To be *absolutely finite* is, obviously, a contradiction and not even an interesting one. And so with "historicism," which itself making non-historical claims, denies that there are any to be made. Of course, the term, "absolute" can be renounced, but then it is hardly worth much talk to show it inevitably emerging under another guise.

Perhaps one point in all this might be of interest to the reader. The term "transcendental" has a variety of uses but in the interest of clarity, a few might be distinguished. Kant, in the modern period, used the term to designate the *a priori* foundation of cognition; that foundation was the *transcendental unity of apperception*. This "unity of apperception" was not an existing thing, least of all a part of nature, but solely a logical function of thought. Thinking itself was a synthesis at very least of subject and predicate, and that synthesis could be accomplished only by that which was the thinking synthesizer. Husserl, on this point closely related to Kant, discriminated the transcendental *ego* as the constitutor of whatever was to have sense to it. The transcendental constitution was either active or passive, but always an *act of the ego*. Since "existence" has already been "bracketed out," the mode of being of the transcendental ego was not considered. Its essence was for cognition basically constitutive and, as for Kant, it was transcendental to anything which it constituted, nature, its own psyche, or anything at all which might have meaning for it.

To descend to my own thought, the transcendental ego which looms large in my writing has indeed these functions of Kant's and Husserl's egoes but in addition, it *is*. Its *mode* of being raises questions which I have considered in virtually everything I have written, and will not weary the reader by repetition here. I identify it with the soul, both as it inhabits the body and as it is in itself, eternally. It therefore has the logical function of being a unity of apperception, as well as the constitutive function of making meaning of what is offered to it. But my own interests focus largely on its life in its existing eternity. In that respect I imagine my view to coincide with that of Descartes, even though his *Meditations* hardly consider these aspects of the "I think."

Mohanty's essay raises yet another topic of the greatest seriousness. How indeed do I reflect upon myself? This reflexive act is, of course, full of perils since that I who reflects is one and the same as the I upon which I am reflecting. And what do I see when I turn my attention exclusively upon myself? In my own case, I very rarely think about myself and when I do, I more or less agree with Sartre, I see nothing special, though I may see it in a new way. But, and each must speak for himself, my own self is in many ways deeply involved in other selves, whom I habitually find more interesting than myself. Autobiography then as a tale of one's life, need not be and rarely is, a meditation on the speaker himself. Even then there is always an implicit listener and so we are plunged inexorably into the society of our fellows. Monologue perfects itself into dialogue, and each I enters into a we, neither losing its identity, nor being encapsulated in it beyond redemption.

III. Ethics

Although I suppose my writings are suffused with my own values, and I would be ashamed if they were not but floated in a value-free gelatine, nevertheless I have not often turned by attention to some separate subject called "ethics." By temperament and choice, I am not in the least a "moralist" and shun those who are. My favorite and final standpoint is transcendental, which, on the present topic, means a preference for *seeing without judging*. This absolute freedom, accessible to anyone, accords to all an essentially equivalent freedom; in a word, live and let live, but while living and letting live, why not also see? And since the present topic concerns human free choice, all are endowed with the choice of making their own lives to whatever extent they can be made, and each, choosing, gets exactly what he chooses, external fate momentarily excluded. In all of this I transcendentally criticize none; if any criticism is to be made, that criticism will be an inherent property of each choice but not from the outside. My thought, therefore, grants total liberty to all; this, needless to say, is no generous gift of mine; it is nothing but the logic of the scene.

If liberty is to be accorded to all, and if I am a person too, my thought also grants absolute liberty to me. This simple syllogism hardly needs belaboring. Hence if each and all are entitled to their passions, so am I. Transcendentalism is not in the least a withdrawal from passion, nor is it in the least an absolutizing of anyone's passions, mine certainly included. This hardly implies that no one should have passions, or that they should ape mine, or that I should not have any at all. But it does imply that the passions we choose be seen in a transcendental light. Would that not enable each of us to enjoy our lives, both loving, hating, and resting in indifference, all without either fanaticism or shame? The view of it all is said to be magnificent.

Some such thing is my particular angle, defended more abstractly in *The Autobiographical Consciousness* (ch's 8, 9 and passim.) In Robert Scharff's subtle and witty essay, concentrating on my blasts in *Public Sorrows and Private Pleasures*, I am gently taken to task for having certain *political* passions which Scharff, I gather, does not share. Good! I welcome *theoretically* a sharp difference of practical opinion, though I may not welcome policies which I deem fanatical or foolish; why should I? All of that is part and parcel of the glorious and hideous tangle of political life. And, obviously, each partisan of any political view, will *act* to put into practice what he supposes best, otherwise the whole thing is in bad faith. But transcendental seeing is not itself a partisan to the fray, any more than Shakespeare, the dramatist, sides with this or that of his characters. He remains behind the scenes, silent and yet the author of all those dramas of passion. So is the transcendental ego when it turns its attention to the life of its own and other's actions. When Scharff regards me as a "maverick," he has hit the nail on the head. But indeed, so is everyone else, Scharff included. To locate one's spirit at the center of received opinions, philosophical or otherwise, is indeed to retire into some calm in the Sargasso Sea where nothing but fetid water and dead organisms circulate about, borne here and there by slight breezes of no one's choosing. Neither Scharff nor I could desire any such thing.

Hugh Curtler finds my excesses "charming," but then he chooses a middle path. I think he understands my own thought very well and makes clear his own choices. My own detestation of moral "principles" he finds somewhat excessive and thinks that various principles can indeed by applied *from time to time*, at the free option of the moral agent. But then, I repeat, what is the value of the "principle"? Curtler, like some others I think, imagines that without principles we would be without "maps and compasses wandering around without guidance." But why is that to be feared, when that is exactly where we are anyway? Or perhaps where we are anyway is indeed to be feared? In any event, the philosophy of moral principles will be of no help whatsoever, since it only throws us back on ourselves choosing *which* philosophy of principles we wish to espouse. In all of this, Hugh Curtler appears gently moderate, a few principles, applied now and then but not too stringently, and I perhaps a madman of anarchistic freedom. But then, even these descriptions are "excessive," and in the long run we live pretty much the same lives, and admire the same virtues. My own dedication to the singularity and dignity of each person is the same as his. If there is any difference it lies perhaps in my refusal to generalize on human nature or each man's assessment of his own and others' lives, a refusal which regards "philosophical ethics" as shambles, as against Hugh Curtler's lingering affection for some systematic ethics if it could be found. I reject his arguments, but not his sensibilities, nor even his anxiety that without reason and its principles, in this area, we are drifting alone on the open sea. I can relish anxiety, yet can one be frozen in a situation which is inevitable and, moreover, the very definition of life? Or, if one does tremble, then indeed that also is an essential ingredient in life not to be obliterated by principles. Rather than squeeze life into moral principles, I would prefer to ignore the principles; but then that is my free option, not in any sense binding on others.

IV. WAR!

I was indeed honored by the essay from my old and very close friend, Errol Harris. I appreciate his hope that on this question, we may have far more argreement on underlying principles than our published writings may suggest; without seeking to be contentious, I, for my part, must even here deny that I *have* any underlying principles; so perhaps we must go even deeper than "underlying principles," wherever that may take us.

But first a small matter to set the record straight, and then on to more interesting issues. One sentence which sticks in Harris' craw is the last in the essay. In my copy it reads, "Wars are not fought to prove courage, but they do prove it all the same." And that is, of course, what I wrote. *To prove courage* is *not* given as a "justification" for war, justifications which, as I see them, are correctly given later by Harris, and even used in his argument that war is indefensible. Wars, obviously, are fought to achieve peace of one sort or another; to wage war for no cause other than exhibiting courage by waging it would, we agree, be seriously insane. And, although men can be found who love war for its own sake, neither Harris, nor I, nor anyone with those few exceptions could possibly share that enthusiasm. That is not under discussion. Nor is the definition of courage attributed by Errol Harris to Plato: "the right opinion about what ought to be feared." How can courage be that when it is not an opinion at all, but rather a disposition of the heart, ready to die from those things it deems more important than its own life?

To get to the heart of the matter, I deny that pacificism, as a principled opposition to all war, is either an honorable or a coherent passion. Harris, while also denying that he is a pacifist in this sense, nevertheless desires more than anything else an opposition to *nuclear* war. That *could* be the end not merely of the present world but any to come on earth. It must therefore never be waged. And, not completely to Harris' surprise I'm sure, I would *agree*. But that is hardly the end of the matter, nor indeed its beginning.

Essential to Harris' plan to make nuclear war impossible, is the dissolution of national sovereignities into a World Sovereignty which, as he rightly says, impresses me as a "monstrous totalitarianism." The details remain to be spelled out, but in Harris' discussion the new World State, with its monopoly of weapons and power, all however under the "control" of constitutions, laws, and public support (can *they* control anything?) would at least prevent "international" wars since they would now be redubbed "civil wars." Somehow hovering in the background of this necessarily truncated argument, lies a picture of something like the United States, perhaps with its bicameral legislature, Supreme Court and Chief Executive. Now, while we agree that our own is one of the best systems *for ourselves*, the analogical transfer of our own system into a world government leaves more than a few occasions for dread. As for the legislature, the low chamber representing population would be a body swamped by the billions of China and India; and is the "senate" to represent what remained of the former "nations"? Here, St. Kitts delightfully floating in the Caribbean, or some other dot in the Lesser Antilles would have a voice equal to that of any other nation. Maybe all that could be fixed up by a new constitution? And the World Court? But it would *interpret* some constitution and bring recalcitrant "nations" to book for their infractions. This can hardly be done by a computer. But these decisions are so much verbiage unless enforced by power, to be located in the Executive. That Executive or Supreme World Power: it hardly requires much imagination to envisage its private dreams. Law, as Errol Harris knows perfectly well, is nothing at all unless enforceable, and that means power and force, as any glance at the revolver of a city policeman demonstrates. These *are* irresistible temptations, not to be curbed by "law" or "world opinion," let alone judicial decision. Power alone curbs power, and when all of it resides in the World Executive . . .?

The "universal city of mankind" which Harris fondly dreams of is, indeed, what he says it is, from my own point of view, a sentimental dream born of noble hopes, but almost wholly unrealizable. It perpetually runs against the solid, a priori conditions of existence.

But, argues Harris, what about the destruction of the earth, within the possibility of nuclear weapons; is anything worth that? No doubt not; or perhaps *very few* values. But, since all concerned parties have given solemn promises not strategically to strike first, the nuclear force serves as a deterrent. This rests not on "promises," but threat. It has so served, and since the atomic bombs in Japan, nuclear weapons have not been used. Has not then this deterrence deterred in spite of Errol Harris' fears? That *war* has not been stopped nor prevented forever is surely too much to ask, and now I refer to "conventional" weapons, which are both used and also serve a deterrent function. No, in my opinion, there will never be "everlasting peace" nor *should* there be on pain of fixing some present political injustice into history forever. These considerations hardly stand in the way of seeking peace, but not at any price, particularly that of *our own* moral or economic deterioration. One effect of the existence of nuclear weapons and their dire potentialities is to virtually paralyze the human mind; *anything* rather than the destruction of the world. But then "anything" versus "destruction" are not the sole alternatives, nor have they ever been. Nor, so far as I can see, even after many readings of Errol Harris' eloquent plea for peace under World Government, need anyone put down his arms; some, we all dearly hope, must never be used; others must be and used with that *courage* with which Errol Harris is so well endowed.

V. SURREALISM

We academic philosophers, suffering as usual from a spiritual *anorexia nervosa*, have left surrealism to "art critics" or historians of

culture who consign it to a peculiar era of post World War I neu-
roticism. And since all that has faded into history, we need hardly
bother with it. And yet does this do justice to an extraordinary
adventure of the human spirit which by no means limits itself to
aesthetic concerns? Surrealism and realism both express spiritual
attitudes which represent fundamental *philosophical* divergencies.

All of this Bill Fowkes knows perfectly well, though he may not
agree with certain of my more extreme sentiments. His own are in
his own book, well on its way to becoming a classic.* Fowkes confined
himself to comment on my book, *A Surrealism of the Movies*. And
then there is a chapter in *Public Sorrows and Private Pleasures* which
goes into the matter in general and is not so restricted to the movies.

Surrealism is, of course, more a *sensibility* than a theory. And why
should philosophy concern itself with sensibilities except that it itself
is based on its own? These are frequently disguised as "assumptions,"
"premises," or the "self-evident." And indeed so they are; but that
hardly removes their character of being *preferences*, preferences of
each philosopher, the American Philosophical Association, librarians,
deans, publishers, "most of us," or some such substitute. Philosophy
so understood is a systematic elaboration and defense of some given
sensibility. Obviously as a general tradition, philosophy is identified
with the rational. Even philosophies of faith, and the absurd, still
have to defend themselves by reason, or they are consigned to
gibberish, or something too personal or autobiographical to be of
"philosophical" interest. But can *reason by itself* ground or defend
its absolute claim without begging the question, failing under its own
canon of fallacies? Reason, in the sensibility of surrealism, is the
very first thing to be thrown out. We are invited to use a variety
of approaches in no way rational: free association, chance, insults,
denunciation, mad love, poetry and freedom.

Further, the reason of traditional philosophy looks *for something*
and seeks to find it; what is that thing but Reality? The correlate to
Reason is Reality, no matter what it is called, or whether it is taken
as factual empirical reality, the everyday world of all of us, or an
ideal reality, that which is fixed in eternity, Platonic Being or even
mathematics. But always Reality. Surrealism, on the contrary, man-
ifests an instant and profound *boredom with Reality*: as its name says
plainly enough, it is after something else, Surreality. Surreality is not
the domain of ethics, science, politics, common sense, or indeed
anything which might be of theoretical or practical value. All of the

---

* William Fowkes: *A Hegelian Account of Contemporary Art* (UMI Research Press, Ann
Arbor, Michigan, 1981)

useful disappears into the domain of the *marvelous,* which must remain the eternal opponent to the true and good. Only a few philosophers escaped their scathing judgment; not surprisingly, Hegel and the Mystics are among them.

If any rational philosophy is to be clear-headed, and take itself seriously, must it not cast a glance at what lies *outside* it, perhaps its most deadly enemy? Surrealism, thus, *must* be of interest to that very philosophy which it despises and which despises it.

In any event, these questions are central to surrealism, and are *expressed* in its manifestoes, its poems, novels, and of course its visual arts. Poetry above all; it remained for a while uncertain whether painting would be appropriate, but Max Ernst among others showed it must be included. Movies came last; could they possibly be a proper medium for the surrealist sensibility? Buñuel's *Andalousian Dog* and Man Ray's films gave movies their right of entry; and, in the end, even the austere André Breton tried out one himself with Man Ray, but it remained incomplete. My own book looks at movies as almost the prime medium for surrealism; but that they might be such remains a "might be" and has to be thought about on grounds more of possibility than accomplishment. The point, then, is that one deepest possibility in movies remains virtually unexplored, drowned in an ocean of realistic bathos, assuredly more popular and forever so; maybe that is best in the long run. Surrealism can never be popular, which is neither to its praise or blame.

And William Fowkes understands perfectly well that the opposition between realism and surrealism in the movies is not conceived as a war unto extinction; the world is large and life is long, and surely there is room for both but not in the same projection room.

His insight into the absolute dissolution of reality to the transcendental ego is right on the point. The transcendental ego in its transcendentality is *not* to be limited by what is, Reality, and perhaps is stimulated into its own life by surrealism.

VI. Memory

Edward Casey has written a most provocative and suggestive essay on memory which deserves a far more detailed examination than would be appropriate to this volume. It would be impossible to discuss the various things said by Aristotle, William James, and Hans Jonas in any finite compass. So I shall limit myself to what Edward Casey says himself here, although he has written extensively about both it and the imagination in professional publications.

I think he understands my own views very well; he half disagrees and half agrees, which is both normal and fruitful. I think we both are in agreement on the overarching roof under which the discussion occurs. The *nature* of memory is a *phenomenological* topic; its *role* in the life of an existing person is *existential*. The present question concerns only its phenomenological essence: what is memory?

Aristotle, James, and Casey all affirm that it is not without mental "images." And so, naturally, the next question is, *what is an "image"?* From the phenomenological point of view, that is an image which, while presenting something definite to the mind, is taken by that mind to be a copy of something else. It is thus *given* a new meaning: that it is not to be taken in itself, but as a "copy" of something else *not* so directly given, although perhaps given on other occasions. Thus a road-map gives me a linear outline of roads which I may take. The map is given, and the roads are also giveable, if I take one or all of them. A portrait of a person is in the same boat; by being understood as a portrait, I see it as a copy of what I might on other occasions see: the subject's living presence. The exactitude of the copy is to no present point, although Casey and Jonas spend some time on the question. What is to the present point is that, phenomenologically, I, having such a presentation, make it, or take it, to be an "image" of what is not given directly in the image itself.

Now one central point in the understanding of memory is whether indeed the remembering mind is confronted with a gallery of "images" some of which it takes to be copies of yet something else more or less resembling them, and then confers upon them the status of being veridical "representations" of something *else*, now forever lost to it because it is past and gone, and thus represented only by these images which, in reverse, are taken to be their representation! Yes, indeed, I regard this as an absurdity, and something which makes memory itself impossible. There is, in fact, no need whatsoever for this apparatus of images. When I see, in the present, something or other, I am hardly seeing its "image." I either see *it*, or I see nothing at all. And when one considers remembering, or remembering imagining, the layering of image upon image becomes stupefying; can one never get to the thing itself? And even with images, are not images copies, creative or not, of something which is given *through* them? There are images, or course, like maps, pictures, or whatever the extension of the term, and they are and give themselves or are given the sense of being an image. But neither present perception, memory, nor imagination can be analyzed into an image-consciousness. With memory, one would have to be conscious both of the image *and* the past of which it is an image. If one is then already conscious of the past, what need is there of its "image"?

Perhaps more importantly, memory offers one of an indefinite number of examples of the unique power of consciousness to reflexively *double back* upon itself, perhaps now in present perception, but also reflexively to become *identical* with itself through the seriatum of time. This reflexivity is not a "hypothesis" to be avoided at all costs, as Casey more or less feels, but simply the *immediate* consciousness of itself as identical throughout temporal dispersion. And it is one more rather dramatic example of the extraordinary powers of the transcendental ego and spirit. And since this self-identity-in-difference in *actuality* is the same as eternity, that term occurs easily as the traditional name for the distinctive mode of being of the self, as well as God. I feel that a good deal of this slips through Casey's view; he prefers "atemporality," a negative term equally applicable to arithmetic formulae, God and the soul, for "eternity." They are not the same. Eternity is an eternity in *actuality*, which *also* relates itself to existential moments in time. This synthesis, which gives Casey much trouble and Casey is not alone, is explicated about as thoroughly as it can be in virtually everything that Hegel wrote. It is either the oscillating either-or of the *understanding,* or the synthesis in actuality of those either-ors which Hegel called Reason. And so Casey prefers "atemporality" to "eternity," the former having nothing but negative consequences, the latter being the very home of the metaphysical actual. Similarly, Casey suggests that the relation between the ego and its multiple acts be thought of as that between a Form and its Contents; but the Form is nothing but a sheer universal, the Contents its particulars, and meanwhile the ego is in no sense a universal but rather the most singular of singulars in our experience.

Nor is James of much help with his effort to connect various moments of experience by "a feeling of warmth, intimacy, etc." all of which enliven his discourse without much clarifying it. With ourselves, we certainly are not in the presence of a "community" of momentary selves, each nodding and recognizing the other with warmth and intimacy, and concluding, perhaps as a questionable "hypothesis', that the we are all one. Hume, Russell and James, at bottom empiricists for all their differences, are alike in their resolute effort to clear out anything remotely suggestive of the metaphysical, religious, or transcendental. If it is brought in reluctantly, it is through some back door and at all costs under other names. James is a bit more liberal, but only at the cost of coherence.

Ed Casey's essay deserves much more than these brief remarks. It is most suggestive. But then all good things must have their temporal end. If the history of philosophy has offered us two thousand-five hundred years of fruitful discussion, what hope is there of terminating it in a few remarks? Or of what value?

VII. Philosophical Vision

Professor Philip Grier's brilliant essay interweaving rational mysticism with ethical considerations could hardly be bettered. As a sympathetic commentary on my own thought, it is perfectly accurate and in some of its formulations far clearer than my own. Grier knows very well what he is talking about, and knows very well how to put it. To the first part I might only add something which plays little explicit part in *Mystical Reason* as it stands. "Philosophical vision," as Grier puts it, is intuition reached by dialectic, and certainly not in a flash. Dialectic or argument can help anyone achieve an intuition, or defend it against objections raised either by himself or others. But, yes, the beginning and end of philosophy *is* intuition, and not a headache resulting from interminable argumentation, most of which is immediately and mercifully forgotten.

Philosophical vision, then, is a mode of "seeing," and not a mode of quarreling. But "intuition" itself would be of little value if not directed: Hegel, no great partisan of intuition, regards it as sliding into "stupid staring" without dialectical direction. And so, what does philosophical vision envisage? That, naturally, depends on the particular philosophy in question. Myself, I would only wish it to culminate in an *intellectual exaltation.* The introduction of that word into philosophy may seem utterly unscholarly and even a surreptitious effort to sneak into an otherwise neutral dialectic some private religious or moral beliefs. That it need not be can be shown by examples drawn from the entire history of philosophy. Unguided thinking or unguided intuition is endless, purposeless, and ultimately a waste of time if not a vice. But a philosophical *exalted* vision is surely one of our most precious accomplishments; there are many and certainly there is no moral or philosophical obligation to "believe in" or pledge one's spirit to any particular one. Even on this ultimate level, "to each his own according to his taste." And, of course, *"de gustibus non disputandum est."* But there is indeed a dispute between the ever living aspiration toward intellectual exaltation, and the fatigue and even despair of an idle inconsequential philosophical thinking.

Grier develops a discussion of personal integrity most subtly, and I wish he had spent more space on it. The distinction between an *ontological* identity throughout time, and a *moral* integrity is vital although rarely noticed by the logicians of neutral entities. If one's identity through time is a *sine qua non* of moral integrity, it is most certainly not its equivalent. Grier argues this and more with utterly persuasive reason.

That I myself am such a person is not for me to say; but how good to hear it said by another in perpetually anxious times!

VIII. METAPHYSICS

William Langan's essay addresses itself to three of my books, *Objectivity, The Autobiographical Consciousness,* and *Mystical Reason,* emphasizing quite rightly their essentially metaphysical obsessions. Those works distinguish the existential and the transcendental, and then, while maintaining the distinction, argue their extraordinary interrelatedness. The approaches both alternate between and also distinguish "phenomenology" and "existential thought," all of which is expressed in Langan's essay.

In the beginning, he draws a contrast between phenomenology and Freudianism. Phenomenology, of course, is directed to the essential a priori corelatedness of consciousness and its object, or the interpretative function of the construing transcendental ego and its construed object. All of this is accessible to the reflective ego itself, and presents itself as the transcendental clarification of the meaning of the world, anything in it or out of it, in a word, of anything that has meaning at all. In this aspect, Freud has no role to play whatsoever. In the quotations from Freud which Langan gives, as well as elsewhere, Freud views consciousness itself not as an agent nor an interpreter of its world but rather an epiphenomenon thrown up by the essentially non-conscious activities of the psyche with its libido, a "seething cauldron of desire." The forces directing human life and thought are therefore sub-, pre-, or un- conscious, and consciousness itself is but a somewhat self-deluded rationalization of these non-conscious forces. The work therefore of psychoanalysis is to make conscious what had been non-conscious, accompanied by the hope that this "clarification" would release the soul of the obsessed or be driven back to its original spontaneity. Now, whatever is to be said of this reinterpretation of the work of consciousness, it seems clear to me that it does not meet phenomenology on all fours. It does not deny the intentionality of consciousness, but does deny the intentionality of its origin, the psyche. That the theory of Freud and his followers is hopelessly inadequate to deal with the philosophical problems it wishes to resolve or even describe, I taken for granted. Freud has never had the lest influence on my own thought and I have never addressed myself directly to the mare's nest of logical, epistemological, metaphysical, and even scientific problems it enjoys living in. Nevertheless, I disagree with Langan in supposing that the fundamental difference between Freud and Husserl lies in a differing analysis of consciousness and its intentionality. It lies, at least for me, in a differing view of the role of consciousness in either life or philosophy. Is consciousness essentially self-deluded or not?

Langan also considers the thought of Kierkegaard, and while I have spent much time with Kierkegaard, and learned from him what I could, I must say I have never had the slightest sense of what Langan's key quotation means. I understand the Danish think it badly translated; I am in no position to judge and end up agreeing with those who think it was intended to be a parody of Hegel at his worst. Kierkegaard is surely one of the fathers of "existentialism," giving "subjectivity" and "existence" their current significance. On the other hand, since I have confessed to something like a total incomprehension of Langan's favorite passage, I must stop here.

Langan's comments on my own rational mysticism I found by and large accurate to my own writing, but then while he is sympathetic to something in them, I sense an irritation with their transcendentality. Although this hardly comes to a head, I sense in Langan's objections a preference on his part for *life!* But that is perfectly *natural* even if indefensible transcendentally. My own position takes no sides on the question; it only emphasizes that it *is* a choice even if not made by deliberation, and for most of us, something more like a consent. But then, the sense of *Mystical Reason*, as Langan says, is essentially to show the coincident identity of the Transcendental Ego, the "wonder of all wonders" as Husserl put it, and the Absolute Reality intuited in the ontological argument. They are one and the same and we are indeed finite, situated gods, and we know it.

IX. LASTLY

Three essays remain, those of Erich Heller, Forrest Williams and William Bossart. Each examines topics dear to my soul; but since they do not direct themselves immediately to my own thought, it would be presumptuous of me to enter into a dialectic with any one of them. Nor do I have the slightest inclination to do so. I profited from all three as a student.

I admired particularly in Erich Heller's Nietzsche essay, what he has frequently been admired for, namely, an indefatigably sympathetic revulsion to what he attends to. No doubt, this is the subtlest approach to the makers of the modern mind: impossible to avoid, impossible to wholly admire; brilliant but fundamentally unsound; saying things never said before, but perhaps which should never have been said in the first place. All of which, to whatever extent it is true, leaves us in a somewhat exhausted, post-febrile state, with a lingering nostalgia for "other times" when we fondly hope, everything was a good deal healthier and one could *sleep* too without shame. I confess to the nostalgia; perhaps Erich Heller does too.

Forrest Williams' essay on Spinoza is something of a small chef-d'oeuvre. I myself have been strongly influenced by Spinoza since I was an undergraduate when Professor Marjorie Grene taught us the *Ethics* at the University of Chicago with an incomparable rigor. Williams is absolutely *right* in his emphasis; few Spinozists realize that his book is called "Ethics" and not "Metaphysics" or "Epistemology." Errol Harris put it well in the title of his recent book, "Salvation from Despair . . ." Of course it is *edifying*, but not by way of exhortation. Forrest Williams demonstrates this in his remarkably sensitive and accurate interpretation. I do not merely agree with it, but have learned much from it with much pleasure.

William Bossart's essay also taught me a good deal. I knew nothing of Hui-Neng, the sixth patriarch of Chinese Buddhism, the founder of Chinese Zen. Nor do I read Sanskrit, hence find some difficulty in understanding such sentences as "An understanding of the relation between *dhyana* and *prajna* also enables us to bring together *sunyata* and *tathata*," no matter how lucidly Bossart has explained it. But this is my fault, following Santayana who read some languages but spoke only his own. The precise nature of the conflict between Zen and Sartre I certainly cannot judge, although I have some familiarity with Sartre, enough to reject a good deal of his "phenomenology" as a forced dialectical construction. In any event, the dispute I found interesting, and perhaps someday I shall be able to speak miscellaneous words in Sanskrit with some confidence.

Again my deepest thanks to all the contributors to this volume for the honor they have done me.

Selected Bibliography of Writings by William Earle

BOOKS

Objectivity (New York: Noonday Press, 1955); second edition, revised (Chicago: Quadrangle Press, 1968)

Reason and Existenz by Karl Jaspers, translated with an Introduction by William Earle (New York: Noonday Press, 1955)

Christianity and Existentialism, with James Edie and John Wild (Evanston: Northwestern University Press, 1963)

The Autobiographical Consciousness (Chicago: Quadrangle Press, 1972)

Public Sorrows and Private Pleasures (Bloomington: Indiana University Press, 1976)

Mystical Reason (Chicago: Regnery, 1981)

Evanescence (Chicago: Regnery, 1984)

A Surrealism of the Movies (Chicago: Precedent Press, 1986)

Imaginary Memoirs, 3 vols. (in preparation)

ARTICLES

"Note sur la Dialectique des Systèmes," *Les Etudes Philosophiques* (July, 1948), pp. 293–296.

"The Ontological Argument in Spinoza," *Philosophy and Phenomenological Research* (June 1951), pp. 549–554; (reprinted: Grene: *Spinoza*, Anchor, 1973).

"Mr. Wild's Ontology and Ethics," *Journal of Philosophy* (October 9, 1952), pp. 672–674.

"The Standard Observer in the Sciences of Man," *Ethics* (July 1953), pp. 293–299. (Some paragraphs reprinted in *Scientific Monthly*, July 1954).

"Anthropology in the Philosophy of Karl Jaspers," *The Philosophy of Karl Jaspers* (Library of Living Philosophers, Paul A. Schlipp, ed.) (German ed. 1957, English ed. 1958), pp. 523–538.

"Implicit and Explicit Phenomena," *Review of Metaphysics* Vol. VIII, No. 3 (December 1954), pp. 211–224.

"Freedom and Existence," *Review of Metaphysics*, Vol. IX, No. 1 (Sept. 1955), pp. 46–56.

"Memory," *Review of Metaphysics*, Vol. X, No. 1 (Sept. 1956), pp. 3–27; reprint: Levensky: *Human Factual Knowledge*, 1971.

"Notes on the Death of Culture," NOONDAY No. 1 (1958), pp. 3–26. Reprinted in *Identity and Anxiety* (1960).

"The Life of the Transcendental Ego," *Review of Metaphysics*, Vol. XIII, No. 1 (Sept. 1959), pp. 3–27.

"Phenomenology and Existentialism," *Journal of Philosophy*, Vol. LVII, No. 2 (Jan. 21, 1960), pp. 75–84.

"Hegel and Some Contemporary Philosophers," *Philosophy and Phenomenological Research*, Vol. XX, No. 3 (March 1960), pp. 352–364.

"Jaspers and Existential Analysis," *The Journal of Existential Psychiatry*, Vol. 1, No. 2 (Summer 1960), pp. 166–175.

"The Concept of Existence?" The *Journal of Philosophy*, Vol. LVII, Nos. 22–23 (Oct. 27 and Nov. 10, 1960), pp. 734–744.

"Being Versus Tragedy," *Chicago Review*, Vol. 14, No. 3 (Autumn-Winter 1960), pp. 107–114.

"Love and Metaphysics," *Experience, Existence and the Good*, edited by Irwin C. Leib. Carbondale: Southern Illinois Press, 1961, pp. 49–68.

"Intersubjective Time," *Process and Divinity*, Ed. Reese and Freeman. LaSalle, Ill.: Open Court, 1964, pp. 285–297.

"What is Man?" *Tri-Quarterly* (Winter, 1965), pp. 67–74.

"Science and Philosophy," *Buffalo Studies*, vol. II, no. 2 (July 1969), pp. 59–67; reprint: *Range of Philosophy* by Titus, Happ (Van Nostrand, New York, 1970).

"Some Notes on the New Films," *Tri-Quarterly* (Winter 1967), pp. 157–164.

"Ontological Autobiography," *Phenomenology in America*, ed. James Edie, Chicago: Quadrangle Books, 1967.

"Political Responsibilities of Philosophers," *Ethics*, Oct. 1968; pp. 10–13.

"Revolt Against Realism in the Films", *Journal of Aesthetics and Art Criticism*, Winter, 1968, pp. 145–151. Reprinted: *Film Theory and Criticism*, ed. Mast and Cohen (Oxford University Press, 1976).

"Paradoxes of Private Conscience as a Political Guide" *Ethics*, July 1970; pp. 306–312; reprint: *Conscience, a Philosophical Analysis*, ed. Donnely and Lyons.

"Notes on the Radical", *Monist*, Oct. 1972, pp. 552–575.

"The Ontological Argument in Spinoza Twenty Years After", Marjorie Grene, *Spinoza*, Anchor, 1973, pp. 220–226.

"In Defense of War" *Monist*, Oct. 1973.

"The Future of Civilization", *Philosophy Forum*, Vol. XI, ed. R. Gotesky, New York, 1973.

"Private Conscience or Myself as Hero" *Conscientious Actions*, ed. Peter
French, Schenckman, 1974, pp. 15–23.
"Phenomenology of Mysticism", *Monist*, Oct. 1976.
"Styled Thought" in *Viva Vivas*, ed. Regnery (Liberty Press, 1976, pp. 25–35.)
"Cinema Banalité and Surrealism", *Quarterly Review of Film Studies*, May
1977, pp. 179–184.
"Variations on The Real World", *Explorations in Phenomenology*, ed. Carr and
Casey, Nijhoff, 1973, pp. 410–422.
"Phenomenology and the Surrealism of Movies", *Journal of Aesthetics and
Art Criticsm*, Spring 1980, pp. 255–260.
"Faces of Being", 7 pp. Introduction to volume of poems by George Strong
(1980, Phoenix Press.)

REVIEWS:

Der Philosophische Glaube by Karl Jaspers: *German Books*. University of Chicago
(March, 1948), pp. 1–2.
The Perennial Scope of Philosophy by Karl Jaspers: *Ethics* (July 1950), pp.
302–303.
Erkenntnis und Erlebnis by Michael Landman: *Ethics* (July 1952), p. 305.
Critics and Criticism, ed. Ronald Crane: *Western Review* (Winter, 1953), pp.
150–155.
A Philosophical Scrutiny of Religion, by C. J. Ducasse; *Journal of Religion* (Jan.
1954).
Personal Knowledge by Michael Polanyi: *Science*, Vol. 129 (March 1959), pp.
831–832.
The Study of Man by Michael Polanyi: *Science*, Vol. 130 (October 9, 1959),
pp. 912–913.
Wahl on Heidegger on Being: The Philosophical Review (Jan. 1958), pp. 85–90.
The Future of Mankind by Karl Jaspers: *Science* (1961).
Ethics and Science by Henry Margenau: *Science*, Vol. 147, no. 3643 (Jan. 8,
1965).
Review-article: *Philosophy of Karl Jaspers: Journal of the British Society for
Phenomenology*, Oct. 1974, pp. 262–265.
"The Rupture between Jaspers and Heidegger," *Modern Age*, Spring 1982,
pp. 197–199.

EDITOR OR CONSULTING EDITOR:

The Monist
Phenomenological Studies (Duquesne University)
Studies in Phenomenology and Existential Philosophy, Northwestern University
Press; Indiana University Press
Research in Phenomenology

Contributors Notes

WILLIAM H. BOSSART is Chair of the Committee on the History and Philosophy of Science at the University of California, Davis. A Fulbright Scholar and a NEH Fellow, he has published articles in aesthetics and phenomenology (with special attention to Heidegger, Kant, and Sartre) and is currently working on a monograph on conceptual frameworks and schematic thinking in philosophy, science, social science, and art.

EDWARD S. CASEY is Professor of Philosophy at SUNY, Stony Brook. His published articles are in the areas of aesthetics, philosophy of mind, and psychoanalysis. *Remembering*, a sequel to his earlier book *Imagining*, is forthcoming. He is presently investigating the role of place in human experience.

HUGH M. CURTLER is Chair of the Philosophy Department at Southwest State University in Marshall, Minn. He is the author of *A Theory of Art, Tragedy, and Culture: The Philosophy of Eliseo Vivas* and has edited several other books. His published essays, mainly in the fields of aesthetics and the philosophy of culture, have appeared in a number of professional journals.

JAMES M. EDIE has twice been Chair of the Philosophy Department at Northwestern University. One of the founders of the Society for Phenomenology and Existential Philosophy, he is now the General Editor of Studies in Phenomenology and Existential Philosophy (Indiana University Press). His most noteworthy book is *Speaking and Meaning: A Phenomenology of Language*. He is presently working on a book on Husserl and another one on the philosophy of the theater.

WILLIAM FOWKES was Assistant Professor of Philosophy at Hobart and William Smith Colleges from 1976 to 1979. He is the author of *A Hegelian Critique of Contemporary Art* and of several articles. In 1979 he made a transition into the business world, and has held positions at Time, Home Box Office, and CBS.

PHILIP GRIER is Associate Professor at Dickinson College. In addition to publishing a number of articles and book reviews, he is the author of *Marxist Ethical Theory in the Soviet Union*, four chapters of which have recently been translated into Chinese.

ERROL E. HARRIS has taught at a number of American and British universities. Recently he retired as John Evans Professor of Philosophy at Northwestern University. Among his many publications are the following books: *Hypothesis and Perception, Nature, Mind, and Modern Science, Revelation Through Reason*, and *Salvation From Despair*.

ERICH HELLER is Avalon Professor Emeritus at Northwestern University. His numerous books include *The Hazard of Modern Poetry, The Disinherited Mind, The Artist's Journey into the Interior, The Ironic German: A Study of Thomas Mann, Kafka*, and (most recently) *In the Age of Prose: Literary and Philosophical Essays*.

WILLIAM J. LANGAN has been a Visiting Professor of Philosophy at Middlesex Polytechnic in London and is currently Professor of Philosophy and Chair of the departments of Philosophy and General Studies at California State University, Hayward. He has written articles on Parmenides, Plato, Nietzsche, Hegel and Sartre, and St. John of the Cross.

J.N. MOHANTY has taught at the Universities of Burdwan and Calcutta in India, at the New School for Social Research and the University of Oklahoma, and is presently Professor of Philosophy, Temple University. He is the Editor of *Husserl Studies*. His most recent book is *Husserl and Frege*.

ASHER MOORE is Donald Babcock Professor of Philosophy at the University of New Hampshire and is concurrently Lecturer at the University of Puerto Rico, Recinto Mayaguez. The author of many essays, including the especially noteworthy "Composition," he has taught at Harvard University, Northwestern University, Penn State University, Ripon College, Bowdoin College, and Osaka University.

DONALD V. MORANO has taught at the Universities of Notre Dame, Tennessee, and Loyola of Chicago. He has published *Existential Guilt: A Phenomenological Study* and essays on existential themes and the philosophy of law. At present he is practicing law in Chicago, where he has been specializing in federal criminal appeals and other post-conviction remedies.

ROBERT C. SCHARFF teaches philosophy at the University of New Hampshire and has also taught at the University of Oklahoma and the U.S. Air Force Academy. He has published articles on Heidegger, Nietzsche, Dilthey, hermeneutics, and comparative philosophy.

FORREST WILLIAMS is Professor of Philosophy at Colorado University in Boulder. He has been a Fulbright Fellow in Rome and has received grants from the American Council of Learned Societies and the American Philosophical Society. With Berel Lang, he is the co-editor of *Marxism and Art*. His numerous articles have been in the areas of aesthetics, phenomenology, ethics, Kant scholarship, and film theory.